Beyond Perception

Finding contentment in a disillusioned world

A Guide to Meditation

Miles Sherts

Beyond Perception

Cover: drawing by Ben Schikowitz
              watercolor by Emma Elizabeth
              author photo by Amy Sherts

Sky Meadow Press
Greensboro Bend, Vermont
www.SkyMeadow.org

ISBN 978-0-9854359-0-5

Dedicated to:

The Faith that Lies Beyond Belief

Acknowledgments

I wish to thank my wife, Cella Sherts, for her steady support and editing, my friends Riva May, Bill Troffer, and Stuart Stotts, for their editing help,and Jenny Thomas, Carrie Abels, and Beatrice Aranow for their editing services.

Contents

The Problem

The problem has become too big to name. I am not talking about your problem or my problem. In fact, that is exactly the problem. We don't yet know how to talk about *our* problem – the one that all of us face together. Let's begin by calling it the problem of our survival. Not our individual survival, but the survival of our species, or perhaps of life itself.

It could be argued that the whole thrust of human civilization, the main point of all of the "progress" that we have achieved in our two hundred thousand years on earth, is to better our chances of survival. Indeed, this seems to be the purpose of life and the primary objective of all living things. Yet, after all this time and enormous effort, we find our survival threatened in more ways than we ever could have imagined.

Our attempts to make life safer and more certain all seem to produce unintended side effects that create newer and bigger threats. Even the most ardent believers in material progress have to admit that our efforts to resolve our insecurity have only made the problem worse. Looking honestly at our predicament, we might do well to stop in our tracks and rethink our entire approach.

A situation like this, where every effort we make to save ourselves seems to put us in greater danger, demands that we at least stop doing what we are doing until we better understand our dilemma. The aim of this book is to get us to do just that – and only that. If we can simply stop for a moment and not *try* to do anything, we may get a glimpse of the problem as it is – *and that would change everything*.

An Impending Crisis

At the dawn of the twenty-first century, humanity faces a looming crisis like none we have encountered before. Any number of impending disasters threatens our future, and we hear of new ones almost daily. None of us like to be reminded of our situation because it seems so overwhelming and irreversible. Yet, without looking at our dilemma directly and honestly, we'll never reach the level of urgency required to find our way out.

Each of the problems that we face today appears daunting, and if we consider them all together the complexity of our situation boggles even the most informed and educated among us. It seems that all we can do is to pick one small part of one problem and spend our lives working to make it better. Yet, this approach leaves many of us feeling inadequate and powerless.

That is why so many of us have either given up hope or are choosing just not to look. And who can blame us? It seems that all we can accomplish are ridiculously small efforts that make insignificant changes. After a while, even the most determined of us are bound to give up and assume that someone else will find the answer, or lose hope that a solution even exists

This book is not going to offer some miracle cure, be cheerfully optimistic, nor predict an apocalypse. It will merely suggest that each of the unthinkable threats facing us today stem from one root cause. And the purpose of all these seemingly malignant obstacles being thrown in our way is to urge us to find that cause.

An old proverb goes something like this:

It is not the mountain ahead that wears you down,
but the grain of sand in your shoe.

If we are honest with ourselves right now, the mountains ahead of us do seem impossible to cross, and our chances of making it through this next period of human history make even the optimists among us hesitate. Yet the very problem may be that we are focusing on the mountains ahead, instead of looking in our own shoe.

The Grain of Sand

While the immediacy of our problems begs for action, it may be wiser now to take a moment to look for the real source of our discomfort and anxiety. Until we understand what is causing us to feel afraid and dissatisfied, despite our unprecedented material abundance and technical capacity, we may never find a lasting solution.

I suggest that the grain of sand in our shoe is simply that we seem to *lack the capacity for contentment*. While our brains have a remarkable ability to process information, and this enables us to manipulate the world around us in astounding ways, few of us are ever satisfied with life. Indeed, it seems that the more we have the more we want. We are caught in a perpetually repeating cycle, chasing one thing after another, only to find that this new thing does not solve our problem, either.

The simple common ingredient underlying each one of these impossible situations lies in our basic human nature. Our primary way of approaching the world is from a place of scarcity and defensiveness. These basic impulses were programmed into us long ago, when we had to defend ourselves against saber tooth tigers and our life was full of immediate danger and uncertainty.

But now, ironically, instead of protecting us our conditioned reflexes are *making* the world increasingly unstable and unsafe for us to live in. These involuntary defenses are no longer serving us and have *themselves* become the source of the problem. Yet, even if we know that our habit of defending ourselves is hurting us, we do not seem to be able to stop ourselves from reacting to the world around us out of fear.

A Way Out

There is a way to change our basic human nature, and this book tells the story about how such a transformation began for me. It is meant to inspire and encourage a similar experience within you. You may already think that you know what this book is going to say. Or you may have given up trying to find answers, because nothing that you have read has ever changed anything. Both of these are true. You do already know what this book is pointing to, and nothing that you read will ever change anything by itself.

Do not believe what is written here. Only keep an open mind and heart, and see if these words resonate with something real and true inside of you. There is nothing you can read that you do not already know, and you cannot substitute someone else's truth for your own realizations. All that my words can do is to awaken a memory or open you to an experience.

However, do not underestimate the value of being reminded. We have fallen asleep so deeply that much of what we know is obscured under thick layers of conditioning. Sometimes another person's words are just what we need in order to remember our own truth and to spark an experience that can remind us who we really are.

Author's Note

When I was a child, I wanted to know every person in the world. I didn't understand that this was impossible. I just couldn't bear the idea that we were each separate and disconnected from the rest, and I felt a deep urge to bring everyone together again. This impulse for unity never waned, and is still with me today. As much as I value my independence, I long for community. I dream sometimes of all of us celebrating our humanity together – united by one purpose.

This book is my way to bring us together. Thinking that you will read this allows me to write and enables me to see my experience from a new perspective. For now it seems that you are really outside of me, we are separated by bodies in space and time, and this is the only way I have of reaching you and remembering that we have always been connected.

Truth

Writing to communicate an experience is like drawing pictures in water. The truth seems to evaporate as soon as I express it. All I want to do is to connect with you and tell you what I see, yet language itself insures that a barrier remains between us. Putting words on a page feels woefully inadequate to express a revelation and seems a project sure to fail.

Still, these ideas well up, begging me to present them. And a line from a once-read poem prompts me to go ahead.

"The secret they say, is doing the wrong things calmly"

I have come to understand this in a way that is truly liberating, and I hope by the time you finish reading this book that you will understand it too.

———————— •◆• ————————

Sources

Much of this writing consists of personal insights. If I know where an idea came from, I will name the source or inspiration as a way of honoring that person and illustrating the connection of teacher to student. If there is no source that I can name, I will simply offer the ideas as they came to me. I do not assume the position of being right or expressing absolute truth. What I am pointing to is beyond right and wrong, and I know that language can only shadow what is real.

Throughout these pages I will refer to stories or scientific theories from our collective human history as a way to make a point or offer a perspective. It is common for authors to credit a source for such examples, however, I usually will not follow this practice. The source for any "factual" information noted is most often the internet, and I invite you to learn more about any of the historical or scientific ideas presented here by looking them up for yourself.

The essential message of this book, as the title suggests, is that truth is not found by distilling different perceptions. This is not to say that we should ignore the practical observations made by science nor the details of our history. I am simply saying that none of these are entirely verifiable because they all depend on perception. And, as this writing will discuss in detail, when we rely on perception to determine what is real, we limit ourselves to approximate knowledge and relative truth.

No Beginning and No Ending

I have attempted to put together a cohesive framework for approaching reality, yet no book can provide the complete explanation that many of us are seeking. As you venture beyond perception, you will see how a spiritual teaching is not a linear process, just as a spiritual path does not begin in one place and take you to another. There is no actual beginning or ending, and any one insight can spark your own epiphany.

I have written this book more as a series of essays rather than one continuous story, so you will hear some ideas repeated in different chapters. I understand that some of you may find this repetition annoying. This is not an oversight, nor is it meant to imply that you are less intelligent. The truth is remarkably simple; however, the process of perception often deeply obscures it. When I repeat an idea, I am merely offering you an opportunity to further digest it or see it from a new angle.

Some of you may choose to read this book from beginning to end and find it helpful to consider the teaching as a whole. Others might find this difficult because the writing is too dense to be assimilated in one reading. Each chapter contains a whole idea in itself and sometimes the connection between chapters may not be apparent. There is no harm in setting the book aside for a while. When you feel adequately stretched, it can be helpful to take a break in order to absorb what you have read.

Words

In this writing I frequently use words like Buddha, God, Christ, religion, truth, reality, spiritual, mind, perception, morality, ego, and self, which are bound to conjure up different ideas for each of us. Some of these words are loaded with significance from centuries of emphasis placed on them by our culture.

This book will be more helpful to you if you allow some flexibility in your interpretation of these words. The point of a spiritual teaching is to enable your perception to change, and in order to do that, you must suspend what you think you already know and open your mind to seeing familiar concepts from an entirely new perspective.

Remember that words are only symbols that we use to describe experiences. They have been in circulation since the beginning of thought, just as the air we breathe and the water we drink has cycled through every living being since life began. The words themselves are not true. They merely *represent* an experience or insight.

What matters is the way in which these words touch you. These words are meant to point to a living experience that is infinitely larger than the concepts themselves. This writing is intended to inspire an experience of your own truth – the kind of revelation that comes before words can form. The aim is to take you beyond perception to a different way of knowing.

1

In the Beginning

The beginning for me felt more like an ending, as a true beginning always does. I was nineteen years old, in my second year of college, when the bottom of my life fell out. It wasn't some great external tragedy that collapsed the underpinnings of my life, but instead a rebellion from inside my own mind.

This made my undoing and subsequent disappearance more difficult for friends and family to understand. There was no external demon pursuing me. My life was going well by any standard of measurement, and no one else could see the internal crisis that was consuming me.

I remember feeling frustrated that I could not focus my mind for more than a few moments. My thoughts were fragmented and I felt drained by my efforts to understand what everything meant. I lost sight of the purpose of education or a career and could not see where my life was going or what all of this was for. All at once, the momentum that had propelled me toward college and life in the adult world just vanished, and I was left stranded with no idea of what to do next.

It was a lonely time for me. There was no one who I could talk to about my disillusionment with the world. All I had to go on was a gut feeling that something important was missing, and it was not something that I could find through more education, romance, entertainment, or success. I just knew there had to be something more than this.

I have not forgotten how strange this unraveling felt to me at the time, and I am well aware of how disturbing and confusing it was to my family and friends. I have longed to explain my sudden departure from school and society, in part to heal this tear in my past, and, perhaps more importantly, to provide a beacon for anyone else who might need to hear, as I did, that there *is* something more. It is a big something, in fact, which few people talk about directly, yet most of us are secretly hoping to find someday.

Life as a Competition

My mother recently made a simple comment that helped put my experience into context. She was talking about my brother signing up his two young children for summer activities such as swimming and tennis, and she said something like "everything here is competitive." She was contrasting her lifestyle with mine, in which competitive activities were noticeably absent.

I then remembered how competition had been the driving force in so much of my childhood. My memory of school and "fun" activities is that they always had a competitive edge. No one presented learning as a means of personal development or as a way to become more conscious or happy, and play was not about the joy of being coordinated or more alive in my body.

As my mother so aptly put it many years later, everything was about winning or doing better than someone else. I don't remember anything that was done for the immediate pleasure of doing it. We somehow had made learning and even playing into stressful work whose only value was in what we could achieve compared to someone else.

Staying in the Track

When I was in fourth grade, my parents and teachers told me that I was supposed to do well in school in order to get into a good college. I dedicated the rest of my youth to this vague idea that I didn't really understand, but which mattered so much to everyone around me. I began to experience education as a kind of treadmill where I always had to run faster to try to get ahead, and the goal we were trying to reach was so far away that no one could actually see it.

I finally reached what I had thought was the end of this treadmill when I was accepted into a good college. I remember receiving my college acceptance letter with great excitement half way through my senior year of prep-school, and feeling this great weight lift off of my shoulders. I assumed that I could relax now and let go of the tension that had been with me since I was ten years old.

As I headed off to college the next year, I anticipated that I would find out what all the fuss was about, and the meaning of these many years of intensive preparation would at last be revealed. Instead, I found myself facing just another school, with no real idea about why I was there. After twelve years of continuous education, I had never developed my own motivation for learning. I had never been taught to see school as something valuable for its own sake, but as merely a means to an end. Now that I had reached that long-awaited end, I didn't know what I was supposed to do with it.

Life Without a Track

When I was young, my father once took me to an amusement park. We got into a model of an antique car that had a real engine, gas pedal, brake, and steering wheel. It was small enough that I could drive, and my father let me take the wheel. I was terribly excited because I could control how fast the car went and steer it myself.

After driving for a few minutes, however, I soon realized that the car was on a track that kept the wheels in line with the roadway. No matter how I turned the steering wheel, the car would always stay on the track. Both my excitement and my anxiety quickly faded as I realized that I was not really in control of the car.

Then an awful realization dawned on me that real cars did not work this way. I understood that driving a real car on a real road meant that there was no track and the person driving *could* go off the road. This thought overwhelmed me with fear, and I could not imagine what it would be like to take on *that* kind of responsibility.

My life up to college had been largely like driving that car on the amusement park track. I had a little bit of control, but not enough to do any real damage, as I was limited in where I could go. Then all that changed. Unlike all the schools I had attended before, college did not automatically lead to more school. College led to life, and life was something that I knew little about. I had always been told what classes to take in order to prepare me for college. Then, all of a sudden, it was up to me to decide how best to prepare myself for life.

While I appreciated the freedom that came with going to college, I had little preparation for the vast array of choices that lay in front of me. I had never had to work to support myself, and had no idea what I wanted to be in the world. Now I had to decide what I wanted to learn and what I was going to do with my life. These seemed like heavy life choices and it all was coming at me a bit too fast.

Taking the Wheel

At the same time that I was feeling overwhelmed with the choices that college presented to me, I felt a new urgency to take life into my own hands. I was beginning to have a sense that I was caught up in a system that had no end. Having been a good student and done what was expected of me for twelve years, I was more than ready to be my own person. I desperately needed to break away from the course that someone seemed to have prescribed for me long ago.

I had pursued math and science in my schooling up to this point because I had been told that I needed to excel in these in order to have a successful career. Now that I could choose my own subjects, I discovered that math and science didn't interest me after all. So, I took classes because I was interested in them, rather than merely to climb higher on some abstract educational ladder.

I signed up for courses in romantic love, women's liberation, communist China, the great philosophers, psychology, sociology, and even bread baking. My interests seemed to circle around all that it meant to be human, and what life was about in the largest and most immediate sense.

I was just starting to have an idea of who I was as an individual, and where my real interests lay, when I began to feel pressure from the school and my family to choose a major. Before the end of my first year in college, I was again being told that there was some future goal that I had to plan for and work toward now if I was to succeed. They were asking me to decide at nineteen years old what I wanted to be for the rest of my life.

I had just discovered the freedom of learning motivated by interest rather than outcome, and the idea of narrowing my focus once again to fit into some predetermined long-term career path seemed unbearable. I knew that I didn't have enough experience to answer this question and I tried to simply ignore it for a while.

Then one day I overheard two senior women at my college talking with great anxiety about their future. Apparently they had both applied to graduate schools and one said to the other, with obvious dread, "I have no idea what I will do if I don't get accepted into this graduate program."

This moment of eavesdropping confirmed that I really was stuck on a treadmill that had no clear end. I realized that I had lived my life up to that point by other people's rules, trying to satisfy other people's expectations. I found the idea deeply disturbing that I was on a track of education that led to more schools, then to some distant, pre-defined career.

This realization was like discovering that the car I was driving at the amusement park was actually on tracks that kept me from going off the road. Suddenly. my longing to make my own choices and direct my own life became larger than my fear of crashing, and I decided then and there that I wanted out.

The Big Picture

I wanted to know why. Why was I here on earth, and what was life for? These questions seemed obvious and essential to answer before I could go further. While some of the classes I took offered a few answers, they fell far short of satisfying my hunger for the meaning of life. Book learning and formal education were too abstract and removed from what mattered the most to me. I was hearing a calling from within the depths of my soul that academic study simply could not address.

My family and friends became worried about me because I seemed so uninterested in doing what they thought was necessary for success and security. They believed that my happiness depended on being able to compete and earn enough money to have social status and wealth. None of the people in my life at that time were as passionate as I was to find out what all this was for. Everyone appeared to be focused on achievement, accumulation, and recognition, and few seemed to question where it was all heading in the end.

My passionate questioning of life's ultimate purpose fell on deaf ears. I felt alone with my questions. It seemed that other people either didn't care, or didn't believe there was a way to discover the meaning of life and had given up asking. People around me seemed uncomfortable with my quest, perhaps because no one had any answers and the search seemed destined only to lead to greater frustration and confusion. They responded by steering me back into the world of competition and achievement. Most of them seem to have settled for the immediate rewards of recognition or financial security and no longer questioned what all of it was for.

The Source of Anxiety

I wanted to know why everyone, including myself, was anxious most of the time. It seemed that this world held so many uncertainties, so much could go wrong, and we were all afraid. The emphasis on achievement and recognition and the clamor for career, wealth, and social status seemed aimed at reaching a place of certainty that would finally put to rest our chronic anxiety and fear of life. Instead of asking what we were afraid of, people were merely attempting to subdue or control their uneasy feelings by amassing as much wealth and power as they could, believing that this would resolve their insecurity.

I could see that it wasn't working. My family had education, money, and social status. The society I grew up in represented the most affluent and well-taken-care-of people in the world, with power and material comfort unprecedented in the history of human civilization. Yet, we were still anxious and afraid and believed that we did not have enough. I recognized that this mad rush to accumulate possessions, climb higher in careers, and attract more social attention had no end to it. There would never be enough to dispel the anxiety caused by life's uncertainty.

As I tried to make sense of this approach to life, things just didn't add up. I saw the world in a fundamentally different way from most of the people around me. It seemed to me that we were unwilling to explore the primary cause of our anxiety and find a *real* solution. Instead, we were simply trying to override the problem by distracting or numbing ourselves from our fear. I knew that, unless I discovered the cause, I would have to spend my life running from uncertainty, as most of the people around me were doing.

Looking Inward

The only thing that seemed clear to me at the time was that the difficulty I was experiencing in relating to the world around me was rooted in my own mind. I had seen how out of control and restless my thoughts were, and how they constantly distracted me and scattered my focus. I began to consider that the solution to my problem lay in understanding and working with my own thought process.

I turned my attention in college to Western psychology and philosophy and searched the writings of some of the better-known thinkers who had addressed the meaning of life and the workings of the mind. I read Descartes, Freud, and Jung, and found their conclusions abstract and circular, always leading back to the never-ending complexity of comparative evaluation and personal judgment. None of the writings of the deepest thinkers in my culture's history soothed my thirst for truth. Thus a growing urgency rose in me to go far away from everything familiar in search of something that would make sense of the seemingly random chaos of life.

I can appreciate now in hindsight how upsetting it must have been for my family and friends to see my fixation on the meaning of life as I was just reaching adulthood. It must have disturbed and frightened them to see me heading directly into my anxiety, instead of away from it like everyone else.

My parents thought that I was throwing my life away and that they had failed in raising me. My college dorm mates labeled me "the thinker," and one of my closest friends left a note in my psychology book saying; "these books are making you crazy." Clearly, they were concerned about me. The truth was, however, that I was much more concerned about them.

Going it Alone

And so it was that I found myself alone among my peers, my family, my school, and the society I had grown up in. I did not mean to reject the people who were closest to me. I simply found myself apart from them because of my need to find a certainty that was bigger than my fear.

I was hearing a calling that no one around me seemed to hear, and somehow, against all odds, I trusted it. At the time people thought I was crazy. Looking back now, people say that I was courageous. For me, it was simply what I had to do because I could not shut out these questions. I could not rest until I got to the bottom of my basic anxiety about life and discovered something that was real and true.

The questions had become a pounding in my mind that no manner of distraction or forced focus could resolve. I had lost interest in school, books, knowledge, careers, and other people's expectations. I knew that I had no real direction and would not find one inside such a society that ignored the questions that had become so vital to me. My only desire was to find someone who knew, or at least could understand my urgent need to know, the ultimate purpose of life.

It became obvious that there was not much support around me for what I was going through. I knew that my sanity and ultimately my survival depended on finding something that I could trust to show me the truth. And I didn't see any hope of finding that within my immediate world. My college roommate recognized what was happening to me and told me there was something called meditation. I didn't know what that was, and he couldn't explain it to me, but somehow I sensed that I needed to find out.

I realized that the only choice I had was to leave, and I did not think twice about it. I left college, my family, my first romantic relationship, and everything familiar, to begin a journey that I am still on today. Looking back now, it is clear that I was embarking on an epic rite of passage – my journey toward self-realization. At the time, I just wanted to get as far away from society as I could in order to sort out what was happening inside me.

A college friend had signed up to go on a term abroad to a remote Asian country, and this piqued my interest. I borrowed her catalogue and read about a program leaving the next semester to some place that I had never heard of, called Sri Lanka. I looked on a globe and saw that it was on the opposite side of the planet and about as far away as I could get from home. That suited me perfectly, and I began to make arrangements to go.

Leaving Home

Aside from the unusual destination, this looked like an ordinary term abroad. Yet, some part of me must have known that I was making a journey of fundamental change and was leaving my life as I knew it for good. In all the inner turmoil leading up to this moment, I had been feeling an urge to change my name. I was named after my father, and now desperately needed to find an identity of my own.

When I arrived at the airport and met the other college students who were going with me on this program, it suddenly occurred to me that they did not know who I was. I sensed that this was the moment, and decided to take my middle name which I had never used before. I will never forget how strange it sounded to hear myself say to my new companions, "Hello, I am Miles."

Up until that moment in the airport, my life had the appearance of normalcy. I was simply a sophomore in college going on a term abroad with a small group of students from other colleges. I knew that this was far from the truth, yet I understood that I could not reveal this to my family, friends, or even to my girlfriend.

I felt one of those pulls from deep within my heart that I could not explain to anyone, and could barely understand myself. I just knew that I had to go, and that if anyone understood that I was really getting out, they would have tried to stop me. It was surely easier to just leave, and not let on that I had no intention to return to a normal life after my adventure abroad.

I knew in my heart that I was desperate to find truth, and that I would go to any length to discover something real. I also knew that no one around me seemed to understand this urge, and so I needed to keep it to myself. I did not want to have to defend my search for meaning or explain it to all the people around me who seemed so invested in fitting in and establishing a place for themselves in this chaotic world.

Letting Go of the Old

Calling myself by a new name proved to be the least of my strange experiences. We had been told that many of the customs in Sri Lanka would be foreign to us and we would often be surprised or confused by the way people lived. They gave us some idea about what to expect, but nothing could have prepared me for how different this new place was.

The first night that I sat down to dinner with my host family, I was surprised to see a linen table cloth, fine china plates, and a vast array of silver cutlery. I was expecting to eat with my bare fingers as our leaders had suggested was the norm here. Instead I was facing a table set with more knives, forks, and spoons than I had ever seen. The food was dished out and my host mother fussed over me in broken English, trying to make me as comfortable as possible. Then I suddenly realized that the room had gone quiet, no one was eating, and everyone was watching me intently.

I thought about this for a moment and it occurred to me that they were all waiting to see how I would eat. I guessed that they were probably used to eating with their hands and had been told that Westerners thought this rude and improper. I imagined that they wanted to eat with their fingers, but were willing to use the silverware if I did, in order to not offend me.

I had been raised not to touch most food with my hands and to always use silverware. I had never simply picked up things like rice or vegetables with my fingers and put them into my mouth, and the thought of it seemed entirely odd to me. Yet, I knew that I was here to shed my past, and was willing to try anything, so I grabbed a bit of rice and wet curry with my fingers and put it in my mouth. At that moment, I felt the whole family heave a great sigh of relief as each of them began eagerly to eat with their hands. None of the silverware was ever touched at that meal, and it never appeared on the table again.

That first dinner experience set the tone for immersing myself completely into this new culture. After some time, it become normal for me to eat rice with my fingers, wear a long cloth around my waist, squat over a toilet in the floor, and walk barefoot. Something began to wake up in me as I felt the earth beneath my feet, saw people growing the food that they ate, and visited with villagers living in simple mud and straw houses.

I went into the fields and watched people harvesting rice by hand and sat with the women in the small kitchens where they cooked the rice in clay pots over a small open fire. I began to understand how intimately connected and dependent we are on the earth and the natural world that surrounds us. I saw that my own culture's dependence on technology had separated us from elements of life so basic that their meaning could never be obscured. As I saw and understood these things, my mind began to relax and settle.

I lived in Sri Lanka for five months, involving myself in the people and culture as much as I could. I loved the simplicity in the way people lived, their child-like playfulness and joy, and the way they valued family and community. All of my notions of poverty were challenged as I recognized that these people, who had so little in the way of material comfort or security, were so happy and content with their lives. This confirmed my suspicions that our Western emphasis on education, career, and material wealth did not finally lead to happiness as it promised.

What Makes Us Happy?

I grew up with the perspective that poverty meant misery and suffering. Our Western society is permeated with the assumption that the worst thing that can happen to us is to not have enough money to get what we need. This fear of being poor is what pushes us, and it was this competitive drive for financial success that made me so uncomfortable in my first years of college. Everyone I knew had a lot of money, yet it was never enough, and no one seemed to be really happy.

In Sri Lanka, the first family that I lived with was among the wealthiest in the country. Compared to my own family at home, however, they lived a remarkably simple life. They had a small car, a telephone, and a flush toilet, but I never saw them use any of these. They traveled by public bus, used a traditional squat toilet, and communicated with people directly in person.

I later lived with a family in a village where no one had a car or phone, and few people had electricity. Most people lived in simple houses with only a few rooms. They bathed and carried water from a community well, cooked on small fireplaces, and slept often in the same room on thin straw mats rolled out onto the floor at night. People walked everywhere they went, often barefoot, and their main diet was rice and vegetable curry with dhal made from small lentils for protein.

According to our Western ideals, these people should have been miserable, *yet they were by far the happiest people I had ever known!* Most of the people I spent time with in Sri Lanka were relaxed and seemed to experience a genuine sense of joy and excitement about life. They had few expectations for things they did not have, and seemed sincerely content with their surroundings. There was always enough food to eat and plenty of time to hang out and be social with each other. They truly enjoyed each other's company and spent most of their time together with family and friends.

I was continually touched and amazed by how warm, open, and friendly the people were. Each family I visited invited me into their home and made me feel like visiting royalty. They fussed over me and insisted on serving me the finest food or drink they had, no matter how poor they were. They offered everything, wanted nothing in return, and seemed to get great enjoyment out of simply having me as their guest.

Perhaps the greatest shift occurred for me as I recognized the simple elements of life that make us truly happy. I saw how important it is to make and eat food together, and how much comfort and security we get out of belonging to a family and community. I realized how good it is to work with our hands, live close to the earth, be surrounded by people who care about us, and not be stressed about having enough or getting more. It gradually became clear to me that these were all things missing from my life at home.

Being Stretched

Many of these new ways came easily to me, perhaps because I was hungry to find meaning in life and ready for change. Yet, some aspects of living in Asia were difficult. Most notably, I was challenged by the lack of privacy.

After some months in Sri Lanka, I went to live with a family in a small village and was given a large room to myself with its own private entrance. I was just settling in on the first night when the door opened and a group of ten or more young men from the village just came in and sat around the room looking at me. No one said anything, and I began to feel very uneasy.

I did not think they meant me any harm, yet I could not understand what they wanted or why they were there. They started going through my backpack, taking each thing out and looking at it with great interest. They laughed a lot and appeared to be enjoying themselves, and I felt increasingly uncomfortable with what seemed like an invasion of my privacy. After an hour or so of this, they suddenly got up and left.

This gathering in my room repeated itself every night for my first week until I finally became so upset that I refused to let them in. I tried to get them to leave by being rude and telling them to go. Yet one young man named Piyadassa just kept coming, saying in simple English that he wanted to be my friend. However rude or aggressive I was with him, he seemed unfazed and kept showing up at my door night after night.

I finally surrendered my privacy, not knowing what else to do, and let him in. I then began to see that he simply wanted to get to know me and his intentions were only to offer supportive friendship. I went through a kind of internal meltdown as I recognized how awfully I had treated him and saw what a kind and generous a person he truly was. I was shocked to see my own fear in stark contrast to his kindness, and ashamed at how fiercely I had tried to defend my privacy for no good reason.

Piyadassa and I soon became the best of friends, and a few weeks later he invited me to stay with him in his parents' home on the other side of the village. We spent all of our time together, including sleeping in the same room, and he shared with me everything that he had. I gradually came to trust him deeply and appreciate a kind of companionship I had never known before.

Discovering the Comfort of Belonging

I have since understood that, for many Asian people, being left alone does not feel good. They don't value personal space and individuality in the same way that we do, and assume that people need companionship in order to feel comfortable. When they see someone alone, they automatically go to join them, as this is what they would want.

This experience revealed to me how deeply our society values personal privacy over friendships, family, and community. I began to see how much of our anxiety and stress is due to automatic defensiveness and self-inflicted isolation. Our emphasis on competition and personal achievement has made it difficult for us to appreciate simple companionship and intimacy.

The price that I pay for personal space is a painful sense of isolation from the people around me. I have been taught to distance myself from other people in order to feel safe. Yet, I really do not want to be alone; and one of my deepest needs is to be joined with others. Most of us feel more safe and at ease when we are surrounded by people with whom we feel a sense of connection and belonging.

When I returned home after living in Sri Lanka, I began to seek out community and a sense of extended family in my life. I determined to live connected to other people and let go of needing so much privacy. However, many years later, I am still astonished at how difficult it is for me and many of my friends and family members to live in harmony together and share space with each other. And each time I have returned to Asia, I have experienced again a bit of the anxiety I went through that first time from not having enough personal space.

In these five months living with families in Sri Lanka, I was profoundly changed. I saw how much of my unhappiness with life at home had come from the assumptions of my culture, and I began to question and let many of these values go. I no longer thought that a lack of material possessions or comforts led to misery, or that individual success or personal security was more important than family, friends, and community.

I had indeed found a place as far from home as I could imagine, and had begun to feel a sense of meaning and purpose that was plainly evident in the rhythm of life lived simply and close to the earth. Yet the most astonishing change lay just around the next corner.

2

Sitting Still

My family had attended a Protestant Christian Church when I was a boy and I had gone to Sunday school and youth groups there. Yet, when my life became overshadowed by the questions of meaning and purpose, it never occurred to me to look to the teachings of Christ for answers. Religion seemed to be a formality that people turned to for a sense of belonging or security, but not a doorway to truth.

I was not looking for religion and had no intention of going to Sri Lanka to find answers in Buddhism, so it surprised me when I found myself being attracted to the Buddhist monks whom I saw everywhere. I noticed their relative ease, sense of calm, humbleness, and simple nobility. There was something inspiring in their presence that made me curious, and I began to visit monasteries and hermitages where they were practicing meditation.

I remembered then that meditation was something I had wanted to experience, and realized that by some miracle I had stumbled into an opportunity. I began to inquire about how I could learn meditation, and eventually I heard about a monastery where foreigners were invited to stay and practice with the monks.

As I told my host family and other people that I met about my aspirations to learn to meditate, I was met with the same puzzling response time after time. People were first honored and excited that I was interested in their religion and monastic practice. Then they told me that I would not be able to meditate because I was from the United States. When I asked for an explanation, they said that the lifestyle I was used to was too fast paced, and I would not have the patience to sit still long enough.

The idea that sitting still would prove too difficult made me all the more determined to try. It was also becoming increasingly apparent in a strange, intuitive way that this is why I had come here. So, when my formal exchange program ended, I extended my plane ticket and arranged to spend an extra month in Sri Lanka doing a silent meditation retreat in a Buddhist monastery. I arrived by bus, checked all my belongings in the office, put on white clothes, and began an experience that would change my life entirely and forever.

Going Inward

One of the younger monks showed me to a small cinder block cell with a cement slab covered by a thin straw beach mat for a bed and a bare light bulb hanging from the ceiling. In broken English, he told me about the monastic schedule. A bell would ring at 4:00 a.m. to wake us up, and a cup of warm rice gruel would be put outside my door.

We would meditate together until 6:00, when we would take our bowl to the kitchen to be served breakfast. The rest of the morning was for silent sitting and walking meditation until we gathered again outside the kitchen to be served our main meal just before noon. After noon, there was no food until the following morning, and we were to spend the rest of the day in silent meditation.

An older monk who spoke a bit of English was assigned to teach me. I realized after a while that he didn't know much about meditation. He was kind and supportive, however, and although he could not answer many of my questions, he kept me supplied with books that described the practice of meditation and the teachings of the Buddha.

Because there was no one to explain things to me in detail, I did not attempt to understand all of the Buddha's teachings, but only tried to grasp the essence of meditation. The simple instructions were to sit upright but relaxed, and focus on the sensation of the body breathing in and out in its natural rhythm.

I could never have imagined how such basic instructions could be so impossible to follow. Trying to sit still and focus on my breath, I began to see how wild and chaotic my internal world was. I was continuously trying to make sense of the fragmented pieces of my life, and my thinking mind never stopped in its frantic quest to work out what some past experience meant. I saw how arbitrary and fickle my thoughts were, how endlessly I planned and rehearsed my future, and how restless and uncomfortable my mind was most of the time.

Realizing the disheveled state of my thoughts came as a shock, yet it also put into perspective my urgency to learn how to focus my mind. I recognized why I had felt so disoriented as I was coming into adulthood, and why I needed so badly to see the bigger picture of life. I began to get a sense of how futile it was to try to sort out life's meaning by thinking about it. I had been counting on my rational thought process to distill the truth. Now I could see that this approach was not making things any clearer and was only adding to my confusion.

I threw myself into the practice, gradually training my body to sit cross-legged for an hour at a time, and struggling to bring my mind back into focus. Meditation was by far the most difficult thing I had ever tried to do, and every day I thought about leaving. I fantasized about of all the exotic places I could travel in my last weeks in Asia, and often thought that I was wasting my time just sitting in this cell and watching my breath.

Yet, something inside me knew that I had to stay. I sensed that the answers to my questions could be found here, if I only could remain still for a while. The pain of my disillusionment with life and my longing to find some meaning kept me there, going inward, when every bone in my body wanted to escape.

Finding Something True

There were many cells like mine in the monastery. Some were occupied by monks, and a few by other curious Westerners like myself. Some of the monks had a steadiness about them, and I found comfort in following their example. The young travelers from Europe and North America seemed to come and go from the monastery at a whim. They did not take the practice of meditation seriously, often broke silence to talk among themselves, and moved on after a few days when it became too hard.

I soon understood why so many people had been telling me that I would not be able to do this. I was not very good at focusing my mind or settling my body, and I often felt frustrated and discouraged, thinking that I would never learn how to meditate. Yet, I found within me a capacity to keep going and not quit. In the end, I think it was simply my determination to stick it out that enabled me to glimpse the truth that I had been so desperately searching for.

While I found meditation extremely difficult, I was also having an overwhelming and uncanny experience of recognition as I read the teachings of the Buddha. Although his actual words were never written down in his lifetime, the recollections of his teachings, scribed centuries after his death and translated thousands of years later into English, spoke immediately to the questions burning inside me about life's ultimate purpose.

I recognized a deep truth in these ancient scriptures and it seemed to me as though the Buddha was speaking directly about my life in this moment. He clearly understood the anxiety inherent in a life where reality is obscured by meaningless thoughts and ego-centered aspirations. I had never heard these ideas before, yet they seemed entirely familiar as if I were simply being reminded of what I had always known.

Instead of presenting his ideas as something to believe in, the Buddha offered the tool of meditation as a way to see for ourselves what is true. The teachings were simply guidelines for a process of inner investigation that would lead to personal insight and revelation. The Buddha taught that this direct personal seeing is the only way to resolve the human dilemma of meaning. He emphasized that truth can only be experienced in this moment now, by each mind individually, and can never be translated into words or passed from person to person.

Because truth cannot exist outside of an immediate experience, I need a way for my mind to look inward and see for itself what is actually happening in each moment of consciousness. This notion was completely new to me and beyond any Western ideas that I had ever known. My mind had been trained to observe the world around me and draw conclusions using my rational thinking process. Yet, I had already lost faith in the process of logical thought to reveal the meaning of life, and this new idea struck a chord in me that resounded throughout my entire being.

The Buddha's idea was so revolutionary, and yet made so much sense. Of course the only time I ever really know anything is when I see it for myself. In all my years of education, the primary focus was on memorizing information so that I could repeat it. It was no wonder that nothing I experienced in school was able to satisfy my hunger for real knowledge. When I understood how passionately the Buddha taught us not to rely on belief or invest in ideas, I felt a certainty about his teaching that allowed me to trust and give myself fully to the practice of meditation.

Learning Patience

Except for group sittings three times a day, and meal times, I was left on my own in the monastery. I dedicated myself to sitting and walking meditation as I was instructed to do. I had never spent so much time doing nothing, and I did not realize how hard it could be to simply be still. I became grateful for my experiences living in Sri Lanka during the five previous months, as they had taught me something about slowing down and waiting.

One time, about four months earlier, I had gone with the father of my host family to mail a package at the post office. We went to a cement building and sat on a cement bench in a room with large openings to the outdoors. It was so hot that day that sweat ran down my face as I sat there. We waited for over an hour, sitting in this stiflingly hot room with no air moving and nothing happening. Then we waited for another hour.

I had never in my life waited so long for anything in such uncomfortable conditions. I knew I had no control over the situation and that there was nothing else that I could do. I remember being so filled with anxiety that I thought I would explode if we waited another minute. I wanted to take charge and make something happen, yet the circumstances were completely out of my hands and I had no choice but to sit still.

We waited a long time more, and somewhere in that last hour, my anxiety suddenly melted away. Something deep inside me just collapsed. To my surprise, I realized that what dissolved was not me, but merely my resistance – my habit of being in control and getting my way. It was my ego that began to break apart, and the result was that I felt more light and free. I had surrendered, and was now all right sitting on that bench and waiting. Nothing had changed, yet I felt relieved and inexplicably free from the suffocating anxiety that had been consuming me just moments before.

A few months later, I was spending my days walking around the countryside with my friend Piyadassa who I met in the village where I first lived. We would visit friends and relatives of his, and always they would stop whatever they were doing, welcome us into their home, and insist on feeding us.

The first time that this happened, I felt honored and sat down with my friend to wait. I assumed that they would be out in a few minutes with some sort of snack or prepared food. Similar to my experience in the post office, however, we waited one hour, and then another, with nothing happening. The people we visited rarely spoke

English, so there was nothing to say and nothing to do but sit and wait.

I could not believe that we waited so long for food. I had grown up with instant food, from the freezer or from a box, ready to eat in a few minutes. As I sat, I became more and more uncomfortable and wondered if hunger or boredom would kill me first. At one point, I could not take it any longer and just got up and walked into the kitchen to see what was happening.

Then things became a bit clearer to me. I realized they had needed to first collect some wood, then fetch water from the well, then start a fire, then wash the rice, and then put the pot of rice on the fire to cook. I soon learned that eating meant sitting in a room for several hours as the rice was slowly cooking and the other food was being harvested, cut, and prepared. Gradually, I became used to this ritual, repeated at almost every house we visited, and learned to be at ease with the endless waiting.

Beginning to See

Learning to wait helped me to sit still in the monastery. However, despite my sincere desire to learn meditation, turning my attention inward proved to be harder than I could have imagined. I was instructed to sit cross-legged on a cushion, and simply focus my awareness on the movement of each breath as it entered and left my body. I struggled for days, first with settling my body and relaxing into long sitting periods, and then with my thoughts, which constantly drew my attention away from my breath.

As difficult as this was, and despite my urgent desire to leave the monastery, I could sense that this was a kind of medicine reaching deep into my being and touching the place that was burning with those impossible questions. For the first time in my life, I felt as if I was getting to the bottom of how and why things are the way they are. I was settling into my body and exploring my own consciousness, and I recognized that this was entirely new territory for me. I had never heard of such an approach in Western society, and I sensed that it just might resolve my dilemma if I stayed on and kept going inward.

After some practice, my body relaxed into sitting cross-legged on the floor and did not hurt so much. I found that I was able to focus my awareness on my breath for more than a few moments, and this allowed me to be aware of things that I had never noticed before. As my mind became more calm and clear I began to see myself and the world around me in an entirely new way. It was as though I remembered why I was here, what I had come for, and what my life was about.

In reading the teachings of the Buddha, and investigating the truth of them for myself, I began to have revelations that brought clarity and light into my mind and dissolved my confusion the way that a breath of air revives a drowning man. I felt this great flood of relief that I had found someone who saw life and the human dilemma the way I saw it, and who offered a path toward resolution. Beginning to see what was true for myself started to answer my questions in a way that no book or teacher ever could. Yet the answers did not come in the way that I had been expecting them.

Focusing Awareness like a Telescope

To the human eye, the moon looks like a pale, flat disc in the night sky with variations of light and dark shading. I could explain to you that the moon is really a round ball and the surface is covered with craters, deep depressions, and mountainous rims. However, if you had never seen the moon yourself through a telescope, this would only be a story that you would either believe or not believe. You would still see just a flat disc in the sky.

The only way that you can really *know* about the moon is through a direct personal experience. You have to see the moon close up to know how it really is, and the only way to do this is by using a magnifying device like a telescope. Once you have seen the moon through a focused telescope, you know for certain what it is like, and beliefs become irrelevant.

The Buddha taught a practice of focusing awareness on a present moment experience, such as the sensations caused by breathing, in order to see more clearly what is real. It is similar to the process of focusing a telescope lens in order to see the moon more clearly. In the Buddha's teaching, he points to aspects of what we call reality, and asks that we look at them through the light of our focused awareness. He suggests that they are not the way we think they are, and gives us some ideas about what he has seen.

He makes it clear that until we see for ourselves what is real, no theory or ideas that anyone proposes can have real meaning or clarity for us. His teaching and practice of meditation is aimed at taking us beyond belief to direct experience, where certainty lies. And he suggests that this is the only way to dispel the haunting fears and anxieties that come from the perpetual uncertainty of life.

If I have a powerful telescope and do not know how to focus it, it has no real value to me and I can't use it to see more clearly. I can see things through it, yet because I have never focused it, I believe those fuzzy images are the way things look in reality. When I learn to focus the telescope and aim it at something like the moon in the night sky, my whole experience of the moon changes because I see it as it is, and not as the distorted unfocused telescope represented it.

The Buddha taught that the mind is just such an exquisite tool for investigating reality, and that we only need to learn how to use it. Our current use of the mind amounts to looking through an unfocused telescope, and the world that we experience this way is but a shadow of reality. Because we have not developed our capacity for direct knowing, we have come to rely on abstract thought to inform us of the world we live in.

This gives is a distorted view of the way things are, and we accept this distortion as real because we have no other references for reality. Yet, this world we see through the distorted lens of perception can never satisfy us because it is based on our own *ideas* about how things are, which is often very different from how they *actually* are.

When I look up at the moon, I see a pale disk of light in the night sky. I might imagine it as a lamp, or plate, or even a round of cheese. I can believe all sorts of things about the moon until I see through a telescope that it actually is a round ball suspended in space.

By continually bringing the mind back to the present moment and allowing all thoughts to pass, I strengthen my faculty of direct awareness. This is a process of focusing awareness much like the physical act of focusing a telescope. This focused awareness then offers me a direct experience of things the way they are, and not the way I think they are.

I begin with observing physical sensations like the breath in the body, and gradually become able to focus direct awareness on the process of the mind itself. In this way I become able to see the source of my consciousness and am not continually distracted by the endless stream of thoughts running through my mind.

The Fog Lifts

Being aware of the immediate sensations of air entering and leaving my body through my nose enabled me to gradually let go of my thoughts and bring my attention back into the present moment. As I learned how to let go of thought I became aware of a steady consciousness that was quite separate from the thoughts which constantly crowded my mind. I could then see what was really going on in my thoughts and recognize how my mind constantly occupied itself with the story of me.

I saw how my mind was often harsh and judgmental, critical of myself and everything around me. It was frequently full of fear and anxiety, neurotically obsessed with danger, loss, and endless longings for things that I did not have. My thoughts would continuously review my past looking for meaning or trying to resolve some traumatic event. Or they were planning every detail of my future, trying to account for all the possibilities, especially threatening ones, and prepare for them.

The more that I was able to just witness my mind, the more I lost interest in its perpetual and chaotic stream of thoughts. I was shocked at how vicious and cruel these thoughts could be, and distressed to see that my mind operated in such an arbitrary way with no steady focus or direction. It just jumped from one thing to another like a small child who has no attention span. I was ashamed to see how fickle my thinking mind was. Despite all of its sophistication and complexity, this process of rational thought *never reached any final conclusions about anything.*

My mind seemed determined to evaluate every aspect of my life, and to my surprise, I saw that it came up with radically different interpretations each time. One moment I would think of my parents as dominating and controlling, and the next moment I would see them as nurturing and kind. A series of thoughts would grow around how fortunate I was to have found my way to this monastery and be learning how to meditate. Then in a flash I would find myself thinking with certainty that I was just wasting my time here and that meditation was useless and would not amount to anything.

Seeing this about my mind was quite disturbing because I had been taught to place such importance on my ability to think and figure things out. I naturally then began to lose faith in the process of reason, and soon became more willing to interrupt my thoughts and let them go in favor of the certain calm and peace of a simple direct sensation, like my body breathing.

As I was immersed in this process of methodically letting go of what I had thought to be my most valued asset – my capacity for rational thought – I became gripped with an intense fear. I saw that I was losing the faith I had invested in my capacity to judge. I could no longer believe fully in the function of reason because I saw that it had no real basis. My judgments and conclusions were all relative, dependent on the thoughts that happened to be dominant in that moment.

In letting go of my attachment to my thoughts and giving up my investment in rational conclusions, I risked losing the very essence of who I thought I was. I could feel my sense of self gradually disappearing, and I had no idea what I would become without my thinking mind in charge of my experience.

At this point, I only had the burning urgency to discover something real to keep me going. I also believed deeply in what the Buddha had discovered and trusted that this was also what I was looking for. It was the intensity of my longing for truth, and the faith I now had in the Buddha as a teacher, that allowed me to pass through this fear and continue going deeper.

The Certainty of Direct Experience

Gradually, like mist rising on a cool spring morning, a new part of me began to awaken. I learned to trust my present moment experience more than my conceptual thoughts *about* that experience. It was like going directly to the source instead of reading or hearing about something secondhand. And it required learning a whole new language – a language of direct experience.

I found that this language was exquisitely clear and simple, while the language of my thoughts was so often complex and obscure. It was just a matter of focusing my awareness on present moment sensations, rather than the images in my mind. As I practiced this, I began to feel an abiding peace and certainty about life.

This creeping certainty was about no particular thing. It was not a specific answer to a specific question, but rather seemed to apply to all questions. When I was simply experiencing my breath without any thoughts about it, the fundamental meaning of life was obvious and beyond question. I knew that I was experiencing something real and true because all of my anxiety, doubt, and confusion suddenly disappeared and what remained was a deep and satisfying clarity that seemed to extend infinitely in all directions at once.

It began to dawn on me that I was actually discovering what I had set out in search of, and I often became giddy with gratitude. When I recognized that the answers were right there in the simple moment-to-moment sensations of my physical body, I laughed out loud with astonishment. I had been trying to figure things out by *thinking* about them. I had invested my effort in cultivating my intellect in the assumption that this would bring me security and peace. And now, it was becoming ever more clear that it was my thoughts that were the *cause* of my great anxiety and uncertainty.

I was learning a new language and connecting with an experience that seemed entirely foreign, though it had been part of my daily life since I could remember. It was a language of direct awareness that only reveals itself when the mind is still, present, and focused. This was the language I had been so desperately searching for to illuminate the truth.

I was slowly replacing my habit of rational thought with an experience of simple, present-moment awareness. In order to allow this to happen I had to let go of my constant efforts to solve my dilemmas and figure out life's meaning. I had to give up trying, and admit to myself that my approach was not working. Along with the great sense of relief that I experienced, there was a certain despair and disillusionment that accompanied this surrender. Some part of my being was crushed, believing this to be the ultimate failure.

I had assumed that the answers to my questions would come from deeply thinking them through to an elaborate conclusion, or from someone telling me what was true. I thought solving a problem was a matter of figuring it out, and that if I became good enough at thinking I could resolve any issue. In spite of my longing to break free, I was still deeply attached to my thoughts. That is why surrendering them felt so heavy and tragic at times.

This process, like any true metamorphosis, was accompanied by a certain amount of internal struggle. I had to give up my attempts to figure my way out, and let go of the only way I knew to try to reach clarity and understanding. I had to admit defeat and allow myself to face my fear of not knowing and having no ideas left to try. Sometimes it felt as if I were taking one step forward and two steps backward as my urge to discover truth crashed up against my terror of losing myself.

The Answers are Gradually Revealed

In the end, my urge to find meaning outweighed my fear, and as I kept letting go of my thoughts, I was astonished by the way the answers began to appear. I could never have anticipated the calm certainty that awaited me as I gave up trying to figure out what life meant. As I grew more comfortable with simple awareness and spent more time focused on the breath coming in and out of my body, a profound and wonderful transformation took place in the way that I experienced myself.

I began to feel large and expanded, and the area that was me seemed to have no boundaries. At times I could not tell where my physical body began or ended. The familiar heaviness of my body and the density of my thoughts began to break apart and I became inexplicably light, buoyed up by some invisible force from below. I felt myself connected to all people and things and could see my life as part of a huge tapestry that was much bigger than my own personal story.

From this new expanded perspective, the dilemmas that I was facing and the enormous questions burning within me appeared small and insignificant. There was a certainty and stability to my being that I had not felt before, and I saw that this absence had been the cause of my distress. I recognized that my anxiety and discomfort came from defining myself in much too small a way. From this new perspective, I understood why I had felt so confused, alone, and desperate for truth.

The questions and seemingly impossible dilemmas weighing down my life simply melted away in the light of my expanded sense of self. When I was only aware, the conflict and confusion in my mind had no meaning, and the answers to my questions were as obvious as the air around me. They had merely been invisible when I was looking for them in the form of ideas that I could grasp and hold on to.

The Paradox of Truth

I had left my familiar life behind, feeling hopeless, and having given up on all the ways that I knew to find out what life was for and why I was here. And in my state of inner turmoil and despair, I became willing to look in the last place that I ever thought I would find the answers. I found what I was looking for in the simple space of pure awareness that exists without concepts, effort, or even understanding. Here, in the cracks *between* my thoughts, in the ordinary knowing that had been with me all along, I suddenly saw what I had been so desperately seeking for the whole time.

The way only became clear to me when I stopped looking for truth where I thought I would find it. I could not imagine any other way of knowing except through my thinking mind. So I first had to see that process for what it is and realize that my rational mind was not able to find truth in the way I was using it.

I had to give up, be defeated, and sink into despair, before I would even consider questioning the process of thought itself. This opened the way for an inconceivable revelation. I realized that once I became identified more with awareness than with my thoughts, *I no longer needed to find the answers to those questions.*

The questions that had once loomed so large and impossible came from identifying myself with my rational mind. As I experienced myself as something larger than this mind and went beyond the limits of perception, the questions and problems that I was struggling with became irrelevant. They simply dissolved in the light of expanded consciousness, and what replaced them was a calm certainty about being alive that could never be in question.

3

The Programmed Mind

The Buddha began his life in luxury and comfort as a prince in a small kingdom in what is now northern India. The story goes that he became profoundly disillusioned and left his palace, giving up his inheritance to become a seeker of truth. After experimenting with different spiritual paths, he finally had an experience that showed him a reality very different from our ordinary one. He discovered a truth about existence that remains hidden for most of us. It is nearly impossible to imagine the magnitude of his discovery. What he experienced changed his entire orientation and transformed his fundamental nature.

He understood that his experience was merely the realization of our human potential and the fulfillment of our purpose on earth. His life set an example for other people to undergo this kind of transformation, and he taught the practice of meditation as a way for us to create the conditions to have a similar experience.

As I explored his teaching through reading and meditation, and began to experience this transformation for myself, the purpose of being alive became clear to me. The Buddha taught that there is a state of being awake or fully conscious that is possible for us to realize. He contrasted this to our normal state of consciousness, which he characterized as asleep, or mechanically programmed.

He described our common frame of reference as *conditioned mind*, meaning that the fundamental way we think is determined by a set of assumptions which most of us take for granted and never question. He explained that there is an entirely different state of consciousness in which the mind is free of conditions and assumptions and is not limited by pre-determined reference points or fixed judgments.

The essence of his teaching is that when we rely on our conditioned mind, we suffer loss and disappointment, our lives feel narrow and limited, and we become enmeshed in a struggle for survival. The way out of this is to allow our conditioning to fall away and our consciousness to change, revealing a true nature that is unlimited and eternal. In this place where the mind is free, there is no suffering, loss, or struggle. He called this state of being enlightenment, and suggested this as the ultimate goal of life.

No Place Like Home

Many of us feel like Dorothy in *The Wizard of Oz* story. Lost and alone in a strange world, we just want to get back home again. The world we find ourselves in has many wonderful and beautiful things, and is also shadowed by seemingly dark and dangerous forces. It is at once whimsical and silly, beautiful and awe-inspiring, and deeply terrifying. We can engage with life and often enjoy the journey, but in the end we mostly want to return to some place that is safe, certain, and familiar – someplace like home.

As a young adult, I became scared that there *was* no place where I could fully rest, free from fear and anxiety. I was looking for this sense of comfort and security in a romantic relationship, family, friends, and achievements. And I found some sense of peace in each of these because they helped me to feel connected and less alone in the world.

Yet I sensed that all of the things I was investing in, thinking they would help me to feel safe, would ultimately fail me. Other people could hurt me, and no one else seemed to care about me in the way that I wanted to be cared for. This is why I was struggling so much with my relationships, my family, and school.

I could see that when I did find real friendship, family, or community, it remained fragile. People eventually die, and situations change. I knew that if I continued to look for a safe home base in this way I would be forever discouraged, simply because *no such place existed in the world around me.*

This may seem to be a tragic conclusion that could only lead to further despair and depression, however, it is not the end of the story. As I stood still for a moment and brought my attention to my immediate experience, the resting place was instantly revealed. It was with me all along, and all I had to do was stop looking frantically for it where it could not be found.

When the Wizard left in his hot-air balloon without her, Dorothy had the heartbreaking realization that she might never make it back to her home in Kansas. Only then was she able to discover that the ruby slippers, which she had been wearing the whole time that she was in Oz, had the power to take her back home in an instant.

And so it is with us. When we have exhausted all other options and it becomes clear that our efforts are not leading us to a place of security and knowing, the way home opens and we recognize an innate certainty and peace of mind that was with us all along.

The solution to our struggle with life won't make sense to us until we give up trying to make sense of it. The thing is that we have to stop using our rational mind to figure it out, so we can recognize that we have another, much more powerful faculty of direct knowing. This is what Dorothy learned when the Good Witch told her to click the heels of her ruby slippers together three times and say "There's no place like home."

Paradigms

In order to understand the Buddha's experience, I find it helpful to use the concept of a paradigm. A paradigm is a context or set of reference points that our conceptual mind uses to frame its version of reality. Most of us don't realize that we depend entirely on a basic paradigm or mental framework to give our lives meaning and orientation.

A paradigm works much like the basic operating system of your computer, enabling the computer to do all the complex tasks it can do. And, like your computer's operating system, it is largely invisible. You become so accustomed to your current paradigm, or set of assumptions about reality, that it disappears from your perception entirely. This is similar to the way the wallpaper or decorations in your home or office become invisible after a time. They are simply the background to whatever else is happening, and you rarely take notice of them.

I had my first computer for almost a year when I experienced some technical difficulties and called for help. The technician on the phone asked me what operating system my computer was using. I told him that there was no operating system – I just turned my computer on and started using it. He corrected me and helped me to understand that the computer had to have a program to do all those functions, and the main program was known as an operating system.

He showed me how to find out which one I had, and soon I understood that a program called Windows 98 was running my computer. I then saw that my computer was just a vehicle or mechanism for the operating system to run through, and it was actually the Windows program that enabled things to happen.

By observing my thoughts in meditation, I realized that my thinking mind operates in a way similar to a computer. It is essentially a mechanism that needs to be programmed before it can do anything. And because the programming is so basic to my existence, like the operating system of a computer, I rarely notice or realize what it is. Most of us use our minds, like I did with my first computer, without any knowledge that they have an operating system or how that system works.

Unconscious Programming

In his teachings, the Buddha points out the existence of our unconscious programming and the consequences of that on our lives.

He describes the common mental patterning or paradigm that most of us share, and suggests that *it is the way our minds are programmed that is responsible for our experience.* Similarly, whatever program our computer is using is completely responsible for what the computer can do. The computer itself has no program and in this sense cannot do anything of its own accord.

A funny story I heard illustrates this point. It seems that a woman was setting up her new computer for the first time and called for technical support. She told the technician that the message on her screen said, "Cannot find the keyboard," so she held the keyboard up to the monitor so the computer could see it. She was complaining to the technician that even though she was showing the keyboard to the computer, it still insisted that it could not find it!

Hearing this story, most of us chuckle because we know that a computer cannot "see" through its monitor screen. We realize that it is just a machine that can only do certain tasks that it is programmed to do. However, because the computer can do so many amazing things seemingly by itself, it was perfectly natural for this woman to assume that her computer could see the keyboard if she held it up.

In a similar way, most of us assume that our rational mind is capable of doing anything, because its capacity for abstract thought, memory, and imagination seems so vast. We can remember scenes from long ago and imagine all sorts of future scenarios with vivid details. We can store endless amounts of information and create seemingly infinite new ideas.

It seems that there is nothing that our rational mind cannot do. So we naturally assign our mind the tasks of running our lives and making us secure and happy, without realizing that these are beyond the scope of its programming. Then we become confused and depressed when our lives remain clouded with struggle and despair.

Looking Behind the Curtain

Many of us been fooled by the fantastic capacity of our mind for conceptual thought and imagination, just as Dorothy and her companions were fooled by the Wizard in the classic movie *The Wizard of Oz*. When they finally meet the great Wizard, they encounter a large, fierce, and threatening face in the middle of a large room behind a cloud of smoke and fire. All of them have their attention fixed on this ominous face and are shaken by its apparent power and authority.

Then, Dorothy's dog, Toto, innocently pulls back a curtain, revealing a small feeble-looking man in a booth in the corner of the great room. This man is manipulating controls and speaking into a microphone, and it soon becomes obvious that he is projecting the image of the great face, and it is not real. As soon as they see that the frightening face is an illusion, their perception changes and their fear turns to outrage and anger as they realize how they were tricked by this bumbling old man.

A similar process occurred when I directed my awareness toward the patterns of my own thinking mind. I began to see that the rational voice in my head was a facade, much like the face of the wizard projected into the middle of the room in the film scene. As soon as I was able to withdraw my attention from the content of my thoughts, I saw their aimless, rambling nature.

I realized that instead of an all-knowing sage, my mind was feeble and fearful, obsessed with reviewing the past or imagining the future. In the light of direct awareness, my thinking mind appeared woefully incompetent, repeating the same ideas again and again without drawing any clear conclusions.

By observing my mind from the perspective of a neutral witness, I gradually began to see that my idea of myself and of the world around me was created entirely by a continuous stream of thoughts that had little bearing on what was actually going on in the present moment. My thoughts were continuously focused on what I had to do to make the world safer and my existence in it more certain. Yet despite constantly thinking about my security, my life appeared to be in perpetual turmoil, and this process never resulted in the stability or certainty that my rational mind promised.

Burying Our Head in the Sand

Most of the people to whom I have taught meditation over the past ten years confess to me at some point that they have an extremely over-active mind. Many of us feel overwhelmed or weighed down by our mind's constant efforts to figure things out. A common response to this dilemma is to numb yourself to the mind's endless chatter through distraction, intoxicants, or medication, in hopes of gaining a moment of peace. Yet, these approaches merely offer temporary relief from a crowded mind and can leave you feeling hopelessly trapped on a never-ending mental treadmill.

This dilemma only appears overwhelmingly difficult, however, because you may not be approaching it in a useful way. Whenever you push against or try to diminish the power of your own mind, you end up in a bind. You are trying to diminish your own conscious awareness, thinking that consciousness itself is the source of your discomfort.

The most common way that many of us try to find peace of mind is to become more *unconscious*. While some of us succeed in obscuring our consciousness for a time behind a fog of distraction or veil of intoxicants, we can never eliminate it altogether. To do so would be to destroy who we are, and thankfully we do not have this capacity.

When confronted with mental or emotional pain, a normal response is to bury our head in the sand like the proverbial ostrich. We tend to think that if we cannot see the problem then it is not there. Aside from its obvious insanity, this approach of *reducing* our awareness by numbing or distracting ourselves diminishes the one capacity we have that can actually resolve our dilemma.

Consider all the ways that you might dull your awareness through drugs, alcohol, stimulants, food, sex, sleep, or medication. While these may work temporarily to ease the stress of an over-active mind, they are merely band-aids covering up the symptoms and making the problem feel less urgent.

I was first attracted to drinking alcohol as a teenager because it seemed to help relieve the pressure of my mind's endless unrest. When I was intoxicated, everything seemed easy and free and I had nothing weighing on me. As soon as the alcohol wore off, however, the incessant questioning in my thoughts and the mounting stress began all over again.

Substances that help us calm our internal mental chaos often become addictions that we become dependent upon. More importantly, however, they undermine our natural capacity for focused attention, which is exactly what we need to reveal and undo the hidden programming that is the cause of our stress in the first place.

Seeing the Man in the Booth

The challenge is not how to diminish awareness or eliminate thoughts. Anyone who has tried knows that these endeavors are impossible. All that we need to do, and in the end all that we *can* do, is to see the programming that is making our mind operate the way it is.

One glimpse of how our mind actually works is enough to begin the process of freeing us from its control. In the same way, all that Dorothy and her friends had to do to break the Wizard's spell was to look away from the captivating face for a moment and see the man in the booth behind the curtain.

The reason that this approach does not occur to most of us is that it does not seem possible. The difficulty in revealing our current paradigm or mental programming, is that we *cannot see it from within the program.* Whenever we engage the program, the program itself becomes invisible *because we are using it.*

In a similar way, as soon as you turn on your computer, it automatically boots up its main operating system and then the operating system itself becomes invisible to the ordinary user. As we automatically engage our thinking process trying to figure our way out of our problems, we never get to see the program that makes our thought process work the way it does. That is why most of us have no idea that we even have a program.

When you are using your computer, you cannot tell what your operating system is, or even that your computer *has* one. One way to see your computer's basic program is to turn your computer off, and watch the screen when you first turn the computer on again. The first thing that appears is the name of the program because the first thing your computer has to do is boot up the program so that it can function. In a similar way your mind first engages its programming before generating a thought, and it is in the moment before the thought appears that you can actually see the program.

The solution to our human dilemma does not involve learning complex formulas or accomplishing difficult tasks. It is, in fact, so simple that we overlook it again and again, just as it never occurred to Dorothy to look behind the curtain in the wizard's room, or that the ruby slippers on her feet could take her home.

My consciousness is being used by a mental program that determines all of the thoughts and images that my mind conceives, and thereby defines my reality. My task is simply to become aware of this. I only have to see for myself the mechanical patterning behind my thought process, and the rest will take care of itself.

As simple as this is, it remains quite difficult for most of us. Because we are constantly using our mental programming to interpret reality for us, it is usually impossible to see the programming for what it is. In a similar way, people could not see that the earth is a huge round ball floating in space, because we were standing on the ball. We were too close to it to see it in its entirety.

A Flat Earth

For a long time, our ancestors believed that the earth was flat because of what their senses told them. Stand anywhere looking out at the landscape and you see a relatively flat earth extending in all directions. Walk anywhere for any number of days, weeks, or years, and aside from going up hills and down valleys, you seem to be traversing one enormous plane.

For many early human societies, it was inconceivable that we were actually living on the surface of a globe so huge that at any given point it appeared flat to the human eye. Without an understanding of gravity, it was impossible to imagine our earth as a ball spinning in space. We naturally made up a story about the earth being a flat plane because this is what it looked like.

The idea of a flat earth is an example of a paradigm. It is a story or image that explains a fundamental aspect of our existence and gives our lives a context. The defining element of a paradigm is that we do not recognize it as merely a story – we believe whole-heartedly that it is real, and it forms the basis for our reality. In earlier periods of human history we made maps of a flat earth, and everything that we thought we knew about our world was based on this assumption. Then this story began to change.

The early Greek philosophers may have been the first ones in Western civilization to suggest that the earth was round. The impetus for this paradigm shift was systematic observation. Thinkers like Aristotle noted the shape of the shadow cast on the moon during a lunar eclipse, and the changing view of certain constellations of stars as one traveled south, and offered these as proof of a spherical earth.

Western history suggests that the shape of the earth was controversial from the time of the ancient Greeks and Romans through the first millennium after Christ. This makes sense when we consider the fundamental re-orientation that had to occur for people to accept the notion of living on a gigantic sphere, instead of a flat plane, as it appeared.

Because our perception of reality relies on fixed reference points, we are usually quite threatened by the prospect of a major paradigm changing. People who first promoted the idea of a round earth were often demonized and persecuted by the authorities of their time. Such a radical notion shook the foundations of their world and the people in power aggressively defended the obvious reality that the earth was flat.

It was not until the first great sailing ships were developed in Europe that we finally gained the capacity to travel around the earth and prove that it was indeed a globe and not a flat plane. The famous adventures of Columbus that resulted in the discovery of the Americas demonstrated that there was more to the earth than anyone in Europe had imagined. More recently with space travel we are able to see pictures of our earth from a distance, and the idea that we live on a ball spinning in space is something we finally can all witness for ourselves.

The Center of the Universe

Another example of a major historical paradigm was our belief that the earth was the center of the universe. From our perspective, it seems obvious that the sun, moon, stars, and planets all revolve around us. We can go outside and look up at the sky and watch this happen. So our ancestors naturally believed that we were at the center of things, until just a few centuries ago.

We now know that when we see the sun move through the sky, seeming to circle our planet, we are seeing an optical illusion created by our limited perspective. This is similar to the way a still train sitting in the station can feel as if it is moving when the train next to it begins to move. We see movement and assume that our train is moving, when it is not.

When we observe the sun, we see it traveling across the sky from east to west each day and naturally assume that the sun is circling around or passing over the earth. Yet, it is not the sun actually moving, but in fact is the earth spinning that makes it *look* as though the sun is moving.

Copernicus is known as one of the first people in Western history to suggest an alternative view of the earth based on his observations and calculations. He suggested around 1515 that the earth orbited around the sun, along with the other planets in our solar system. His ideas were supported by Galileo a century later when he was able to see what was happening in space through his newly-invented telescope.

It was inconceivable to most of humanity then that the earth was rotating around the sun, along with a host of other planets, and that we were only a small particle in an immense universe of many solar systems and galaxies. This notion was likely considered too absurd to merit any consideration, or too threatening to the dominant paradigm of the day to allow. Galileo's ideas conflicted with those of the all-powerful Catholic Church, and he was tried for heresy and sentenced to house arrest for the rest of his life.

This historic tragedy offers a clear example of how we become entrenched in our paradigms and resist any changes to our basic view of reality. It also demonstrates how dependent we are on having a fixed story that explains the world around us and our place in it. When that story is challenged, our reality seems threatened and we react to bolster and defend it. In this way we continually keep ourselves stuck in our *ideas* about what is real, instead of seeing reality directly for ourselves.

Paradigm Shift

An important lesson to learn from both of these historical examples is that *paradigms shift*. Our current view of reality is always just a theory – *it is not real*. Eventually, all of the paradigms or frameworks that we use to understand reality change. Basing our experience of reality on a paradigm therefore *ensures* that our lives will feel unstable because there is nothing absolute or real supporting our existence.

In both of these classic examples of major paradigm shifts, it is clear that our mistaken assumptions were due to the limits of *perception*. We trusted what we could see, not realizing that we were seeing an illusion caused by the inconceivable magnitude of the earth and the universe around it. And it was a new tool or capacity that we developed which finally expanded our perception and enabled us to see what was really happening.

A paradigm shift does not create a new story. It reveals a truth or reality that was always present, yet was merely not visible to us before. In the case of our discoveries about the earth, we simply could not see what was real until we developed sailing ships capable of circling the earth or telescopes able to see the other stars and planets clearly. Nothing changed in reality, but our new technologies enabled us to see our situation from a broader perspective. As a result, our *experience* of reality changed dramatically.

Looking back at our history can remind to us to question our basic assumptions about reality today. Given our past experience, it is entirely likely that we are still living with false beliefs about ourselves and our world. Any belief limits us because beliefs are based on our interpretations of our experience and not on what is actually happening. Relying on perception to interpret reality for us creates a sense of insecurity in our lives because we do not have a way to know for certain. We also feel a sense of being constricted, as we are limited within the confines of our paradigm.

A paradigm, like a computer program, enables me to do certain functions, yet it also *limits* my capacity to just those functions. A computer can be programmed to do an amazing array of tasks, yet the more that I use them, the more I come up against the limitations of the program. A computer screen cannot recognize an object such as a keyboard, as the woman in the previous story finally realized.

My deepest longing is to be unlimited and unrestricted. And my beliefs about reality always confine me to the limits of my understanding. Some of the sailors in the early sailing ships that explored the great oceans were reportedly terrified of falling off of the edge of the earth. It is easy to see how such a fear would limit their explorations and confine them within a world created by their illusions. Until I allow my perception to be altered by reality, I am stuck in a limited world of beliefs and ideas, assuming that my very survival depends on holding on to what I *think* is true.

Limited by Our Own Beliefs

Another important lesson to learn from our history is how major paradigm shifts are usually met with strong resistance. Despite clear evidence that shows us that we are wrong, human beings tend to cling to old beliefs to the bitter end. This is an inherent part of the way our minds are programmed, and points to a paralyzing aspect of perception. We tend to believe the *ideas* that we have about something more than our *actual direct experience* of it. We cling to familiar beliefs, thinking they are real, even when a new experience shows us the contrary.

People did not want to believe that the earth was round, nor that our planet revolved around the sun, because these realities challenged common beliefs that were based on common perceptions. Everyone could see that the earth was flat and the sun went around the earth. Few of our ancestors could stretch their perception enough to imagine that they were seeing an illusion. By clinging so tightly to their ideas in this way, they blinded and limited themselves.

Our true nature is unlimited, and any paradigm or finite definition of reality ultimately causes us to feel trapped and constricted. The Buddha pointed to our conditioned mind as the source of our suffering because we end up feeling stifled by it. In my late teenage years, I felt an intense dissatisfaction and internal pressure that was a result of me bumping up against the limits of my mental conditioning again and again. It felt like being inside a tight box, and all I wanted was to get out.

Many of us feel a sense of our lives being restricted by something and want desperately to be free. This sense of being trapped often accelerates in adolescence because that is when we come up against the edges of our programming repeatedly and feel the tightness of the box that our beliefs have created. That is why teens and young adults often become rebellious and act out in ways that hurt themselves and other people, such as being reckless with sex, alcohol, drugs, or violence. They are pushing back against whatever they think is limiting them in their attempts to be liberated.

Many of us continue this reactivity in some way throughout our lives. We often think that it is our parents, teachers, boss, spouse, government, church, or another group of people who are trying to control us. We then either lash out against them or become passively resistant, filled with resentment and anger toward whatever seems to be confining us.

You may be convinced that the pressure holding you down is coming from some outside force that is trying to limit you. It often seems so obvious that someone is restricting your freedom and happiness. Yet, it is not any of these imagined enemies that are really causing you to feel so boxed in. It is your own limited beliefs and blind determination to hold on to them that creates the constriction that you feel.

Consider for a moment that the edges that you keep bumping up against may come from an unconscious mental program that you are continually activating without knowing that you are doing so. This is hard to conceive, and I am not asking that you believe it. I am merely suggesting that you investigate this for yourself and see what you discover. If it is indeed a pre-determined mental framework that is causing you to feel powerless, this is actually good news, because it means that there is something you can do to free yourself.

———————— •◆• ————————

Take a moment now to notice some beliefs that are present in your mind. You are probably either agreeing or disagreeing with the ideas that you are reading here, and contrasting them with your own version of how things are.

Instead of focusing on the ideas themselves, notice the tension around your efforts to establish truth. Become aware of the struggle to reconcile competing ideas. See if you can feel the frustration and sense of futility that often accompanies this endeavor.

Now, let it all go. Allow the tension to simply fade away and surrender to not knowing anything for a moment. In the pause before you return to your judgments again you may feel uneasy.

You may also notice a bit of serenity and open space in your mind. If you do, allow yourself to breathe and relax into it.

———————— •◆• ————————

4

Waking Up

A spiritual teaching like that of the Buddha works to free us by revealing the paradigm or mental programming that we are using. It does nothing more than this, for to do so would only be to create a new paradigm. The essence of spiritual liberation or enlightenment is that *we do not require a paradigm or conceptual framework* in order to create a context for our existence. Our existence simply *is*, and does not need proof, explanation, or support of any kind.

Perhaps the defining characteristic of life is consciousness. And what distinguishes human consciousness from a computer is that we can function perfectly without a program. Most of us do not realize this yet and are living our lives entirely under the influence and limitations of a prescribed mental framework. The program has become so familiar that we no longer notice it, and we have become so dependent upon it that we cannot imagine life without it.

I often use my mind in the same way that I use a computer. Although the personal computer has only been widely used for the past fifteen years or so, many of us have become dependent on them to manage our daily lives. In a similar way, the thinking mind with its astonishing capacity for unlimited abstract thought and imagination has come to dominate our existence.

I tend to rely on my rational mind so exclusively that I am often not able to separate myself from my thoughts. The French philosopher Descartes, who was a defining voice in Western civilization, famously declared; "I think, therefore, I am." Most of us cannot distinguish *ourselves* from our *rational thought process*, and this is exactly the source of our problem, according to the Buddha.

Longing for Freedom

As a young man, I recognized a deep, unfulfilled longing that could not be soothed by anything in the world. No manner of pleasure, distraction, material comfort, wealth, or fame seemed likely to reach that deep hollow and fill it. Many of us are unwilling or unable to face this longing directly because we have no idea how to resolve it. We may have tried at some point to address our primal discomfort, yet our attempts usually fail miserably, and even the most optimistic among us become hardened in our belief that there is no cure.

This empty feeling was simply my innate longing for freedom from my mental programming. Until I decided to recognize this longing for what it was, and stopped trying to make it go away by feeding it candy or giving it trinkets to play with, my life contained a certain amount of despair and impotence. I became caught in an endless loop where all of my attempts to free myself fell short and I unconsciously affirmed the hopelessness of my situation again and again. This naturally led to chronic depression or anxiety from which I could get only temporary relief through addictive behaviors or medications.

The hard part of freeing ourselves is that we each have to activate the process on our own. We have to develop our capacity to see what is happening inside our own consciousness in order to recognize that we are bound by our mental programming and not by the circumstances of our life. This, however, is all that we have to do. Once we see our conditioning for what it is, our natural desire for freedom becomes awakened and takes over. A wild animal has only to recognize that it is caged, and then every fiber of its being wants to find a way out.

Of course this is different for an animal that has been raised in captivity. For domesticated pets, the cage that they live in is their world. The thought of getting out may not occur to them, or may even be frightening, because the cage is all that they know. And this is more like our predicament. We have lived with our programmed mind in charge of our life for so long that we can't remember any other way to be. The thought of doing without it frightens most of us, and we cling to our thoughts as an animal might cling to its cage, even when the door is left open and it is free to leave.

Yet, deep inside each one of us is a memory of freedom that we cannot erase. This vague notion haunts us and shadows our lives with a sense of confinement that we can't ever be quite sure about. We usually blame our limitation on factors outside of us that are beyond our control, and spend our lives fighting with or trying to escape from these. However, if we can just glimpse the patterned programming that controls our mind, we have a chance to see that we are imprisoned by nothing more than our own habits of thought.

Caught in a Virtual World

Perceptual mind is merely a mechanism for processing information, much like a computer. They both use a program that turns raw data into images or concepts. While these images may look and feel entirely real, they are only a *representation* of reality. I have become so used to filtering sensory experience through perception that I rarely even notice it happening. I only see the final result, which is an idea or belief about the way something is, and I often mistake this for the truth.

The basic problem with this dependency on rational thought is that it often does not correspond with what is actually happening. I often live, therefore, in an illusory world constructed by my mental images. This keeps a distance between myself and reality that limits me and results in chronic frustration and anxiety.

My idea of what is true usually does not match up with my experience, so I am continually trying to change what *is* happening to make it look more like what I think *should* be happening. The result is a perpetual struggle in which I seem to be constantly at odds with life.

Many of us sense that there is something false about the world, yet we can't quite put our finger on it. We know that something vital is missing, but we cannot say exactly what. We then try to fill our lives with an endless variety of new things and experiences, trying to find that missing piece.

As this process fails again and again to satisfy us, we become increasingly frantic to fill the void within, and often sink more deeply into despair. A closer look at how the mind creates the images that we mistake for reality may help us to understand what is happening.

The Mechanism of Mind

A computer is capable of amazing tasks. It can hold unlimited amounts of information, compare them in any conceivable way, and generate detailed images that appear astonishingly real. And the entire mechanism behind this capacity is a simple contrast between two fixed reference points. The whole digital system, which has so greatly enhanced our capacity for storing and transmitting information, is based on comparing the number one and the number zero, in infinite combinations.

If we look at how the rational mind works, we can see a stunning similarity to the digital system that computers use. As a computer requires a program, the rational mind requires a paradigm. The basis of both the digital system and our mental framework is contrasting two opposites. As we see in the digital world of computers, by using the tension or contrast between the numbers one and zero, it is possible to encrypt, organize, and transmit an infinite variety of data and images.

The polarity that our mental program uses to construct thoughts and images is established by a constant process of evaluation that occurs in our rational mind. The thinking mind is continually comparing opposing ideas such as good and bad, up and down, dark and light. The poles or opposites have to appear absolute for the mind to use them as a basis for perception. So we tend to solidify our basic values into finite reference points, and our whole conceptual reality formulates around these.

The basis of perception is the contrast between something that is absolutely good and something that is absolutely bad. Therefore each one of us is continuously establishing and reinforcing a basic value system, or designation of right and wrong. We each have some idea of what these are for ourselves, and we maintain them as pre-determined reference points so that we can formulate clear images and opinions.

Once we designate right and wrong, these arbitrary designations tend to fade into the background of our mind and, although we use them as the basis for each thought or idea, we pay little attention to them. That is why paradigm shifts are so disturbing to us. Our whole system of establishing what is real depends on reference points that are fixed. When these fixed reference points change, our image of the world that we based on them essentially crumbles.

The big paradigm shifts that I've described from our recorded history have been about significant physical reference points like the shape of the earth, and the place of our planet in the solar system. The paradigm shift that the Buddha describes, however, has to do with an entirely different realm. This is the realm of consciousness and the reference points that we use to establish our concept of ourselves.

The Limitations of Rational Thought

Our Western scientific method of careful observation has lead to amazing discoveries about the nature of the world we live in, yet we have not found an effective way to apply this process to our own consciousness. The closest we have come is our science of psychology. However, this science can never reveal the programming behind our rational mind *because it utilizes this programming*. As soon as we use the program, we immediately limit our capacity to see the program itself. In a similar way, we cannot see the earth as a round ball in space while we are standing on the earth.

While traditional Western psychology can describe many of the patterns of the mind and detail their results, it cannot offer a real solution to the problem of human suffering because it fails to recognize the underlying cause. That is why our use of psychiatry has focused on categorizing mental illnesses and developing drugs to control the symptoms, instead of actually healing the mind.

The more practical applications of psychology such as psychotherapy focus on analysis and behavior corrections that are getting closer to the real problem, yet are still limited in their effectiveness. While some Western therapeutic approaches recognize our underlying mental programming as the fundamental cause of our emotional pain, they often cannot free us from this programming entirely because they are working within perception. Most of these methods rely on some kind of diagnosis which engages the rational mind and thereby obscures the mechanism it uses.

The Buddha developed his capacity to look inward to his own consciousness, and in his determination to see how this process worked he found a way to use his mind *without engaging the programming of the mind*. The tool that he offers for this purpose is the practice of meditation in which we simply disengage from each thought as soon as we notice that we are thinking, and redirect our attention to a physical sensation happening in the present moment. By doing this over and over again we develop a field of awareness that utilizes our consciousness, but does not involve conceptual thought.

The Buddha's teaching invites us to look at the very nature of a paradigm and question our dependency on establishing points of reference in order to formulate ideas about our world. He suggests that the only purpose for these references is to enable the mind to manufacture its own version of reality. This means that we live in a world of our own making with no foundation that is real. And this explains the vague existential anxiety and sense of emptiness that permeates most of our lives.

The Buddha offers the tool of meditation to cultivate awareness so that we can observe our mind continuously attempting to create its own reality. He also offers us the reassurance that we do not need to make up images in order to exist or function in the world. He suggests that without any paradigm we return to our original state of wholeness. And it is this completion that finally satisfies our deepest longing, bringing the peace and contentment that we are searching for.

What is Progress?

In contrast to the Buddha's focus on observing consciousness and examining the basis of thought itself, Western science has focused primarily on understanding our physical world. By strengthening our capacity for perception, the scientific process has enabled us to better understand material things. Galileo learned how to construct a telescope that allowed him to see for himself that the sun did not revolve around the earth, as it appeared to us, but rather the earth revolved around the sun. This was a radical revelation that eventually changed our whole concept of our place in the universe. He and his predecessor Copernicus are sometimes credited with beginning modern science.

We have a long history in Western civilization of great thinkers and scientists who helped us to gain mastery over the world of matter. It seems that our strength has been in learning how things work around us, and as a result we have become a dominant culture capable of controlling vast amounts of resources for our own benefit. Yet now we are facing the stark realization that instead of securing our future, our attempts to manipulate and control our world may be leading to our own destruction.

We cannot blame great thinkers like Copernicus, Galileo, Newton, or Einstein for the mess that we find ourselves in. They were merely trying to reveal the truth about our world, and respond to our innate human longing to know what is real. The problems that we face now are caused by what we have *done* with the information that our scientists gave us. Their discoveries have often been used to accumulate power and assert control in an effort to contain our chronic fear and insecurity, instead of simply expanding our understanding of life and increasing our awareness of truth.

While we normally view a scientific discovery as an expansion of our understanding and celebrate it for the increased awareness and knowledge that it offers us, we invariably use most new information for the purpose of making money, controlling our environment, or dominating other people. Our new discoveries are usually channeled into technology intended for use in industry or war.

It should be clear to us by now that our capacity to dominate our environment and other people through our use of technology has far outpaced our understanding of life. While we have dramatically increased our ability to change the world around us to suit our desires, we have not managed to mature much beyond our basic animal instincts.

We may adopt certain rules and moral codes that dictate how to behave in a more civilized way, but as a culture we have not done the inner work of becoming more conscious. The result is that while we can harness tremendous power, we lack the spiritual maturity to use it wisely. This explains why we find ourselves on the brink of a total catastrophe brought about by our own material "progress."

Inner Development

Our Western civilization is tragically lacking in the realm of inner development. While we have access to great spiritual teachings such as those of Christ, we have used them mostly to concentrate power in the hands of a few individuals, much as we have used the discoveries of science. The Catholic Church became a dominant institution in Europe and the New World that rivaled the great monarchs and was focused primarily on accumulating power and control, rather than teaching the message of Jesus.

While Western culture has been fixated on exploring the natural world and utilizing its resources to develop personal empires, people in some parts of Asia have been more interested in exploring the inner landscapes of human consciousness. These people saw their frontier within their own mind and developed elaborate ways of understanding and harnessing the power of consciousness itself.

The Buddha was a defining part of this rich heritage of inner development and he left behind detailed maps and instructions about how to navigate the world within us. Five hundred years before Christ, when early Western philosophers like Pythagoras in ancient Greek and Rome were discussing the shape of the earth, the Buddha was teaching people in ancient India how to focus their awareness in order to see clearly what was happening within their own consciousness.

While our Western scientific discoveries have revealed astonishing truths about our world and enabled us to accumulate great resources, they have not changed our basic mental programming. This is why, despite all of our material advancement, our lives are still full of illness, stress, and danger, and we seem to have ever more to fear.

The discoveries of the Buddha, however, centered on transforming the mind. As he learned to focus his awareness in the way that we might learn to focus a telescope, and pointed his focused attention inwardly toward his own consciousness, he discovered an astonishing revelation about his own reality. Just as Galileo saw the moon and sun and other planets in our solar system from a new angle through his telescope, the Buddha saw his own mind from a new angle through his focused awareness.

The Buddha experienced what is perhaps the most fundamental paradigm shift – a change in his basic consciousness. This happened when he witnessed his own mind from a new perspective and saw clearly the mechanism behind his own mental thought process.

He then realized that he was *not* this mechanical process of contrasting one thing with another, and he existed entirely apart from his perceptions. His revelation is similar to the way our experience of the moon changes once we see it for ourselves with a telescope. The old assumptions tend to fall away more easily once we have the means to see reality as it is.

The unique aspect to this spiritual paradigm shift is that it concerns our own identity. It is a revelation about *who we are*. As such, it directly answers the existential anxiety about our place in the world that troubled me as a young man and disturbs so many of us deep down.

The Buddha's teaching suggests that our deep-rooted fear and uncertainty about life is caused by not knowing who we really are. Having such basic knowledge obscured predictably leads to a sense of discomfort and uneasiness about life. And the solution, as he discovered, is to use our own capacity for awareness to look directly at the nature of our innermost being.

Being Asleep

It became clear to me in that monastery thirty-five years ago that we in the West desperately needed the kind of wisdom that the Buddha has to offer. I had gone to the East searching for meaning and a way to understand the essence of life itself. And I stumbled upon a living teaching and practice whose primary purpose was to empower me to see for myself the nature of reality.

As I practiced meditation daily and the sensation of breath moving in my body became a steady field of reference, I began to recognize that I was awakening from a dream. I saw that the frustration and anxiety that had launched my quest came from the sense that I was living in an artificial world. Everything appeared fake, I deeply longed for truth, and my foremost desire was to be real. I resonated with the notion that the world around me was some kind of facade, and I felt an urgency to get to the bottom of it.

The Buddha used the idea of waking from a dream throughout much of his teaching. When we are unconsciously following a pre-determined mental pattern, as most of us are, it is like being asleep. We fall into patterns of thought and behavior that are determined by our assumptions, and they become so familiar that we no longer question or even notice them. In this way, we go through the motions of our life automatically, without questioning the basic premise.

As the saying goes, we are creatures of habit. This is obvious if you watch how animals or children behave. They are often slow and cautious in trying something new; however, once they get used to doing something in a certain way, they tend to repeat that behavior over and over again. This is why it is so important to train children or animal pets when they are young. The habits that we learn as we are growing up tend to be the ones that stick with us for our entire life.

The reason that we are creatures of habit is that our perceptual mind is set up to work within programmed patterns, just as a computer is set up to work with software. Rational thought requires a recipe or formula in order to function, and instinctively mechanizes everything we do. We love to use our minds in this way because we don't have to think about what to do next. It is like pushing a button on our computer, washing machine, or coffee maker. The machine does its function and we are free to do something else.

Perceptual mind is inclined to go on automatic whenever possible. It will make a system out of everything and find a mechanical way of approaching tasks because that means we don't have to pay attention. Once it figures out an automated way of doing something, the perceptual mind is free to wander in the ocean of imagination and memory.

We develop habits of thought and behavior because it seems to make our lives easier. Notice how you approach your life as a routine, doing much the same thing in the same way day after day. You may like to sit in that chair in just that way, eat that food, and wear those clothes. And notice how you feel when something disrupts your routine and makes you change the way you usually do something.

These habitual routines often give you a sense of comfort and security. They are predictable and easy and you usually feel safe in them. Yet, they also tend to deaden you because you don't have to actually *be there* for them to go on. You can go about the day with your attention off in some other place and time.

The result of operating within set patterns like this is that life takes on a vague fuzziness. Everything begins to feel superficial and false. You do not value your own presence and things seem to go on around you without needing much of your attention or care. You can end up feeling that your presence is not important, your life feels increasingly more empty and hollow, and you do not understand why.

Our use of technology tends to increase our capacity to function automatically. Most of our newer tools enable common tasks to happen without us having to think about them. We often value the ease and freedom that this seems to give us, yet we can end up being profoundly confused about our purpose. As technology enables more everyday tasks to happen without us being there, we find ourselves increasingly wondering about our place in the world.

When you follow the conditioned program of your mind and fall into habitual patterns of day to day living, you are "asleep at the wheel" of your life, and experiences pass you by like scenery on the highway. The programming of your mind automatically removes you from direct experience by making mental images out of sensory data. It is like going on a car trip and taking a lot of pictures without getting out of the car. You experience the journey through pictures instead of actually being there. This can result in feeling lost and alone, removed from direct experiences, and only knowing about life through hindsight.

Becoming More Awake

The alternative to this is to become more awake. Waking up is not an abstract ideal or final destination. It is what you are here to do, yet it is not a goal to achieve some time off in the future. Waking up can only happen in this moment, and it happens by simply being present with what you are doing now.

In each moment you are either more awake or more asleep. There appears to be a gradual process of becoming more awake that allows for you to do it in your own time. Yet, in reality, time is not involved and there is no learning required. Unlike any other achievement that we know, waking up is not a step-by-step process that the perceptual mind can direct and measure, and this is what makes it so difficult.

None of your learning patterns apply to waking up. Waking up is a decision that you make to be present, when you reach the end of your tolerance for living life from a distance. You don't learn *how* to do it. There isn't a way, there is only the will. When you want to wake up and be real more than anything else, it begins to happen by itself.

Think about waking up from a dream that you are having when you are asleep at night. There is no way to *learn* to wake yourself up, or to practice waking up. The fact that you are asleep means that a part of your consciousness is not present – the very part that you would use to learn something or make something happen. Once you realize that you are sleep-walking through your life, you have to find another way to wake yourself up. If you think of it as a skill that you have to perfect, you end up merely prolonging the dream.

The Buddha taught the practice of mindfulness, which is simply bringing awareness to everything that you think or do. Waking up is just paying attention to your moment-to-moment experience and becoming more aware of what is actually happening now.

———————— •◆• ————————

Notice where your feet are right now. Where are your hands? Where do you feel pressure or tension in your body? What position is your body in, and how does it feel?

Take a moment now, close your eyes, and merely notice what you can feel in your body in this moment, without drawing any conclusions about it.

———————— •◆• ————————

Chances are that you were surprised by what you noticed. Perhaps you had a tight neck, or your feet were crossed, or you were twitching your hands. When you notice the physical sensations that you are having in this moment, you are becoming more awake. You are noticing experiences that are there, but you were not aware of. This is waking up. It is simply seeing what is right there in front of you, and has been all along.

If you were paying attention to your mind, you also probably noticed a running commentary about what you noticed in your body. Your mind might judge your body as fat or your posture as poor. It might diagnose the tension you noticed in your legs and begin planning what to do about it. It may have evaluated you and begun making comparisons with other people around you.

If you get caught up in these thought streams you become lulled back to sleep. You stop noticing the way your legs, fingers and face feel, and begin living again within the abstract images in your head. They are difficult to resist because the mental images are often so much more complex and colorful than the direct experience of feeling our body from the inside. As long as you believe that the images in your mind are more real than the sensations in your body, you will continue to fall back into the programmed patterns of perception and become more asleep.

The practice of meditation is merely a way that you can begin to recognize your direct experience and distinguish it from your mental conclusions *about* that experience. The more that you bring your attention back to an actual experience, the more you get used to living in the moment and rely on your senses, rather than your mental images, to inform you about what is real.

5

Seeing Beyond Perception

Most of the things that I think I know about my world are a result of the way my mind processes information through perception. Perception is a mechanical way of taking in sensory data, comparing it with other data, and categorizing it. This process perpetuates itself repeatedly without end in my effort to understand the world. Yet, the "understanding" that I achieve in this way is superficial at best. I only know something relative to something else and can only define it in relative terms such as "more" or "less."

My thinking mind is continuously occupied with this process of refining raw experience into concepts or ideas, and then projecting these onto the world around me. The mind does this so rapidly and completely that it produces the experience of a seamless world within which the personality I call "me" lives. I engage my mind in this way often, without ever questioning the entire premise, because I think this is necessary to achieve an understanding of myself and of my world.

I rarely notice that the process never reaches a definite conclusion about anything. I end up with vague notions or theories about the way things are and settle for these as truth. Meanwhile, my life is fraught with an undercurrent of doubt and uncertainty because the conclusions that I come up with to explain the world *keep changing.*

Caught Up in Illusions

Perception works much like an old reel-to-reel film projector. The film itself is just a series of still pictures on a long plastic tape that are run continuously in front of a lamp that projects the images onto a screen. The result is a moving picture which looks so realistic that I can become caught up in it as though it were actually happening.

As long as I look at the screen, I am likely to get drawn into the story and forget that I am merely watching a movie. This is the excitement of a good film. I react to what happens to the characters with genuine emotion and feel that I am part of their lives for a moment. Yet, if I stop the projector and look at the film itself, I only see a long string of still pictures and the story vanishes. It becomes obvious then that the characters that seemed so alive and real were only an illusion projected onto the screen.

In much the same way, by stringing together an endless procession of comparative evaluations, my perceptual mind creates the illusion of a world that appears very real. Yet, just as a movie is an illusion of reality made up by a continuous stream of images, the world that I see is merely a projection of a continuous stream of thoughts. This does not mean there is no world, or that I do not exist. It simply means the world is not as I see it, and I am not as I see myself.

This is not such an outlandish conclusion if we consider the model of reality presented to us by modern physics. The current theory is that all matter is made up of tiny particles that we cannot see, called atoms, which are constantly in motion and consist mostly of empty space. We have used this model to understand how our own body is built from microscopic genetic codes called DNA, and to create the massive release of energy in nuclear bombs. Yet, just as it is difficult to imagine that we are living on a giant ball in space, it does not make rational sense that solid objects such as a rock, table, or our own bodies are really made up of tiny moving particles.

It is difficult for our perceptual mind to see the ephemeral nature of matter. Without the use of a powerful microscope we cannot see the tiny particles that make up solid objects, and atomic theory remains an abstract concept for most of us. In the same way, we may consider the idea that the world around us is merely an illusion projected by our thoughts, yet few of us actually experience this.

I am not trying to get you to believe in this idea, but rather I want to prompt you to test it out for yourself. The value of a self-awareness practice such as meditation is that it enables you to see how an uninterrupted string of thoughts distorts your direct experience and creates your own version of reality.

Finding Stillness

As the practice of Buddhist meditation has been adapted from the monasteries of Asia to our Western culture, it has taken the form of intensive retreats that last anywhere from a day to three months. Seven to ten days is a typical length of time for a meditation retreat in the Therevadin Buddhist tradition. Often referred to as Insight Meditation or Vipassana, this type of retreat involves following a schedule of sitting and walking meditation periods, interspersed with meals and personal time. The conditions on a retreat such as this include silence and no eye contact, and thus create a perfect laboratory for observing the mind.

When I first tried meditation, I was often overwhelmed by the chaos of my thoughts and the idea of stilling them seemed impossible. Many people new to meditation find that, instead of getting more quiet, the practice seems to make their minds more active. More likely, you have gotten so used to ignoring the constant chatter of your thoughts, or distracting yourself from them, that you simply do not realize the volume of your background commentary until you are still and quiet for a moment.

In a similar way, I often do not notice the ticking of a clock until I sit quietly. As I set myself up for a period of meditation, I may think that the space is perfectly silent. Then, a few moments into the sitting, I notice a tick-tock sound that did not seem to be there before. Sometimes a simple background noise like this that I ordinarily don't notice can sound like thunder in my ears once everything else stops moving. When I sit still and quiet myself, I suddenly become more sensitive and aware of things I didn't notice before. And that is exactly the point.

Shutting out the World

A common way of dealing with things that bother us is to shut them out. The process of perception affords us an extraordinary capacity for denial that enables us to simply ignore things that we don't want to see or hear, and this is how many of us try to cope with the chaos and confusion that we commonly encounter in life.

When I am confronted with something that I don't like, I often turn away or distract myself with something else. This is why those of us living in big cities often become so calloused and aloof. There are so many unwanted sounds, smells, encounters with people, or visual images creating so much cacophony around us that we become increasingly shut off and numb in an effort to protect ourselves.

Notice how often you may distract yourself with music, television, movies, video games, radio, cell phones, email, text messages, or whatever draws your attention away from what is happening in your life in this moment. It is common now to see people going about their lives with tiny speakers plugged into their ears or constantly looking at a screen, instead of taking in whatever is going on around them. Our amazing electronic devices greatly enhance our capacity to create a virtual world, and we can easily become lost in this world.

Shutting out your mental chatter or external interference in this way requires that you shut yourself down and become less sensitive and aware. While this strategy may work in the short run to give you a bit of peace, it eventually wears you down as you become more and more insulated from life and isolated in the self-contained bubble of your own world. You become less tolerant and require more protection in order to function. And eventually you can feel so disconnected from your surroundings that your life loses all sense of meaning and purpose and you feel afraid and anxious most of the time.

This was the state I was in before I left for Sri Lanka, and I knew that I had to do something about it. I could tell that I was becoming more numb and closed off from the world, and I could not just ignore that and go on with my life.

When I returned from Sri Lanka I eventually met up with my former college roommate who had suggested meditation to me. I explained all that had happened and what my life was about now, hoping that he would understand something about the transformation I was experiencing. After I had explained my new direction, his first response was, "Why would you want to become more sensitive in this world?"

My friend understood how harsh and abrasive the world could be and he was coping with this, as most of us do, by shutting himself down and becoming less sensitive. Becoming more sensitive meant to him simply getting more hurt or being more overwhelmed.

Seeing Through the Illusion

It may seem as though television, computers, or other digital electronics are the problem as more people become addicted to them. Yet all these devices are doing is furthering our capacity for living in a world created by our imagination. Take all of these away and you are still left with your own mind doing exactly the same thing on a more subtle and less visible level.

The problem with living in a virtual world defined by the thoughts in your mind is simply that it is not real. Imagine that your life was merely a projection on a movie screen. Much of the time you might be engaged and you would forget that it isn't real. Yet your life would always have a feeling of being make-believe and temporary, and you would never have a sense of fulfillment or completion. You would also likely sense how fragile and fleeting your world is, and this would undermine your life with a constant sense of insecurity.

The Buddha highlights our fundamental discontent or existential anxiety and suggests that our suffering comes from mistaking our thoughts about ourselves and our world for the truth. This creates a sense of vulnerability and futility that we usually try to cover up either by enhancing our ego or ignoring our fear and insecurity. Yet all this effort does not resolve our basic uneasiness because it does not address the superficiality created by investing our thoughts with reality.

One way to find a genuine resolution to anxiety is to look directly at the problem instead of away from it. Consider that the problem could be in your own mind, and not caused by something outside of you. This is a big step for most of us and cannot be achieved by merely understanding the idea. It is possible to see for yourself that stress originates within your own thought patterns. And this is exactly what the practice of meditation can show you.

When my life feels hectic, it is easy to imagine how nice it would be to get away from it all and go someplace where I have no responsibilities except to take care of myself. I may fantasize about a remote tropical island, or a quiet meditation retreat where there are no pressures or distractions. I tend to assume that my problems in life are caused by what is going on around me, and if I can step away from all that for a moment, I will be at peace.

Yet, when I do manage to get to such a vacation spot or retreat, my experience is usually quite different from what I imagined. I soon discover that my life is just as full of chaos and stress as it was before, and my mind cannot let go of the problems that I tried to leave behind. Even if I succeed in letting go of my familiar problems, I soon begin to feel anxious about my immediate surroundings and create a whole new set of difficulties for myself.

If I pay attention, it becomes obvious that I have a *mental habit of anxiety and fear* that I cannot easily let go of. While this may at first seem to be a discouraging revelation, it is in fact the beginning of finding a real solution. I first have to see how I habitually create struggles for myself in my mind before I can find a sustained sense of peace. On a meditation retreat, this is often the first thing that I notice.

Letting Go of Thoughts

As I sit, my body upright in a relaxed and alert position, and try to bring my attention to bear on the simple sensations that accompany my natural breathing, I begin to be aware of my mental habits in a new way. It becomes quickly obvious that my mind cannot stop thinking, even for a moment. If I have the idea that meditation is about stopping the mind, I can easily see myself as failing and eventually give up in despair. Yet, if I consider that the practice is not about *making* something happen, but simply about being aware of what *is* happening, I can stay with it, knowing that there is no end goal aside from my own presence.

Bringing my attention back to my breath again and again simply gives me a new reference point that is not a thought or idea. Instead of referring constantly to what I *think* about something, I learn to come back to a tangible present moment experience that does not require interpretation – it just *is*.

Allowing a sensation to simply *be* is revolutionary. I normally run every experience through the filter of my conceptual mind without being aware of what I am doing. I have become so entrenched in the world of perception that I often only pay attention to the conclusion my thinking mind comes up with, and rarely notice the direct experience that preceded it.

My immediate experiences come to me through the sensations of touch, smell, sound, taste, and sight that precede my thoughts. This sensory information appears to be so simple and ordinary that I normally disregard it as meaningless and irrelevant. I look instead to the elaborate images and ideas that my mind generates, assuming that the meaning of life lies in them. This is like getting lost in a computer game or movie, and looking to these alluring dramas to fulfill myself.

Because I have become so addicted to the dramas created by my imagination, it takes a while to take my attention away from them. This is why a simple practice like bringing my attention back to the breath over and over again can be so difficult - and so useful. Each time I interrupt a thought, and refocus my attention on a present moment sensation, it diminishes the power of my thinking mind to lure me into its stories.

I remember distinctly the moment that I was able to consciously let go of a thought for the first time. I was trying to focus my awareness on breathing and suddenly realized that I was deeply engaged in a thought and had lost track of my breath entirely. I redirected my attention to my nostrils where I had been instructed simply to feel the air moving in and out, and was able to connect with my breathing again. I then noticed that I had let go of the thought that had been so compelling just a moment ago, and was amazed to realize that the images and ideas simply vanished!

Up until that experience, I had practiced a fierce allegiance to my mind, always tending my thoughts and trying to bring them to some conclusion. I assumed that this was the way in which I would piece together a whole story that would finally make sense out of all my random memories, emotions, desires, and fantasies. When I realized that I could simply interrupt a thought and let it go, and my world did not fall apart, I was astonished.

Becoming the Witness

As I learn to focus my direct awareness through a practice like meditation, I gain the capacity to witness my thoughts instead of being caught up in them all the time. Meditation is not trying to force the mind to be still and quiet, but merely being with my mental process just as I learn to be with the breath coming in and out of the body. The practice teaches me to observe all sensory experiences with neutrality, as just phenomenon with no particular meaning or relevance to me.

I begin by observing the sensations of breathing in sitting practice, and then learn to focus on the sensations of my feet and legs moving and touching the floor in walking practice. Gradually I expand my focus to include all the physical sensations of seeing, hearing, smelling, touching, and tasting. And finally I include my thoughts as just another sensation coming and going.

Usually I am so identified with my thoughts that observing them impartially is impossible. That is why it is useful to begin to meditate using simple physical sensations as the primary object. I am learning to merely observe without reacting or formulating an opinion about what is happening, and it is much easier to do this in the beginning with sensations like breathing which I do not invest with so much meaning. As I develop a capacity to witness physical sensations and mental images without reacting to them, the restlessness of my body and clamor of my mind gradually begins to subside.

Stilling the Water

Imagine that your consciousness is a clear lake and your thoughts are the waves caused by the wind. As long as the wind is blowing, you cannot see below the surface of the water because it is covered with ripples. You naturally would focus your attention on the surface of the water because that is all you can see. If the wind dies down, however, and the surface of the water becomes still, you can then see deep into the lake and all that is underneath the surface becomes apparent.

As long as the wind is blowing, there is nothing that you can do to make the ripples on the surface of the lake go away. You cannot push them away or force them to flatten out. All your efforts to still the water in this way will only make more waves. To flatten out the surface of the lake through some mechanical means would require an enormous effort, and as soon as you became exhausted and stopped, the wind would make waves again. The only thing that stills the surface of the water in a sustained way so that you can see through it is when the wind stops blowing.

In a similar way, there is nothing that you can do to still your body or quiet your mind. Any efforts to force your body to sit still or push your thoughts away only result in more tension and agitation and make it impossible to see into your own consciousness. It is your attention to your thoughts that stirs them up and keeps them going continuously, just as the wind stirs the surface of the lake. Then all that you can see is your own thoughts because the consciousness beneath them is obscured.

All that you can do to enable yourself to become aware of what is going on beneath your thinking mind is to allow your thoughts to subside by withdrawing your attention from them. Just as the lake becomes calm once the wind stops, your mind becomes calm once you take your attention away from your thoughts. Turning your attention away from your thoughts is like taking the wind away from the lake. The surface instantly becomes smooth and clear, and then you can see through it.

It doesn't require effort to do this in the way that you are used to applying force or using your will to make something happen. You cannot use these familiar means to quiet your mind because anything that you *do* will make more disturbance. Quieting the mind is an *undoing* or letting go of making anything happen. It is so difficult simply because most of us are not used to letting go of control in this way.

Meditation does not require learning anything new or becoming better at doing something. It simply requires a clear intention and desire for peace. Once your thoughts no longer command your attention in the way that they do now, you naturally let them go and the mind becomes still. You begin this process simply by becoming aware of your thoughts and seeing how arbitrary and fickle your rational mind really is.

———————— •◆• ————————

Take a moment now to close your eyes, sit back, and relax your body. Breathe deeply into your belly a few times, and let go with each out-breath.

Now, begin to notice the thoughts coming into your mind, without reacting to them. Don't try to do anything except to recognize each thought as it comes.

When you become aware of a thought, bring your attention back to the breath in your belly. Notice your belly rising and falling with the in-breath and out-breath.

Notice what happens to the thought. Where does it go?

———————— •◆• ————————

This exercise introduces you to the simple practice of awareness of breathing. More detailed instructions will follow later in this book. For now, simply notice the momentary disorientation and sense of stillness that happens when you let go of a thought. With practice, this spacious presence can be available to you any time that you focus on it.

Distorting Reality

A meditation retreat is designed to create a neutral space around you so that you can see how your mind is constantly interpreting your experience. The idea is to create a blank screen with few familiar external reference points, so that you can get a better look at what the mind is projecting. In the tradition of Insight Meditation, retreats are held in silence with no eye contact between participants. With no verbal or visual exchanges, there is little of the usual information to base evaluations on, yet most people continue to make up judgments and opinions about everyone and everything around us.

With practice, I can begin to *see* the thoughts in my mind instead of becoming absorbed in them. The person next to me moves their sitting place in the meditation hall and I think that they don't like me and are trying to get away from me. Another person seems quite disciplined about their practice and I compare myself with them, concluding that I am not very good at meditation. If I can notice the process of my mind, instead of getting caught up in the content, there is a great opportunity to see how my mind distorts experiences and fabricates stories like this that have no basis in reality.

If I pay attention in my daily life, I can see the mind's patterning as well. I may be driving in traffic when another driver pulls in front of me, and I think that they don't like me or are trying to get back at me for something that I did wrong. If I step back from my thoughts and observe the pattern behind them, I see how my mind draws convincing conclusions about things it knows nothing about.

I have no idea why the person in the retreat moved away from me, or the other driver cut me off. Most likely, the other person was not paying attention to me at all. When I judge the quality of other people's meditation by the way they sit or walk, I am simply constructing my own reality. I have no way to know what is going on inside another person's thoughts. In these situations, my mind is making stories up out of pure imagination. Yet, the stories are so convincing that I often end up believing them.

A man once came to see me for meditation instruction. He had learned to sit in the Zen Buddhist style and had perfect form. He could sit cross-legged in full lotus position for an hour without moving a muscle. When I asked him what was going on in his mind, he told me that his thoughts were all over the place. He confessed that he had put all of his effort into looking like he was good at meditation, yet he had not done anything to focus his mind, and inside he was as scattered and confused as ever. Someone sitting with him on retreat could easily conclude that he was much better at meditation because he sat so perfectly, yet this was far from the truth.

When our ancestors believed that the earth was flat or the sun revolved around the earth, they were being fooled by their perception. Just so, we are being fooled now by our perception that the thought stream running through our mind is representing reality. Many of us are so dependent on using thought to define our experience that we can no longer tell the difference between reality and our thoughts *about* reality.

Deluded

Mistaking our thoughts for reality leads to a tremendous amount of suffering and dysfunction in our lives. Because we cannot tell the difference between something that *we think* is happening, and something that *is* happening, we react to events that are not really occurring. If I cannot separate what really happened from what I think happened, my life becomes a tangled web of distortions and I become caught in an endless series of reactions that do not address my real concerns or needs. This is the plight most of us find ourselves in, and it is why the Buddha taught that we are deluded and our delusion leads to suffering.

I may be sensitive about not being included because as a child I thought that my parents did not listen to or value my input and I was repeatedly treated as if my ideas did not matter. If my wife makes a major decision without asking me what I think, I can easily jump to the conclusion that she is excluding me. I then may make up a story about how she does not value my input, and this in turn triggers my old feelings of hurt, frustration, and anger.

I would likely become upset and accuse her of shutting me out, or I might treat her in a similar way to "show her how it feels." As we all know, these common reactions of blame and retaliation wreak havoc with personal relationships and often lead to painful struggles that end up damaging the trust and intimacy between people. In this way, we can end up tragically destroying the very relationships that we cherish the most, and cause ourselves great loss and suffering.

This common experience in relationships is the result of not being able to tell the difference between my conclusion about what happened, and what really happened. The actual event that triggers an emotional explosion is often innocent and benign. My wife probably forgot to tell me, or simply thought that I would not be interested or have the time to discuss such details. She would likely be surprised and hurt by the intensity of my emotional response, and could easily react defensively herself. In this way, these simple misunderstandings can escalate into destructive conflicts between people.

We normally try to remedy such difficult situations by assigning blame or trying to determine whose story is correct. We tend to focus on who is right and who is wrong to help us sort things out. Yet, this approach only gets us further into conflict, as each of us believes that we are right and the other is wrong, and both of us struggle to defend our position.

When we try to figure our way out of a conflict, we often dig ourselves in deeper because we unconsciously refer back to the basis of perception – the idea that someone is right and someone is wrong – which is where the conflict started in the first place. In this way, our perceptions do not resolve our struggles – they *cause* them. And if we continue to trust our perceptions, we may continue to feel overwhelmed by life's seemingly irresolvable conflicts.

6

Religion and Spirituality

After my initiation in the monastery in Sri Lanka, a great fire had been ignited within me. I saw that it was possible for a human being to become complete, and understood finally that this was what I was here to do. I recognized the man who was called the Buddha as a person who had done this, and he became a role model for me.

I became curious about who Christ was as soon as I returned from my time in Asia. Having seen him only through the eyes of formal religion, I had no idea about his true message. I had learned of the great atrocities committed by the Christian church over the last centuries, and had good reason to suspect anything related to Jesus. Yet, as I learned more about him and his teachings, I was astonished to realize that he had an experience much like that of the Buddha, and that their teachings were entirely similar. The only differences I was able to find were ones of language and context.

Misunderstanding God

Christ used the idea of God to designate the infinite creative intelligence that we are all part of, while Buddha expressed the same concept as an infinite, spacious emptiness. This demonstrates the limitations of language to express what we can only know through direct experience, and shows how words can only approximate truth. Another difference seems to be that while the teachings of Jesus became systematically buried beneath layers of institutionalized religion, the Buddha's message remained more intact and accessible, in part because the practice of meditation was kept alive.

Using a term like God to describe the ultimate intelligence behind all life is certainly a practical and simple way to discuss reality. Yet, it is also invites misunderstanding as we see repeatedly in the history of deistic religions. Many of us feel uncomfortable with the notion of an infinite intelligent source that is beyond our capacity to define or describe. So we usually picture God as a supreme version of ourselves with all the inconsistencies of human behavior, and tend to limit our idea of God to concepts that are familiar to us.

When we use a word like God, we usually formulate an image, like an old man with a long white beard, which obscures the experience of infinite intelligence that the word is trying to convey. The Buddha merely sought to eliminate this possibility by calling ultimate reality emptiness. What he meant is that it is entirely empty of concepts or anything that our rational mind can recognize. God, or the infinite source of life, is essentially *beyond perception*.

I imagine that the Buddha chose not to use the word God to describe our ultimate source, and instead used the idea of emptiness, because emptiness or void leaves no room for human concepts to fill in. As soon as we name something, we think that we can know or understand it through our use of concepts and ideas. Yet, the absolute source of life can never be understood in this way, and to try to do so only ends up reducing it to an artificial façade.

A Sacred Map

I wondered why the teachings of Jesus had not jumped out at me when I was going through my deep searching before I left for Asia. Jesus was certainly a familiar figure, however, nothing of the magic or power of his teaching came through to me. All I could see then was the heavy morality and rigid formulas of the church, and this did not interest me at all.

I realized that Jesus' teachings had become so encrusted within the religion of Christianity that the essential message in them was obscured. I began to see how the Buddha's teachings were also obscured by the religion of Buddhism that dominated the culture of Sri Lanka. Yet, because these religious beliefs were not my own, I was not weighed down by them and could more easily see and access the original underlying message.

Both of these teachers, Buddha and Christ, focused their teachings on the ultimate meaning and purpose of life. They each gave us a map showing a way out of our human predicament. They both recognized and taught that ultimate fulfillment and freedom lay beyond the realm of perceptual mind. Yet, until I realize that I don't need it, perception seems to be the only way that I have to navigate here. So the maps are essential because they make the way visible to perception.

A spiritual path is a way of cultivating the conditions within my mind to have an experience. As such, it is like a map showing me how to get to a certain destination. Just as it takes some time and effort to understand and use a map, it may take some time and effort to understand and use a spiritual teaching. Yet, the point is never to become an expert on the map. The point is to have the experience that the map is pointing to.

These maps show us a way out of our world of conceptual thought, yet they have to work *within* this world in order for us to understand them. The challenge of a spiritual teaching is to engage us in our process of comparative evaluation long enough to convince us that the very process that we are using to understand the teaching is the source of our problem. A true spiritual teaching therefore aims to make itself unnecessary. Once you reach your destination, you no longer need the map, and the idea is to let it go.

Spiritual Experience

When I think of spiritual experience, my conceptual mind can only imagine a superlative sensory experience. In the beginning, I was expecting a dramatic moment accompanied by flashing lights and thunder claps. I assumed that a spiritual experience must be an extraordinary event that overwhelms all of my senses. Yet a true spiritual experience is usually more subtle than this, and when I was looking for a dramatic event I was often disappointed.

A spiritual experience happens when my paradigm or context for reality shifts, and I see common everyday things from an entirely different angle. It is really just seeing what has been there all along, but was obscured by the process of perception. Because I am not used to seeing beyond perception, it can seem like there is nothing there at first.

Imagine walking into a dark room after being out in full sunlight. At first you cannot see anything and may think that the room is empty. Your mind often then "plays tricks on you," and soon you are imagining all sorts of dangers lurking in the darkness. It is common to become afraid in the dark because you cannot see what is there, and your impulse may be to leave the room or turn on a light.

However, if you stand still and wait a moment, slowly your eyes adjust to the darkness and you begin to see objects in the room. After some time, you can look around and see everything that is there clearly. Nothing has changed. It is just that your eyes slowly adjusted to the darkness and then you could see what was actually there, instead of what you imagined was there. This is what a spiritual experience is like and why spiritual growth is often referred to as becoming more awake.

In a similar way, I often feel some fear and apprehension about swimming in a pond, lake, or ocean if I cannot see what is under the surface. I love swimming on a hot day more than anything else, yet I still feel some anxiety about entering the water if the surface is choppy. I cannot help but imagine large water creatures that might be waiting to devour me, or sharp objects underwater that might tear at my skin. Yet, if the water becomes still and I can see into the depths below, my fear disappears immediately because I can see what is there.

Perception obscures your natural inner vision so that you cannot see anything at first when you turn your attention toward your own consciousness. It is common to become uncomfortable or afraid of the enormous emptiness that you find when you try to look beneath the constant chatter of your mind. You may imagine things that are not there and feel lost in the vast emptiness, missing the familiar references of ideas and judgments.

Yet gradually, by practicing awareness, you become able to see your internal landscape just as you can see around a dark room once your eyes have adjusted, or look into the water when the surface is calm. Meditation practice is similar to staying still in a dark room and allowing your eyes to adjust to the darkness, or waiting for the wind to stop so that you can see underneath the surface of the water. By withdrawing your attention from your thoughts, the surface of your mind becomes still enough to see clearly what is beneath.

If you can relax your impulse to assign some value to every experience, your frantic thinking begins to subside, your mind becomes calm and clear, and you can finally see what is really there. When you see clearly what is happening within your own consciousness, your anxiety and confusion in life disappear because you know reality for yourself without the need for perceptual mind to interpret it for you.

The Origin of Religion

This direct seeing is the experience that the sacred maps are pointing us toward. Only this can free us from the belief that our mental images are real. Most of us resist or avoid this experience because it is so foreign and we have not yet learned to trust it. Our perceptual mind would rather study the map because this is what it knows how to do. It understands symbols and models, but cannot relate directly to reality. So we tend to cling to the map and mistake the map itself for the destination that it aims to guide us to.

Our sense of loss and confusion here demands that we find something solid to cling to for comfort and safety. Our perceptual mind tries to remedy this dilemma by creating a continuous story of a self that appears real and true. And the cornerstones for our sense of self are a set of values or ideals. If you look for what defines you as a separate person beyond your body, you will find a matrix of beliefs. This is as close as perception can come to the truth. And this is how religion is created.

Religions usually begin with a teacher who gives us a map that contains information that we need to resolve the struggles that we face in life. Yet, as I have been describing, the map points to a destination completely foreign to us. And as much as we want to be healed and complete, we are often afraid to leave the comfort of our familiar territory.

The territory that we are familiar with is defined by our process of perception. So we tend to stay within the comfortable realm of perception and create a set of beliefs and ideals out of a spiritual teaching that we can access and control with our conceptual mind. This is like using your car to go somewhere, yet remaining in your car once you get there because it is more comfortable. Most of us have had moments when we wanted to, or actually did, stay in our car when we got to someplace new and unfamiliar. Yet, sooner or later we realize that we did not drive all this way just to stay in our car, and we finally step out to experience our new surroundings.

The Limits of Religion

Organized religion is one of the primary ways that we try to remain within the familiar territory of our thoughts. A religion is a set of beliefs and ideals that define our world and our place in it. Religion attempts to explain where we came from, why we are here, and where we are going when we leave here. It offers us a set of rules to follow and gives us something to measure ourselves against. As such, it provides a context or paradigm for our lives here on earth.

Buddha and Christ never intended for their teachings to become a religion. The Buddha taught consistently that belief in a set of ideas would only obscure the experience of enlightenment. He advocated believing nothing until we could see it clearly for ourselves. Neither of these teachers appear to have written down their teachings, perhaps because they did not want their words to become a fixed reference point for perception.

I have been emphasizing that truth cannot be conveyed in words and has to be experienced directly by each of us individually. This may be why the teachings of both the Buddha and Christ were not recorded during the lifetimes of these teachers. They both understood that people would inevitably mistake their words for truth. History suggests that the Buddhist and Christian scriptures that now form the basis for these religions were not written down until decades or centuries after these teachers were gone.

Once we understand the process of perception, it is easy to see how our mind would naturally create a religion out of a spiritual teaching. In fact, the only thing that perception *can* do with such a teaching is to formalize it into a set of abstract ideals. We then make a formula out of these ideals that our programmed mind can adapt to. In this way we further attach ourselves to our mental programming, rather than becoming free.

When we try to apply religious ideals to everyday life, they do not translate well into all the mistakes and imperfections that seem to infuse the human condition. So we end up with a set of impossible rules which we measure ourselves and everyone else against. These ideals seem to offer a stable reference point, yet they merely feed the mind's habit of comparative judgment and give us another means to limit, and thereby diminish, ourselves and other people.

The Longing for Certainty

Perception creates an image of reality by contrasting opposite values. The basis of perception is therefore an absolute right and absolute wrong which requires a clear division between these polarities that is beyond question.

This is the origin of morality, and it typically falls within the realm of religion because religions attempt to define reality for us.

Morality establishes a distinction between what is good and what is bad that applies to all people at all times. The problem with morality however, is that in order to work as a reference for reality, it has to be accepted by all of us. Everyone has to agree on what is right and wrong, and there has to be some clear way of knowing the difference.

Without an absolute way of distinguishing good from evil, we naturally make reference to other people. The more people that believe something, the truer and more real it appears to be. So we end up caught in this struggle to convince more people to believe the way we do, and we constantly make divisions between the believers and the non-believers, thinking that this will make things clearer.

People who are passionate about their religion often try to convert other people because they want others to benefit from their beliefs. Yet, an underlying motivation behind the zeal expressed by religious fundamentalists is to strengthen their own belief system and bolster their certainty by attracting more followers. That is why there is so much conflict between people of different religious beliefs. If other people disagree with our religion or morality, it can threaten our certainty, create insecurity, and cast a shadow on the stability of our world.

Values Change

The problem with trying to create certainty within this perceptual world is that all knowledge is derived by comparisons, and no absolute measurement exists. We cannot ever be sure about the difference between right and wrong because there *is* no way to determine these once and for all. Everyone's perception of what is right and wrong is slightly different, and they change with the circumstances. So religion ends up basing its morality on relative and arbitrary reference points that eventually change, and this leaves us just as uncertain as we were before.

The Catholic Church is perhaps the most authoritarian religion in our Western civilization and once was a dominant force in the world.

The Pope is the head of this church and has the capacity to make decisions about what is right and wrong that many people believe in and adhere to. The Pope is supposed to represent God and as such his decisions about morality are beyond question. Believers in this religion need this in order to gain a sense of certainty about the world.

Yet, oddly enough, the values of the Catholic Church can change. What once was wrong, can be determined right, just by the Pope saying so. Earlier I described how the Catholic Church convicted Galileo of heresy and sentenced him to house arrest for life because he asserted that the earth was not the center of the Universe. In recent centuries, several Popes have renounced this condemnation of Galileo and declared him a great man for his contributions to modern science. And a few years ago, the Pope decided to erect a statue of Galileo inside the Vatican.

Morality and Hypocrisy

More disturbing than its inconsistency is the way in which morality breeds hypocrisy. While most of us might agree that rules are necessary to create order and safety in society, few of us like them and we all try to get around them at times. Morality is often used to point the finger of blame at other people for not following the rules in order to better hide our own transgressions. A universal value system like this lends itself to proving our innocence by making other people look guilty.

Organized religious groups have often committed some of the most brutal acts of violence and oppression against humanity. This is a natural result of needing other people to share our same beliefs and values in order to validate that we are right. In our own Western history for example, the established Christian Church has been responsible for violence against people of the Muslim faith in the medieval Crusades, and against women who followed pagan practices during the witch hunts of Europe and colonial America.

Throughout our history, religious missionaries have initiated genocide as they tried to eliminate indigenous people's spiritual traditions, lifestyle, and language. The Christian Church in North America forbade the essential practices of many Native Americans, such as the sweat lodge ceremony, and took their children away to be stripped of their own language and culture and forced to conform to ours.

A horrifying example of hypocrisy in recent times is the revelation of widespread sexual abuse and child molestation perpetrated by Catholic priests. This represents a contradiction on a scale that is beyond imagination. The people invested with the authority to uphold the strict moral standards of the Church used their authority to violate those whom they were supposed to protect.

The Catholic Church presents sexual desire as inherently shameful, holds its priests to a standard of celibacy, and employs guilt to control the sexual impulses of its members. Meanwhile, those in positions of power used their authority to satisfy their own sexual desires in perhaps the most brutal and damaging way possible – forcing children against their will. No one could fathom that vulnerable and impressionable children could be traumatized in such a way. And it turns out that when these truths were revealed within the church, the higher authorities who could have done something to correct this brutality instead acted to hide it and protect the perpetrators.

These are not reasons to condemn the people involved or judge anyone as evil. However this should wake us up to the hypocrisy that inevitably accompanies morality. When we try to limit the harm done by our individual egos by measuring each other according to a static set of rules, we merely encourage denial and rationalization which further obscures reality.

Trying to establish who is right and wrong simply does not work as a way to make our lives more safe or secure. Morality has never been the source of unity and stability that it promises to be, and has instead caused more pain and suffering in our world than we can imagine.

The Shadows of Morality

I had a shocking experience in my own life that brought the contradictions of morality into view. I was applying to work at a large Buddhist retreat center and was being shown around an enormous old building by the staff. This center had a strict policy of no sexual activity in the building, and in the custom of this particular Buddhist tradition, the subject of sexuality was generally not discussed. The teachings seemed to suggest that the best way to handle sexual feelings or thoughts was to avoid them altogether.

I was going to work in the maintenance department and was asked to get to know the various utility rooms in the basement. There was a catacomb of large rooms under the building that contained furnaces, water systems, and workshops smelling of old grease and oil. I was fascinated by the dark and dirty atmosphere of these cavernous old rooms.

In contrast to the bright and cheerful sunlit halls of the meditation center above, these caves contained a musty earthiness that appealed to me. This is where all the basic elements originated that made our life upstairs so clean and comfortable – water, heat, and electricity. This place seemed somehow more real and authentic, and I enjoyed exploring it.

As I wandered through one of those rooms, however, I stumbled upon an earthy reality that I was not prepared for. I looked into a waste paper basket and found a pornographic magazine depicting sadistic homosexuality. There were pictures of naked men tied and gagged in brutal ways while other men had sex with them.

I had never seen anything so disturbing in my life, and to find it here in this building left me stunned and confused. As I sat with this, I understood how trying to contain our ego by establishing strict rules merely results in furthering denial. In this case, as with the

Catholic priests, someone's dark impulses were literally forced underground by a policy that left no room for a more natural and healthy expression of sexual energy. When we label something as bad or wrong, often the only thing we accomplish is to encourage people to hide it. When we try to control something like sex using shame or guilt, it often expresses itself in darker and more destructive ways.

The Authority of God

Most of our efforts to find a fixed reference point here involve some person or group claiming moral authority. Many of us have come to expect those in positions of authority to tell us what is right and what is wrong, and we often look to them to determine these reference points for us.

The ultimate authority figure that is frequently referred to in these situations is God. We want a super-parent figure who can establish the rules of the game. We seem to need this idea of a supreme being who is in charge of all of us who can ultimately determine right from wrong. God then becomes a larger-than-life figure who passes final judgment because we need someone greater than any one of us to draw the line.

As we can plainly see, this approach leads to perpetual conflict in our world. God never materializes in a physical form that all of us can recognize, so we end up fighting over whose God is the real one. And God never seems to speak directly to all of us at once, so we only have someone's interpretations presented as God's word.

The concept of a singular all-powerful God has become such a tragic source of conflict because different religions assert their particular version of good and evil as having been decreed by God. This may work to create a sense of stability within an individual culture or religion, but it only causes tension between all of the different cultures and religions that make up humanity.

This way of trying to stabilize our world ultimately leads to more struggle and ends up dividing us and pitting us against each other. We often find ourselves in violent conflict with each other to see whose version of God's rules will win. Far from making the world more secure, the notion of God as the supreme judge that is often employed by different religions has resulted in never ending violence and perennial war between us.

Fundamentalism

A natural outcome of our attempts to solidify duality is fundamentalist thinking. If ideals are the only reference that we have here, then fundamentalism is a natural way to make them appear absolute and solid. Fundamentalist thinking happens all the time and is not limited to religion. It is simply an attempt to unify the world by establishing a belief system that labels something as right and something else as wrong and applies to all people in all situations. This habit is so ingrained in our thought system that it may be difficult at first to understand what I am talking about.

How else could we navigate life except by trying to sort out right from wrong? This question itself points to how completely we are embedded in perception. We cannot conceive of any other way to approach life than by learning to make constant distinctions and sort things out according to these fundamental polarities.

Anytime that I label another person, culture, way of thought, or belief as wrong or bad, I am acting out of fundamentalism. My perceptual mind is required to set up this opposition in order to verify my own innocence. I have to have someone else who is evil to compare myself with so I can know that I am not that. This is how the paradigm of comparison between two opposites works. Tragically, it means that I always have to have an enemy and someone to call bad, so that I can be assured of my own rightness and goodness.

The actual outcome of fundamentalist thinking, religious belief, and morality, is not peace, love, and stability, but rather conflict, hatred, and war. In order to maintain a religious or fundamentalist foundation I have to separate myself from everyone who does not believe the way I do. This way of thinking automatically divides the world into those who are right, and those who are wrong. Anyone who does not agree with me must be wrong in order for me to be right. And this naturally leads to the kind of endless power struggles that commonly plague humanity today.

The Buddha wasn't Buddhist and Christ wasn't Christian

Inspired teachers like the Buddha or Christ warned us against fundamentalism. The Buddha taught us never to rely on beliefs but only to keep investigating the truth through the practice of direct awareness until we see for ourselves what is real. Christ told us that we needed to be like little children to enter the Kingdom of Heaven. Both of them were directing us to give up our reliance on rational thought and admit that we *do not know*. They each suggest that it is only in the emptiness of not knowing that we have a chance to see the truth that lies beyond opinions.

Buddha and Christ each had been raised in the context of a religion. Buddha was raised as a Hindu and Christ as a Jew, and their experience of awakening showed them the difference between religious belief and direct experience. They both broke from their inherited religions to teach that direct experience was the way to become fully conscious, and suggested that belief in religious ideals only served to maintain the mind in its unconscious sleep state.

Christ was not a Christian, and Buddha was not a Buddhist. These labels did not come until much later when there were enough people following their teachings that others needed to call them something. People who were still dependent on the process of perception took these teachings and formulated them into new religions. And when they tried to frame these teacher's words as absolute truth, they only obscured the original maps that the teachers left for us.

A religion is a set of ideas that define our reality in absolute terms in order to give us something to hold onto within the fickle and ever-changing world of perception. Religious beliefs attempt to solve our problem of not knowing who we are or why we are here by giving us a story. The story only serves us when we believe in it without question, and this is how religion often uses the concept of faith. Faith in this sense is belief in a "pre-scribed" set of ideas about how things are.

Religion and Culture

Religions tend to form the core of our mental programming, and are often the basis for different cultures. Culture could be described as a fabric of beliefs and customs which define a group of people, often in a specific place. It is a kind of paradigm or basic operating system, and as such remains largely invisible to us until we step outside of it, or until it shifts. In Western culture we are in the midst of a major cultural shift from Christianity or Judaism to science as our primary religion or way that we explain our world.

Most of us don't usually think of science as a religion, and instead tend to focus on the differences between science and religion as we navigate this period of cultural upheaval. Yet, many of us believe in scientific conclusions and have faith in them as a way to explain our world and understand our place in it, just as we have in the past with religious stories.

We usually have difficulty seeing our own religion or culture as merely a paradigm or mental framework. We believe it is the *truth* because that is the only way it can serve as a basis for our reality. It is often easier to see the superficiality of this approach when we look at other people's religions.

When we look at the some of the religious beliefs of older and simpler cultures they often appear to be arbitrary, childish, and too far-out to be credible. For example, we often consider that some ancient cultures were ignorant and superstitious because they assigned personalities to objects that we consider to be inanimate, such as the sun, moon, rivers, rocks, wind, clouds, or trees. Their stories often personified animals, plants, or elements of nature and gave them human characteristics. We tend to laugh at the stories that they tell to explain how the earth was created or people came into existence, because they sound like fairy tales to us.

Yet look at the way that our primary modern Western belief systems such as Judaism, Christianity, or science explain the world and our place in it. The book of Genesis in the Old Testament of the Bible describes a creator God who made the earth and all life forms in six days and shaped man out of clay and woman out of a bone from man. This God, which we cannot ever see or contact directly, then rules over us and judges us like a supreme monarch, using a system of justice, reward, and punishment which none of us seems able to fully comprehend.

Our modern scientific theory of the origins of the universe and life on earth is even more fantastic. It describes a world in which all matter and energy was compressed into an infinitely small particle sometimes referred to as a "singularity." Presumably, this tiny particle contained everything we know, including all matter, time, space, and consciousness itself. Then, for some unknown reason, this particle exploded in a mysterious cataclysmic event called the "big bang," and out of it came the raw materials for the entire universe as we know it, including ourselves.

The popular theory of evolution goes on to explain that life on our planet began as separate elements crystallized and came into contact with each other when the molten ball of gases and minerals slowly cooled over billions of years. Somehow, out of this mixture of essential elements, life emerged in the form of single-cell organisms which became increasingly complex over time and mysteriously developed conscious intelligence.

Seen in this light, our own modern religious or scientific beliefs seem no more sophisticated or accurate than those presented by earlier societies. In the end, they are all merely ideas that try to explain our reality and give meaning to our existence. We invest in these ideas, making out of them a religion or paradigm in our attempt to know the truth. Yet, believing in something is not the same as seeing it for ourselves.

A Spiritual Journey

The teachings of Buddha and Christ presented a radical departure from the established religions of the cultures that they each lived in because they pointed away from belief and toward direct experience as the way to certainty. The simple idea that both of these teachers demonstrate is that *belief can never provide certainty.*

Belief is the way our minds try to solidify an idea and give it the *illusion* of certainty. Yet no amount of belief can answer our hunger for truth. Only direct experience can do this. And that experience is outside the realm of our perceptual abilities. So we have to learn to go beyond perception to be able to access our capacity for direct awareness. And this is what a spiritual teaching is designed to show us.

Both the Buddha and Christ intended to leave us a map or spiritual path to facilitate our own ability to see the truth. They knew that the truth we long for is not an idea or concept and cannot be found in beliefs. Both of them tried to direct us away from religious belief and toward developing our own capacity to see reality directly for ourselves. They each knew that this was the only way in which we could become complete and awake.

A spiritual path uses the concept of faith differently from a religion. This kind of faith is the willingness to set aside all beliefs, concepts, and understandings, and *not know anything*, in order to allow the truth to be revealed directly in this moment. In Christ's teachings, this has often been translated as revelation, and in the teachings of the Buddha it has been called insight.

Revealing Your Primary Assumptions

Take a moment now to become aware of one your own religious beliefs. You may not recognize them as such and believe yourself to be free of fundamentalist ideals. Yet, this habit comes with the territory of perception, and most of us carry an invisible framework by which we measure all of our experiences.

———————— •◆• ————————

Think of some ideal that you hold as right or true. It may be a belief associated with a religion or spiritual teaching, or it may simply be "the way something is" in your mind. An example would be the idea that "religion is good" or "religion is bad."

You will know when you have found one because your mind will "click" into it like your computer boots up when you press the start button. It will feel familiar and almost transparent at first, and often will only become visible when you hold your attention there for a moment.

Don't focus on the belief itself, but rather notice how your mind tends to stick there, and you cannot easily disregard this idea or consider a contrary one.

———————— •◆• ————————

If you were able to feel the "groove" that your mind locked into, you might have noticed both the sense of stability and certainty it gave you, and the sense of limitation and constriction that accompanied it. This is the essential nature of religion, and it is an inevitable result of our exclusive dependency on perception to interpret reality for us.

7

The Only Way Out is Through

As I entered college, the passageway into adulthood in Western society, I began to experience the uncertainty and anxiety that naturally accompanies a world created by perception. In this world, which most of us mistake for reality, everything is known by comparing it with something else. Nothing stands by itself and there is nothing fixed, solid, or permanent to hold on to.

I was being encouraged to focus on some distant accomplishment that seemed to promise security, yet my attention was on the chaos and disintegration that was apparent all around me. I was at the end of my rope. I could no longer endure struggling to drown out the uncertainty by building a stronger ego, establishing more beliefs, learning more information, or trying to secure a good job.

I didn't believe that my father knew what he was doing, or why. He always said that his goal was to earn a million dollars. I asked him once what good a million dollars would be to him after he died. He said that he didn't know, and he didn't care. This was too much for him to think about.

He just wanted to believe in something that he could hold on to and measure himself by. A million dollars felt real to him. It would mean that he was somebody and had done something important. He never got his million dollars, and he died thinking that he had somehow failed in his life.

I knew that I was being offered a good education so I could get a good job, so I could earn good money, so I could have a sense of security and comfort in this unpredictable world. And I reached a point where this thinking made no sense and no longer motivated me. I wanted to get to the bottom of the anxiety and find out *why* this world contained so much uncertainty and seemed so threatening. I sensed that somewhere there had to be real security, and I was determined to find it.

Pain as a Motivation for Change

Common in stories of spiritual awakening is a descent into despair and hopelessness, referred to as the "dark night of the soul" by the Roman Catholic mystic, Saint John of the Cross. It seems that we have to use up all of our other options before we are willing to look deeply inside ourselves for the answer. As I sank into a desperate state of confusion and uncertainty, my whole being became focused on finding a real way out. When the mind is one-pointed like this, the way becomes visible.

Looking back now, the risk that I took was worth taking, yet I could never have been sure of this at the time. This is how crisis, disillusion, or disintegration can be viewed as a positive force. It requires that we go where we previously resisted going, and that we see what we refused to look at before. The reality of our situation here is that we can never know this ahead of time. That is where true faith comes into play. Faith is finding a small glimmer of trust within ourselves that allows us to risk everything for something which we can never be sure of in advance.

I was willing to risk everything familiar to find something new because the pain had become too great for me to bear. When I try to describe this pain to people, some look at me blankly and have no idea what I am talking about. I was not suffering from a physical ailment, nor did I have any obvious emotional crisis. My pain was the kind of existential anxiety that most of us barely recognize or understand. That is why no one around me seemed to be able to relate to what I was going through.

We have so little understanding of this kind of mental suffering that most of us assume the anxiety shadowing our lives is to be avoided by ignoring it, covering it up, or distracting ourselves. We develop a great capacity to deny our own and other people's chronic fear of life because we believe that this is the best way to deal with it. We want it to go away and don't know how to effectively accomplish this, so we simply pretend it does not exist.

A spiritual path is essentially a choice to resolve this pain by going through it, instead of trying to avoid it. To advance spiritually, you do not have to harden yourself or create more pain to endure, as some people believe. You can grow by simply being present and allowing the predictable pain that is there in everyday life to be felt.

Try facing discomfort directly and meeting it without turning away. Look sincerely for the roots of your pain and don't settle for blaming it on circumstances beyond your control. In this unlikely way, your perpetual unrest becomes the best motivation that you have to reach completion and experience fulfillment.

Living in this world feels unsafe and uncertain. If we are honest with ourselves, all of us can recognize a sense of anxiety deep inside. I felt this as a young man and could not ignore it. And I made a radical and seemingly irrational choice to *go into it* to find out what was causing my insecurity.

I wanted to get to the root of my discomfort, and believed somehow that it *could* be healed. I believed, as I think we all do in the depth of our hearts, that there *is* something that is solid and real and does not change. I went in search of this because nothing else made any sense to me, and I could not rest until I had found it.

Nothing to Hold on To

During one of my traveling adventures, I was taking a public bus up a winding mountain road in Nepal. The bus was crowded with people carrying all sorts of things like chickens, goats, and bags of grain, and it was hot and stuffy inside. I noticed some young men climbing out the window and disappearing onto the top of the bus, and my curiosity got the best of me. I poked my head out to see what they were doing, and they motioned to me to join them.

This was an old yellow school bus, probably from the United States, and the windows were barely large enough for me to squeeze through. I got half way out, realized that there was nothing to grab hold of, and wondered what I would do next. In a moment someone reached down to offer me a hand up and soon I was settled on to the top of the bus with a dozen other people enjoying the fresh air, sunshine, and beautiful mountain views.

The top of the bus was slightly curved and I noticed to my surprise that it had no rack or railing. In the middle was a set of five or six large metal containers that looked like the five-gallon milk pails I had seen in old photos of early American farms. A rope was tied around the milk pails, and everyone on the top of the bus had a hand on the rope to steady themselves. I inched my way over and got a grip on the rope myself, and instantly felt more secure.

This road was narrow and winding and the bus was constantly swerving hard in one direction and then the other. I looked down at one point and gulped as I realized that the road dropped off onto a steep mountain side. I had managed to settle my nerves and was feeling fairly comfortable with all of this until the bus took a particularly sharp turn. All at once, the cluster of milk pails in the middle of the bus roof started to slide a bit to the side.

I had assumed that the milk pails were attached to something that was part of the bus and that I was holding on to something solid and secure. I began to feel a sense of panic as I realized that nothing on the top of this bus was actually tied down. There was nothing to hold on to up there that would not move. I thought of the long drop off the side of the road and felt the fear rising in my belly. This put a whole new perspective on my situation.

Learning to Let Go

Our life here is like my experience on top of that bus. We grow up as children assuming that someone knows what is happening and has everything under control. We believe that our parents, family, friends, house, school, or possessions are permanent and will not change. Even if these things around us seem unstable at times, we have our sense of self to cling to as we go through life. In just this way I held on to the rope around those milk pails on the bus roof because it seemed to offer security.

As we grow up, we naturally try to find something fixed and permanent in our primary relationship, career, family, house, or surroundings. Or we tend to become fundamentalist in our thinking and try to create a fixed point out of a religion or set of beliefs. Even if we have nothing else to hold on to, we believe in our sense of self as the one thing that is permanent and does not change. We invest so much importance in our ego or individual personality because this often seems to be the only thing we can really count on in life.

At some point, even the most stable parts of our life begin to shift, just as the milk jugs moved on that roof, and we realize *there is nothing to hold on to here*. There is nothing here that we can anchor our lives to which does not change. Parents, relationships, career, money, possessions, our body, and even our personality, are all temporary and we cannot depend on them to give us a sense of certainty. Most of us glimpse this from time to time, although few of us want to acknowledge it or face this reality directly because the thought of our predicament is terrifying. So we often deal with the inherent uncertainty of life by pretending that things are not the way they are.

Once the milk cans started sliding on that bus roof top in Nepal, there was no way that I could pretend that things were secure. The situation was obvious and immediate, and I was afraid. I started to tense up with anxiety as the metal pails slid across the roof, and I looked around at the other people on the bus top to see their reactions. I noticed to my surprise that they calmly readjusted themselves and did not seem the least bit worried. I marveled at this and decided to do the only thing I could do, which was to try to relax myself and enjoy the ride.

This is ultimately the only thing we *can* do about life. We can get angry or tighten our grip on the people and things around us, but this does not change the fact that everything here is relative and subject to change. We can deny the situation and pretend that it is not so, but we only make ourselves more ignorant and blind. Or we can look honestly at what is happening, realize that everything here is impermanent and subject to change, and find the courage within us to have faith that things will work out, even if we cannot see how.

Something broke open for me on that bus top as I realized there was no point to my fear and anxiety. If I continued to tighten, I knew that I would become overwhelmed with worry and defeat myself. I could see that holding on tighter to the ropes around the milk jugs would not make me any safer, and I had to accept that for the rest of that bus ride there was nothing to cling to that would not move.

The situation was unacceptable, yet there was nothing that I could do about it. So I did the only thing I could do, which was to surrender my fear. Then, to my astonishment, I really enjoyed the rest of the ride. I did not give the situation another thought and merely took in the incredible beauty of each moment, grateful that I was alive to experience it.

The North Star

In James Michener's book *Hawaii,* he describes a fictionalized account of how the early Polynesian islanders of the south Pacific may have discovered and come to inhabit the islands that we now call Hawaii. This story beautifully illustrates our search for certainty in the midst of a world where everything changes. I retell it here in my own words.

———————— •◆• ————————

The people of the South Pacific knew how to navigate small boats in the waters between the islands they inhabited that were scattered across a wide expanse of open ocean. They used the stars to help them, and because all the stars that they could see in the southern hemisphere moved in the sky through the night, their capacity to navigate in the open ocean was limited.

A time came when the Polynesian islanders were compelled to seek for new lands outside of their familiar territory. Perhaps it was over-population, a natural disaster, or an ideological divide. Whatever the motivation, it was clear that they needed to find a new home or perish. So a larger-than-normal sailing craft was built, and a crew prepared to sail beyond the known waters in search of new lands.

Imagine these people setting out in a small sailing vessel in the open ocean beyond any known reference points. They found themselves surrounded by open water with no land in sight and nothing familiar to help locate their position and guide them onward. Everything around them was constantly moving and changing – the water, air, sun, clouds, sky, and even the stars at night. Their feeling must have been one of complete loss and disorientation.

Then, after many days of sailing in the open ocean with nothing to guide them, one of the sailors cried excitedly to the others that she had found a star in the night sky that did not move. She had been watching this star, which had appeared on the horizon earlier that evening, for some time. She discovered that while all the stars in the sky appeared to move and shift their positions through the night, this one remained fixed. They all watched for a while to confirm what she had observed.

For the rest of their journey, the sailors kept their eyes on this fixed star and were able to navigate their vessel in a steady direction by following it. The fixed star enabled them to move a great distance in a straight line, and eventually find the islands of Hawaii which lay far to the north of their South Pacific home.

This star, of course, was the North Star, which was not visible to the Polynesians until they reached a point far enough north of their familiar waters. Once they found the North Star, it provided the reference that they needed to navigate across the distance of ocean to find the islands which would become their new home.

A World of Constant Change

Our world of perception, which most of us call reality, is like the experience of these sailors in the open ocean once they left their familiar territory. Everything around us appears to change and move and we have no fixed references with which to orient ourselves and choose a direction. Everything here gets old and sick and eventually dies. Nothing remains constant, and as soon as we get attached to something, we become afraid of losing it.

My father was very sick some years ago and as the family gathered around his hospital bed on what turned out to be his last day, I noticed a profound sense of disorientation. My brother, two sisters and mother, all of whom were normally quite sure of themselves, seemed a bit lost. No one really knew what to do or how to be.

The next morning my father died and the family gathered again around his body, except for my youngest sister. I could tell when I saw her later that day that she was deeply disturbed by my father's death and did not know how to be with it. As I thought about this, I realized that there is no way to understand or accept death. It is impossible to make sense of the fact that a person is here one moment and gone the next. If we let ourselves face the reality of death, it is a profoundly disorienting and disturbing event.

Like the stars in the Polynesian's sky, there is nothing we know of here that does not change. As a result of this, we often feel lost and experience ourselves wandering aimlessly, never getting anywhere. For the human mind, this is a source of great anxiety and often leads to a sense of depression. We long to be connected to something that does not change and will provide stability, certainty, and guidance. And we spend most of our energy trying to find something constant and certain that we can hold on to.

This is how I felt when I found my way to the small Buddhist monastery in Asia. I was completely lost, and I longed with all my heart for something true that I could use to guide me. I thought that I was looking for a person who could tell me the truth, and that the answers I was seeking would come to me in the form of ideas. However, the Buddha's teaching and the practice of meditation pointed me toward a signal within myself which I had not noticed before. I learned to trust a knowing that came directly from awareness rather than from my rational mind. And this knowing became my North Star.

We tend to trust our thinking mind more than anything else to guide and direct our lives. We don't realize that all of our thoughts are relative and are not based on anything fixed or stable. We think that we can find something certain in our values of right and wrong, and base our entire reality on these polarities.

Yet, as much as we want our values and beliefs to be absolute, these ideals remain arbitrary and subject to change. Trusting our judgments to guide us would be like the sailors from Polynesia out in the open ocean trusting the constantly moving stars to guide their way. To do so would mean sailing aimlessly with no fixed direction, and would likely result in a scattered and useless voyage.

These sailors knew enough about the constant movement of the stars not to trust them to find their way. They waited without any security, not knowing what would happen next, until finally the North Star appeared. In the same way, once we recognize that the basis for rational thought is constantly shifting, it is wise not to look to our judgments and conclusions to guide us.

Rather, we need to muster the faith to wait for something to appear that we know to be true and constant. We need to be like that small boat on the open ocean, and trust that a true reference point will somehow reveal itself.

The Still Point

Like the Polynesian sailors finding a star in the night sky that did not move, I discovered a still point of reference in my world through the practice of meditation. I realized to my astonishment that the one thing that did not change was *my own presence*. Whatever event or story is playing out in my mind, part of me is there simply witnessing it without comment. Wherever I go and whatever I am doing, I am there, and a part of me is conscious and aware.

I was so used to my own presence that I took it for granted, and rarely took notice of it. It had always been there, and would always be there, and was so ordinary and familiar that I never gave it any value. In fact, I spent much of my life trying to obscure my own presence and dull my awareness, because I could not distinguish these from the mental clutter that was consuming me. I was looking for something grand and magnificent to solve the riddle of life for me, and never once considered that I would find the answer in simple attention.

Suddenly realizing that I carried the most accurate and reliable compass inside me was like Dorothy in Oz realizing finally that she had been wearing the magical ruby slippers the entire time. I had been searching for this fixed point of reference *outside* of myself, in other people, ideals, accomplishments, material possessions, or recognition. Even as I embarked on my quest and left behind my familiar world, I was convinced that I would find a person who would finally show me reality. I never imagined that I would find what I was seeking *inside* myself, and that I had carried it with me the whole time.

The Buddha made it clear that believing in his words or making a fixed set of beliefs out of his teaching would not help us and would only perpetuate the illusion of reality created by our conceptual mind. He suggested that the certainty we long for is to be found only in our present moment experience, unfiltered by thought or judgment.

The practice of meditation is simply coming back to an immediate experience without adding any concepts or images. As I do this again and again, I increase my capacity to rest in awareness and relax my compulsive habit of filtering every experience through conceptual thought.

It begins as a small part of my experience, and increasingly I spend more and more of my time just being conscious and aware. As my awareness becomes more steady, a certainty arises that dispels doubt and confusion and anchors my life in the present moment. This eliminates the need for anything outside of me to hold onto for support and allows me to be genuinely free and content.

———————— •◆• ————————

Close your eyes for a moment and feel the breath pushing up against your belly. Let go of your thoughts and pay attention to the gentle rise and fall of your abdomen with each breath.

Imagine that this simple awareness is beaconing you – calling you to be present and inviting you to notice what is occurring in this moment.

Consider that this beacon, which is always there, may provide you with exactly the fixed reference point and guidance that you have been seeking in your life.

———————— •◆• ————————

The Cherished Mind

Letting go of familiar habits is hard. I had come to love my mind and how it could conjure up images at any moment about any subject. I was fascinated by thoughts, and resisted the notion that they were misleading me. I had invested heavily in my capacity to figure things out, believing that this would resolve my troubles. I had been through fourteen years of intensive schooling to learn how to use my intellect. I saw my thinking mind as a knight in shining armor riding in to rescue me from my despair. I hated to consider that it was instead an imposter, leading me further and further away from reality.

From the place of neutral observation enabled by an increasing field of awareness within me, I could see my thoughts and perceptions whirling around in all directions, creating a storm of emotional drama that I easily became caught up in. The stories that unfolded in brilliant complexity in my mind as I sat in meditation all had me as the central character. I saw how I was drawn into them like a moth to a candle flame, unable to resist remembering, analyzing, and planning my own life. And once I became involved in these thoughts, I saw how my experience of life became a wild emotional roller-coaster ride.

I recognized that my mind was obsessed with my own story and could not stop thinking about it from every possible angle. This seemed to be its purpose and I realized that I had been counting on it to resolve my life's struggles and dilemmas. I was convinced that if I just thought long and hard enough about my life I would be able to make sense of it. My strategy had been to try to complete each thought and in this way to finally figure out the meaning of life.

Yet, I had become exhausted and overwhelmed by the complexity and impossibility of this task. I recognized that it was not working and I needed a completely new way to proceed. From the still point that I found in meditation I was able to see the insanity of my own thought process, and to begin to let it go. This is the aim of awareness practice. It is simply a tool to allow us to recognize what is happening so that we can make an informed choice about where to place our attention.

The Buddha said that we are like children playing with our toys in a room in a house that is on fire. I did not want to give up my toys. I loved my thoughts and wanted to play with them forever. It came as a shock to see that they were hurting me. It was like finding out that my therapist was selling my stories on the internet. I did not want to believe it at first, and as the truth slowly dawned on me I was struck with a deep sadness and grief. I knew that I had to let go of the only real friend I thought I had, and I did not know what would replace it.

Once I saw how arbitrary and chaotic my mind was, and how circular and desperate its process, it became easier to let it go. In contrast to the dramas endlessly spinning in my head, I found the steady calm awareness of each breath to be a relief. I recognized that my thinking mind was not solving the problems which it promised to take care of, and instead it was continuously creating *more* problems. So I began to lose interest in the story of me, and chose to put my attention on much simpler and more direct experiences. I found peace and security in the feeling of my feet against the hard floor, or my breath gently pushing my belly up from the inside.

Dissolving the Illusion of Self

Despite my grief and my fear of the unknown realm I was entering, I believed that I had found something which I could finally trust to lead me to reality. The only thing I could do now was to go deeper into the Buddha's teaching and develop my practice of meditation. I considered the Buddha's suggestion that my mind is creating an *illusion* of a real world with me as a real person in it, and this notion began to turn me inside out.

The last thing I would ever have thought to question was the reality of my *self*. The idea of me as a separate mind and body named Miles was such an obvious, familiar, and ordinary part of my world that to question it seemed absurd. In a similar way, questioning that the Earth was flat or the Sun revolved around the Earth once was unthinkable. Looking back on those historical times, we marvel at how people could have been so sure, and so wrong, at the same time. We wonder at their resistance to question or investigate beliefs that we now know were mistaken.

The Buddha is reported to have challenged his students to find this thing called a self. He urged them to look deeply for any tangible evidence that such a self exists. He wanted us to see what he had seen – that this precious idea of a self that we take for granted is merely a grand illusion made up by our conceptual mind.

Something in me recognized this idea as soon as I heard it, and wondered why I had not thought of this on my own. Yet, I could not have come up with this question because the thought of my self not being real would never have occurred to me. I was so convinced that my mind was showing me the truth that I could not imagine reality any other way.

Once the suggestion was made, however, I began to doubt my own perceptions and question the most fundamental assumptions that I had about my own identity. As I applied awareness to my own thinking mind, I could see that my thoughts seemed to center around a singular theme – the notion of Miles as a fragile, independent person having to protect and provide for myself in an often hostile world. My mind made *everything about me*. This pain in my knee was *my* pain, and the person talking in the room next to mine was disturbing *my* meditation.

I began to see that each of the thoughts flashing through my mind contained a piece of a story about me. Each thought applied in some way to my personality and related to me as the center and focal point. As I watched more I could see how my thought processes were actually *creating* a person called Miles moment to moment. Instead of reaching for some noble truth, all of the endlessly repeating stories going through my mind were merely providing a backdrop for the drama of my personality.

One thought would be about the relationship I had left behind, and the next would be about what I would do when I returned home. Then my mind would zoom to a memory of being hurt when I was six years old, and the next instant I would be wondering what would be served for lunch. On and on this thought stream went, creating and recreating the story of me from every possible angle.

I began to notice how this continuous thought stream painted a picture that was absolutely convincing. There was no end to the concerns, problems, and crises to be faced and overcome. The story had moments of great achievement and great tragedy. There was glory and defeat and mystery all woven together with a dynamic tension and the sum of my life seemed to hang in the balance.

It seemed as though my mind was determined to evaluate every detail about me as if it were compiling a great file that would eventually determine my right to exist or not. Every aspect of me was being continually reviewed, judged, and compared with evaluations of other people. Yet, I could not see the overall objective of this process. It seemed that there were endless lists and comparisons and examinations with no final conclusion to any of it. The closer I looked, the less I could find anything solid about my own identity. All of this endless comparison and evaluation seemed to amount to nothing.

The words of the Buddha began ringing in my ears. *"I challenge you to show me the self – find one thing that is solid and real about yourself that does not change – Where is it? – What part of your self can you prove is real?"* I remembered Descartes' axiom, "I think, therefore I am," and suddenly began to realize that our whole struggle here is merely to validate our existence. I realized that this struggle had brought me here to this monastery in a remote corner of the world, and was now forcing me to confront the very basis of my own identity.

Free Fall

Questioning my own reality brought me the greatest fear I have ever known. I suddenly felt as though there was nothing beneath my feet to stand on. Without my familiar story, I felt entirely naked. I would experience myself without a context or an identity for a few moments, and then would instinctively leap back into the stream of my thoughts.

Once there, I could comfortably reminisce about my past and plan my future as I always had done. Yet, the comfort of this old habit began to wear thin. More and more I noticed how confining and rigid this place was. There was no room for expansion and creativity, and fear seemed to be the underlying force behind all of it.

I began to realize that I had a choice to make. I could stay within the comfortable and familiar thought patterns that I could now see were weaving a continuous story of the life of Miles. Or, I could let go of my thoughts and enter a space of direct awareness where there was no story of a self engaged in the struggles of life. I was terrified by the emptiness that I found beyond my thoughts. Yet I was more afraid of not finding the truth that I had come so far to discover.

When we try to let go of something that we cherish, it is helpful to find something else to replace it with. In order to get beyond the thinking mind, we need to have a point of reference that does not involve thought. The Buddha taught the practice of meditation as a way to develop a new reference point. The rhythmic breathing of my body or the hardness of the floor against my feet became my basis, instead of the constant thought stream running through my head.

I was beginning to have an experience of presence where my thinking mind was not in charge. Aside from the moments of sheer panic, I noticed a sense of true freedom and an incredible feeling of lightness. There was an inexplicable knowing which answered all the questions I had been so desperately asking. I marveled at how something so simple and ordinary as feeling my legs touching the floor or being absorbed in the sensations of my own breathing could answer questions that my mind had struggled with for years. I was losing myself, and becoming happier and more certain about life than I could ever have imagined.

8

The Struggle to Be Somebody

The Buddha suggests that we are using our thinking mind to create an illusion of something solid within a constantly moving world. A primary way that we do this is to make up a personality which appears to be fixed, real, and stable. It seems to offer us a firm platform in a sea of constant flux and change, and we cling to it as we would a life raft in the open ocean. None of us remember creating our self, and so we assume that it has been with us all along. And the one thing that we seldom do is to question the reality of this self, because it only works if we believe in it wholeheartedly.

Our concept of ourselves as separate individuals could be considered our fundamental paradigm. In Western psychology we sometimes use the word "ego" to represent this sense of self. The primary problem with the ego or personality is that it is not stable or solid. It is not based on anything actual that does not change. We have to keep creating and maintaining it so that we can present it to the world as authentic and thereby validate our existence.

In this strange paradigm of a separate self, the main way that we know who we are is to be recognized by other people. The ego has no real source and cannot validate itself, so we rely on getting attention from others for self-assurance. We find ourselves then in this impossible situation where we are all lost and trying to validate our existence by gaining the approval and recognition of other lost people. This explains the sense of chaos, confusion, and futility that often permeates life.

The Paradigm of a Separate Self

On a silent meditation retreat we do not speak to each other or have eye contact. This takes away one of the primary sources of the ego. Without getting recognition from other people, our personality begins to unravel because it has no reference points. That is why being around people without speaking or looking at each other can feel so uncomfortable at first.

This kind of intentional solitude is a powerful medicine to help me identify with something other than my ego. Once I get used to it, the silence offers a wonderful freedom. I don't have to be anybody or try to get other people to recognize me, and I begin to discover a source within myself that is much more reliable and sustainable than other people's approval.

It often appears that the ego is my source and it is the ego that maintains me. In reality it is exactly the opposite. My struggles in life are *to maintain the ego* because it has no real foundation and cannot stand on its own. I mistake my personality for who I am and then I end up enslaved to it, having to keep it alive in order to assure my own survival. I spend most of my time and energy trying to enhance my sense of self by creating a persona that other people will notice and value.

When feeding the ego becomes my primary task, I end up competing against others for recognition and life becomes a stressful contest to see who can be seen as better. I continually have the sinking feeling of failure because no matter how much recognition I get, it never seems to be enough. Someone else always seems to be more important, attractive, or worthy.

The root of our word "person" and "personality" is the Latin *persona*, which means mask. Establishing myself as a person in this world is very much like putting on a mask. I often sense that I am faking it and not being real. And while I may be able to create a powerful personality that gets attention in the world, in the end it always feels hollow and does not satisfy my longing for authenticity.

It is not possible to make the ego real or permanent, and many of us live with a haunting sense of failure and incompletion. It is as though we are trying to breathe life into a wooden puppet that we have made, and it simply cannot work.

Maintaining Our Self

——————— •◆• ———————

Watch your mind for a moment and notice how it refers everything back to yourself.

As you are reading, you may be thinking about how this book relates to your own story. You might be judging and evaluating this writing and deciding if you agree or disagree with these ideas. You may be comparing yourself with me and contrasting your life story with mine, trying to decide who is better or which one of us is right or good.

——————— •◆• ———————

This constant stream of comparisons and evaluations is how the ego tries to build itself and maintain the illusion of an individual personality who is different from everyone else. Your mind is constantly evaluating and comparing you with other people, and judging you and them by some fixed ideal or standard.

You may notice that this process never stops and is quite exhausting. It is like being on an endless treadmill, trying to reach a point that keeps moving further away. Most of us keep going because we don't see any alternative. We think that if we give up trying to make something of ourselves we will fail at life and everything will break down.

Notice that the promised goal of becoming somebody is always off in the future, with many steps to achieve before its attainment. Your only chance of completion seems to be to stay on the treadmill and hope to get to the end some day, and you may never think to question the entire premise.

Despair and exhaustion is an inevitable outcome of blindly following this program. Anxiety and depression are the natural result of relying on a personality to form the foundation of our being. This is because no matter how hard we try, we never seem to come up with anything solid or real that does not keep changing.

Some of us throw ourselves into this struggle with all our might and thrash away aggressively trying to gain as much power and control in the world as we can. We think that dominating other people or getting them to believe in us is the way to ensure our place. Given our belief that it is our personality that makes us real, this option makes a lot of sense.

In this paradigm, conflict with opposing forces is a requirement to establish our identity. We have to compare ourselves against someone who is wrong, to know that we are right. Imagine the consequences of a world full of people, each of whom believes that in order to establish our identity we have to make someone else wrong. We each are struggling to be right and good and special, and our main way to measure this is to compare ourselves with someone who is not. So we find ourselves in endless conflict, with each of us trying to be better than everyone else simply to verify our own right to exist.

Some of us give up trying to be the best, and find our identity by being nice and getting people to like us. We often submit to the will of others, thinking that we can win their approval and recognition in this way. While this option may seem nicer, more socially acceptable, and less destructive, it is simply a more disguised way to feed the ego.

In this approach we often identify ourselves as the innocent victim of some evil aggressor. We use the sympathy of others and a sense of moral superiority to build up our sense of self. Yet, our personality is still in control and we still think that being recognized by others as special is the only way to validate our being.

Disengaging from the Self

The Buddha teaches that this approach does not work and will never reach a conclusion. He suggests that we can simply step off the treadmill, and once we do, everything will look different. He offers a way to do this, by disengaging from the entire thought stream that is trying so hard to create the image of a separate self that has to fend for itself in a threatening world.

The main difficulty that we have in doing this is the inevitable sense of failure and vulnerability that comes from giving up trying to be somebody special. We have made the impossible task of creating our own identity into some kind of noble endeavor, and taught ourselves to believe that if we abandon the struggle we are worthless.

Our struggle to maintain our self-image is fueled by our fear of mental collapse, depression, or nervous breakdown. We know intuitively that if we stop shoring up our ego, it will crumble. And we assume that if our ego dissolves, so do we. This is why it usually takes a total failure of our current life situation before we are willing or able to give up our attempts to fortify our identity in the world.

In our Western society, this kind of mental breakdown or instability is what we tend to fear the most. We have no way of understanding that the failure of our perceptual mind can lead to a transformation or increase in consciousness. So we exhaust ourselves trying to keep our ego alive by desperately competing with each other for recognition. The only way that we have to keep our illusion of self going is to push ourselves toward greater and greater achievements. And there is no end to this process. Nothing we do ever seems to be enough because we are trying to create a basis for something that is inherently *not real*.

The Buddha offered a way out of this bind by allowing the ego to collapse while at the same time rooting our existence in something actual, such as the simple sensations of the body breathing. This is entirely different from the mental breakdown that so many of us fear.

It is a gradual letting go of our dependency on our rational mind by replacing it with a steady field of awareness. We learn to ground ourselves in our own presence, rather than in our personal story.

This is the process of spiritual awakening or becoming more conscious, and a practice such as meditation creates the context for this transformation to occur. In returning to a present moment sensation again and again, I gradually become identified more with simple awareness and less with my conceptual world. As ideas and images lose their sense of reality, the sensations in my body and the experience of simply being conscious becomes the foundation of my existence.

Keeping the Form Simple

The desire for a special self is a difficult impulse to break, and the capacity for the ego to formulate around any basis is astonishing. I have developed such a knack for building a personality that I can adapt it to any conditions. It is no wonder, then, that when I learned to meditate, I began to formulate a new self-identity around it.

My life made a complete turnaround as a result of discovering the teachings of the Buddha. I was headed for a professional career and had been taught to value myself by how much money I could make, how much education I had, or the importance of my position in the world. Suddenly, none of that held any interest for me.

I thought I was free, but my ego had another idea. When I made a radical life change, so did my ego. It said, "Oh, now we are going to be spiritual? O.K., I can do that too!" I found myself trying to appear calm, cool, collected, wise, and a bit removed from the world.

My ego became fully engaged in the pursuit of not having an ego, and got pretty good at it. I quickly learned how to hide my aversion and greed and present myself as free, open, and awake. It is not that I wasn't becoming those things, or that they weren't worthy pursuits. It is just that I was *trying* to become them. Instead of letting go of me, I was reinventing me in a new form. I was unconsciously fueling my desire to become something, while I believed that I was disengaging from this very process.

Most of us have a fierce allegiance to the ego and are afraid of letting it go entirely. When we take up a spiritual path or follow a particular teaching, we often unconsciously put our efforts in service of our ego again, and merely create a *new* identity. We can easily imagine ourselves as the one practicing meditation or enduring hardships for the sake of spiritual achievement.

This is why the idea of spiritual practice at all is so tricky. As soon as we are *doing* something, we engage our unconscious programming. There is a kind of focused effort and clear intention that is required to transform our consciousness. It seems necessary for most of us to have some form to follow. We need some practice or discipline to challenge our dependency on the conceptual mind. Yet, the form has to be so simple and empty of meaning that we cannot become attached to or identified with it.

I have tried many different forms including no form at all, and have found that the simple form of meditation taught by the Buddha works best for me. The only task is to focus on the sensations of each breath coming in and out of the body, or each footstep touching the floor and lifting up again. It is so simple that there is no way to make anything out of it. I cannot become an expert breather, sitter, or walker because these things are so ordinary, they are happening all the time, and anyone can do them.

The challenge is to keep the practice simple and immediate, and not embellish it with personal style or infuse it with meaning. There is no meaning in the breath. Being aware of breathing does not mean thinking about it or trying to understand it. Paying attention to a bodily sensation like breathing is merely a way to focus the mind on something actual, instead of something that we perceive or *think* is actual. Meditation is simply a tool or mechanism to help us let go of the past and future and be in the present. Meditation itself has no meaning, and there is no value in being a "good meditator."

The Urge to Be Special

I remember the night that I returned home from Sri Lanka to my family in the United States. I was quivering with excitement and anticipation, and filled with anxiety as I imagined trying to describe everything that I had been through. I had changed so much in those six months away that nothing felt familiar any more. I was a new person with an entirely new perspective on myself and the world, and I was still only nineteen years old.

I desperately wanted to talk about my experience with someone familiar. Although I was now aware of the ego's game of seeking approval from others, the urge for someone to validate what I had been through was still compelling. Of course, I turned first to my parents and siblings, hoping that they would recognize my epiphany.

I sat in the living room of my parent's home with all of my family there and began to tell them my story. I wanted so badly for them to understand what I had learned and was eager to describe each of my experiences in detail. Yet, it all must have sounded so foreign to them and been too far beyond anything that they could understand. I will never forget my disappointment that evening as I was excitedly explaining the miracle that had happened to me, and one by one each member of my family fell asleep.

I saw then that I was alone in the world, caught between two of the most different cultures I could imagine, and having just begun to see the astonishing truth about life. It was an uncomfortable and exciting place to be – full of grief and uncertainty, while also ripe with possibilities. I sensed that I had to leave behind everything familiar and give myself to this new path. And I knew that there might be no one to oversee my journey, give me guidance, or ensure my safety.

I had no interest in rushing out to find other people who knew about meditation or were on a spiritual path. I did not want to become part of a group, since it seemed to me that this would only encourage the creation of a new identity. Yet, I struggled with a sense of isolation and still longed for someone to recognize what I had just gone through.

I felt different from everyone around me. I had been through an experience and seen things about myself that no one else seemed to be aware of, and this seemed to set me apart from others. I had seen the nature of my mind and was aware of its program of trying to become somebody. Yet, I was not free from its magnetic pull.

I saw myself as special because of my extraordinary experience. I began quietly to think of myself as having been selected for this exclusive process of awakening. This gave my ego a boost and once again gave me a place in the world. In this way, I was unconsciously using the teachings, which were meant to liberate me, to further ensnare me in the idea of a special, separate self.

Reinforcing the Illusion of Self

I was caught going in circles within perception, thinking that I was following a spiritual path which was leading me out. I was so taken with the Buddha's teaching and awestruck at how the experiences I had in meditation so thoroughly answered my questions, that I mistook this set of directions for the awakening that they were pointing to.

I had been searching for a handle on the world. I desperately wanted to find a way to make sense of all the chaos and confusion I saw around me and find my place in it. I knew that the Buddha had done what I needed to do, and was overwhelmed with gratitude to discover his map. Yet, instead of simply following the map and finding the nature of reality for myself, my perceptual mind took a hold of it and used it as another means to measure the world around me. As many of us commonly do, I made a religion out of a set of simple instructions.

The Buddha's teachings became the basis for evaluating everything that I encountered. I developed an unconscious set of criteria based on the monastic form that I had been taught. I compared this new form with other places, people, and teachings. If they measured up to what I thought spirituality was supposed to look like, then they were good. If they did not, then they were bad.

I did not go so far as to call myself a Buddhist, or join with other Buddhists. However I went on a personal campaign, categorizing everything as right or wrong according to what I believed the Buddha was saying. In this way, I further divided and polarized my world and strengthened this new self-image I had as a spiritual person.

I thought that I needed to do this in order to delineate the path and make it clear in which direction to go. I had no idea that I was merely building a new ego in order to gain a temporary sense of security and certainty in my life. I could not see that I was further isolating myself by dividing my world into an "us and them," and rejecting what did not fit with my new standards. I really believed that this was what the Buddha wanted me to do. Without these new criteria for evaluating the world, I thought that I would be lost again.

Thinking I was following the right path meant that I had to judge other ways as wrong. Seeing the practice I was doing as good meant seeing other forms as bad. This way of thinking seemed to be reinforced when I later joined the staff of a large retreat center where this form of Buddhist teaching was the primary focus. We tended to look upon other spiritual paths as corrupt or inferior as a way of strengthening our identity and establishing a sense of belonging with each other.

One Way

I became fundamentalist, narrowing my world to one way that I thought things should be, and suspicious about anything that did not fit into my new model. While this approach may have helped me to stay focused and not get distracted, it meant that I was missing the essence of the Buddha's teaching. I was rooting myself deeper in my perceptual mind instead of learning to function without it.

Some part of me felt torn about this approach from the beginning. I naturally found myself wondering about other spiritual teachers and paths and wanting to understand how they all fit together. I resisted the approach of narrowing and turned away from teachers or students who seemed to be dogmatic or absolute. At the same time, I doubted myself and wondered if I was just too undisciplined or loose.

This process took many years to unfold. Over time, it became clear to me that I had limited myself and my thinking in a way that was not healthy or true to the Buddha's teaching. I began to explore different teachers who offered different paths, yet all the while feeling a bit uneasy about not being true to *my* chosen path. However, a persistent voice kept telling me to let go, open up, and stop being afraid of making a mistake.

As I did this, my mind began to heal on a profound level. I was able to see how my fear of straying from the straight and narrow path had been keeping me stuck. I was excluding things that did not seem to fit into my idea of what was spiritual, and reinforcing the idea of me being separate from the world. As I stopped doing this, I realized how simple and immediate waking up really is, and how difficult and complex I had been making it out to be.

Waking up requires that we limit the ego in some way, so that we are not caught up in its illusions and can see what is real. Getting distracted by different approaches can keep us rooted in perception by never challenging us to surrender on a deeper level. And committing to one method or path can help to go deeply into the process of letting go and shedding layers of personality.

However, religious fundamentalism is not the way to do this. Using a spiritual path to establish a set of rules with which to judge ourselves or other people simply feeds us back into the perceptual mind's original framework of right and wrong, and does nothing to free us.

Practice Without a Goal

It took years of practicing meditation on my own, and remembering what had driven me to find this practice in the first place before I began to understand that there was no *reason* to meditate. If I was doing the practice to become enlightened, to get somewhere, or to be someone, I was merely creating a new context for my ego. This was difficult to accept because I had no experience in doing something for no reason.

My mind was programmed to achieve goals, and this is what had always served to motivate me. Even though being present with no future or past now made more sense to me than any worldly goals, the mechanism of trying to attain something in the future was still my default way of framing life. Unconsciously, I was still trying to get somewhere else.

The problem with goals is that they are always off in the distance. By setting a goal, I re-establish myself as a person living in time with a past and future, and in this way create a new foundation for the ego. Spiritual practice is elusive because I have to find a way to motivate myself toward greater consciousness without making that into a goal.

It can help to simply pay attention to the stress of struggling to be somebody in the world. As soon as I am trying to be or do something, the struggle begins again. Spiritual practice is about sensitizing myself to this tension so that I feel the pain of it immediately. As soon as I feel this discomfort, I take it as a signal to let go and surrender.

In this way, the discomfort of building an identity in the world and looking for validation from others becomes my motivation. Instead of trying to find peace by finally getting enough recognition in the world, I find peace by dropping my desperate attempts to enhance the ego, and begin to let go of my sense of self entirely.

In the end, the only reason to meditate is because there is nothing else to do. Nothing else gives me the same sense of peace and taste of reality. I go inward into the vast emptiness because it nourishes me to go there. It is like going to the well of life. If I am wise, I realize that I need to go there often and drink deeply.

Finding Your Source Within

The loneliness that permeated my life when I returned from Sri Lanka was made more harsh by my father's complete disapproval of my newfound passion. While my mother was clearly mystified and confused, my father was adamantly opposed to my attraction to the teachings of the Buddha and the practice of meditation. He saw it as a complete waste of time and I quickly recognized that there was no point in trying to explain it to him.

My father was a goal-oriented man, driven by the urge to be someone and make something of his life. To him the idea of giving up goals and undermining the ego's aspirations was blasphemy. I realized with great sadness that he would not be able to understand my new direction and I had to give up seeking his recognition.

I left again shortly after I returned home from Sri Lanka, to live on the other side of the country from my parents. I knew that I needed space to explore my new path without having to explain it to anyone, and thought that putting three thousand miles between my father and me was one way to do this.

Eight years later, I moved back closer to my family because I realized that I had unfinished business with my father which I had simply postponed for a while. I knew that I had to face him and work through some of our differences directly in order to complete the process of transformation that I now knew was my purpose here.

One day when I was reflecting on how different I was from my father, I realized that he was actually a strong proponent of everyone finding their own way in life and disliked conventions as much as I did. I remembered when he would sail in races and I used to go with him as his crew on our small Sunfish sailboat. At the start of each race, there were twenty or so sail boats all crowded together, heading in the same direction. Then my father would inevitably turn our boat and head off alone in his own direction, trying a completely different tactic than everyone else.

I was amused as I remembered how strongly he advocated for us to be our own unique person, not constricted by a job, a family, a church, or anyone else's expectations. My father never liked conformity and taught us to be as independent as possible. Yet, he could never come to recognize that I was doing exactly as he suggested because my direction was so different from anything he had ever imagined.

As I faced my father's rejection of my spiritual aspirations directly, without trying to defend or explain myself, I realized that I was learning to rely on my own inner strength. I had wanted my father's approval, as any child does, and when it became clear that it came with strings attached, I knew that I had to let go of wanting my father to believe in me. I had to learn to believe in myself instead.

Letting Go

One of the main functions of meditation practice is to continually expose any unfinished business so that we can let it go. When we sit still for a moment, everything that we have been holding on to comes to the surface trying to get our attention. All these memories or future fantasies want us to pay attention to them and *do* something about them. They all seem to require mending or enactment, and we quickly become overwhelmed by the endless volume of stuff that we have to take care of.

I have a tendency to want to hold on to things, thinking that someday I will return to repair or re-use them. I have lived in one place now for over twenty years, and my home includes a large old barn. It has been easy to stash things away that I no longer use, thinking that someday I will get back to them. What happens, of course, is that over time the piles mount and the idea of sorting through them becomes overwhelming. In the end, holding on to all this stuff can end up suffocating me and weighing me down instead of nourishing or supporting me.

It is the same way with our mind clutter. Many of us have a habit of holding on to past hurts, losses, or great achievements, thinking that someday we will resolve or re-live them. Meanwhile we experience new ones every day, and never seem to have the time or energy to sort back through all the old ones and deal effectively with them. So our memories pile up like the stuff in my barn, and eventually they can overwhelm, exhaust, and deplete us.

Meditation practice is a means to let go of all these thoughts that you don't need. It is a bit like compressing the files on your computer, or cleaning up your desktop or hard drive. If you don't do this regularly, your computer begins to slow down because its memory is crowded with odd bits of information. The mind is similar and requires regular clearing in order to function well. So meditation is a way of cleaning the mind by simply letting go of everything that you do not need in order to function in this moment.

Spiritual practice is also about not adding anything. This is difficult for most of us because our conditioning and habits are about getting things, and learning how to hold on to them. We have invested in the notion that we need to get more in order to be happy, so this is what we know how to do. The act of release is actually quite easy, and requires much less effort than grasping or clinging. Yet it is so unfamiliar that we often have no idea how to do it.

Meditation is simply the practice of letting go of everything, and allowing what *is* to be. As soon as you add more structure or form you risk acquiring a new identity. It does not take great intelligence to learn to let go. Letting go is not something that you can strive for or accumulate. It always occurs in the present moment, and the result is always a lightening and sense of release right now. There is nothing to learn about it that you don't already know. It simply takes willingness, patience, courage, faith, and persistence.

There is no place for achievement in spiritual practice, and no future goal to attain. You don't need complex rituals, formulas, or practices to learn to let go. And there is no way to measure your achievement and evaluate your progress.

You only need to pay attention and know where your awareness is in this moment. You are either present, letting go of the past and future, or you are not. You cannot accumulate moments of presence to add up to some final completion. All that you can do is develop the habit of release, so that you are free of your mind's baggage more of the time.

———————— •◆• ————————

Take a moment now to release some of your accumulated "baggage." Close your eyes, relax your body, and notice what thought comes to the front of your mind. Then imagine that thought "popping" like a soap bubble would burst if you touched it with your finger, and watch it disintegrate.

Notice what happens next.

———————— •◆• ————————

9

Under a Trance

Most of us are familiar with classic fairy tales and myths that get passed down from generation to generation. No matter what culture we come from, there seem to be these old stories that are told and retold. A favorite theme in these tales is a villain with magical powers casting a spell on the hero of the story.

Often, the people under the spell forget who they are and have to live with certain conditions that are difficult and make their lives painful. These heroes live their lives thinking this is just the way it is, having forgotten about the spell entirely. The tension in these stories revolves around the people under the spell somehow undoing the dark magic so that they wake up, remember who they are, and can resume their normal life.

While these stories may appear to be pure fantasy, there is a reason that this theme of being cast under a spell comes up again and again. It is a perfect metaphor for our human condition. We think that we are living our lives in a normal way, while we are really under a trance induced by our perceptual thoughts. We are literally under the spell of our thought patterns, and we allow them to define and limit our lives in a way that causes us to suffer.

I know that this idea may sound absurd. However, the nature of a spell is that the people under it have completely forgotten their true self. We forget that the spell ever happened and think this is just the way things are. We don't see the spell at all until we are out of it, just as we do not realize that we are dreaming until we wake up.

Another way to think of a spell is a *paradigm* or *mental program*. Remember that the nature of a paradigm is that it defines reality for us, remains largely invisible, and we believe wholeheartedly in it. In order to work, the paradigm has to remain entirely beyond question.

There are people who know about our trance and have told us clearly that we are dreaming and need to wake up. They include many of our great spiritual teachers like the Buddha or Jesus, as well as ordinary-looking people who are with us today. Their message is clear and consistent. Yet, in our entrancement, we often cannot hear their teaching or it makes no sense. Even if we do recognize some truth in their message, we usually formalize it into a religion or set of beliefs which merely perpetuate the trance.

Our resistance to change is so strong that we frequently become threatened by some people's attempts to reveal the truth to us and try to get them to stop by punishing or even killing them. Consider what happened to visionaries such as Jesus, Galileo, Gandhi, or Martin Luther King, Jr. The message of these teachers challenged the way that many of us see ourselves, and upset the dominant paradigm of the day so much that someone felt compelled to silence them.

Breaking the Spell

All that is required to break the spell created by our stories is to look away from them long enough to recognize what is actually happening in this moment. We simply have to interrupt the trance so that we can see our dream-state for what it is. In a similar way, all that Dorothy and her companions had to do to realize that the Wizard image was not real was to look away long enough to see the man behind the curtain. Once they saw the man speaking into the microphone pretending to be the Wizard of Oz, they were no longer entranced by the ominous face in the middle of the room because they could see that it was not real.

All that a teacher or savior can do is to direct our attention away from our thoughts to the mechanisms that our mind uses to *create* our perceptions. They can tell us where to look to see the "man behind the curtain" creating all the complex ideas and conclusions that we think are so real.

The Lion Who Thought He was a Donkey

A teacher I met in India, named Poonjaji, once told this story to illustrate our human predicament:

———————— •◆• ————————

There was a man whose business was washing people's clothes, and he kept some donkeys to help him carry the laundry. Each day he would gather people's clothes in the village, load up the baskets on the backs of his donkeys, and take the clothing to the river to wash it.

One day the man heard some hunters shooting in the jungle near the river. He went to see what was happening and saw that they had shot a lion. He then heard something whining nearby and discovered a baby lion in the bushes by the river, crying to be fed. He took the lion home with him, kept it warm, and fed it milk from his donkeys.

The baby lion survived and lived with the washer-man, growing up among the donkeys. He learned to eat grass and hay and sleep in the barn as they did. And when the lion was big enough, the man put baskets on his back so that he could carry laundry back and forth from the river along with the donkeys. As he reached maturity, the lion felt longings he could not explain for something he could not imagine. All the while he felt a strange restlessness, but there was nothing to do about this, so the lion went about his day, assuming that he was a donkey.

Things went along like this until one day a wild lion came to the river to drink and saw the donkeys, the lion, and the man coming to do their work. The wild lion was outraged. Why was this full-grown lion carrying baskets of laundry and eating grass *like a donkey*? He rushed out of the jungle to confront the lion, demanding to know why he was acting like a donkey.

The lion that had grown up with the donkeys had no idea who this other creature was and what he was asking him. He explained that the wild lion must have made a mistake because *he* obviously was a donkey. He pointed to the other donkeys to show how he was just like them, and went back to munching grass and carrying laundry.

This made the wild lion furious and he grabbed the donkey-lion by the scruff of his neck and dragged him to the river. He held the lion's face over the river and showed him his reflection in the water. He then made the lion who thought he was a donkey look at him, and then back at his own reflection. It slowly dawned on the donkey-lion that he did not look like a donkey at all, but he looked like this creature in front of him who called himself a lion.

The wild lion exclaimed passionately, "See who you are? You are a *lion*, not a donkey! Your place is in the jungle roaming free, not here by the river, tethered to a rope, eating grass and carrying baskets of laundry!" And so the lion finally saw who he was, and with a roar he went off into the jungle to join the other wild lions.

———————— •◆• ————————

This story illustrates how deeply deceived we can be by what we see around us and how that informs who we think we are. It is meant to get us to look at our invisible conditioning and question our most cherished assumptions about ourselves and our world.

Our tendency is to take stories like this and use them to support our ego. We might think that it is about being held captive by someone who is tricking us for their own benefit. Then we spend our lives looking for oppressors and trying to fight against them. We assume that the help we need is for someone to rescue us from our evil captors, just as the Jews of ancient Rome assumed that Jesus had come to vanquish the Romans and liberate the Hebrew people from enslavement. But this is missing the point.

All we get when we overthrow the people who seem to hold power over us is that someone new becomes the oppressor. Look at the communist revolutions throughout history and it is apparent how the oppressed people merely become the oppressors once they have a chance to gain power and control. Or consider the United States, where a popular revolution freed the people from a distant monarchy and gave birth to a new nation founded on the principle of democracy. And now, the ideal of a government "of the people" is usurped by private corporations who concentrate wealth and power to serve their own needs, just as the authoritarian monarchies of Europe and the Catholic Church once did.

In this story the man who kept the lion was not trying to trick the lion. The lion was deceived *by his own misperception*. He only saw donkeys around him, so naturally he assumed that he was one of them. In a similar way, we only see the world around us through the filter of our preconceived ideas, and so we believe that this is reality. No one is trying to trick us. We are deceiving ourselves, just as we once believed that the earth was flat and the sun rotated around it because this is what we *saw*.

It is our limited perception that causes the illusion of our separate, individual self. We simply cannot get past the images that we see of separate people with separate bodies, each of us having to protect and provide for ourselves. It never occurs to us that we are each a part of one great organism or intelligence because we can never *see* the whole in its entirety.

The deeper point of this story is that by believing our conclusions about reality, we confine ourselves to a life of pain and isolation where we get old and sick and die. We assume that this is our fate and there is nothing to be done about it. In a similar way, the lion confined himself to a life of servitude as a donkey. No one is putting this curse upon us. We are limiting ourselves and creating our own suffering by remaining within the narrow confines of what we believe to be true.

This does not mean that we are doing something wrong and need to condemn ourselves. It is simply that we believe what we see through the filter of our mental framework and do not know that there is anything else. Most of us are like the lion who thought he was a donkey. And like that lion, our truest feelings may be the deep restless longing that we feel sometimes for something important that we cannot quite remember.

As much as I may wish to be rescued, neither God nor an enlightened teacher can go into my mind and interrupt my thought process in order to free me from my trance and show me what is real. To do so would violate my innate sovereignty and reduce my capacity for consciousness, which would diminish the whole. Thankfully, nothing and no one is capable of diminishing the whole of what all of life is together.

The tough part is that I have to see through the illusion created by my perceptions *for myself*. This is an inside job that no one else can do for me. I have the inherent freedom to engage in the imaginary world of my conceptual mind as long as I want. The only real consequence of choosing to do this is my own discomfort and unhappiness.

Entranced by our Own Thoughts

The idea that we are under a spell, or deluded into believing that we are something different from what we really are may sound too unlikely to be taken seriously. Yet, many of us can admit to a deeply unsettling sense that our lives are not under our control and we are somehow being confined. Rarely do things happen the way that we want them to, and we seem to be confronted with endless obstacles which keep us from getting our way or being happy.

As I mentioned earlier, we frequently blame our difficulties on some person or situation that we think is trying to hurt or control us. We start out blaming our parents, siblings, or teachers, and then it is often our boss, employer, or government who we think is controlling us. It is normal for us to have a list of enemies who are trying to harm us and against which we have to fight for our survival.

If we don't view other people or institutions as having power over us, we often assume that God is an all-knowing being who is measuring and controlling us, who has the capacity to either reward or punish our behavior. We may not believe in God as such, yet many of us feel oppressed and downtrodden much of the time and assume that there is some great power controlling our fate.

In the fairy tales, it is usually a wicked witch or evil magician who casts a curse on an innocent victim. Deep down, many of us harbor some resentment toward a vague almighty being who seems to be out to get us and make our lives miserable. Or we assume that we are being punished in some way for our private sins.

Our idea of a savior or benevolent God is someone who will defeat our enemies, break the spell, and free us from our entrapment and misery. Many of us are waiting for such a hero to swoop down and save us. Yet the nature of our condition is that we are *willingly under the spell of our thinking mind.*

There is no villain here, but merely the irresistible power of attraction that our private thoughts hold over us. Just as we can easily become addicted to television, movies, video games, or reading fictional dramas, many of us are fundamentally hooked on the endlessly changing evaluations and conclusions projected in our mind that continuously weave the story of ourselves.

If you want evidence of this, simply try to disengage from your thoughts for just a few moments. This is what the practice of meditation is about, and explains why most of us find it impossible to do at first. Our thoughts are too compelling, and we have become too enamored with them to easily let them go. The first thing that we notice when we try to meditate is that our thoughts overwhelm us and we cannot escape from them. This may seem like failure, yet it is a vital first step. We have to see how powerless we are to control our thoughts before we can muster the courage and intention to do something about it.

Losing Interest in the Drama of Me

The power of meditation to transform your consciousness does not come from willing away your thoughts or forcefully controlling your mind. You may achieve some moments of stillness from doing this, but these are fragile and easily broken. When you engage your will to try to meditate in this way, you merely feed the process of perception that generates thought in the first place. You are *trying* not to be interested in your thoughts, while at the same time you are entranced by them. This is like arm wrestling with yourself. It pits one part of you against another, and creates an intolerable inner tension that eventually snaps and leaves you back where you started.

You finally let go of your attachment to your thinking mind *when it no longer interests you*. This is how you recover from any addiction. As long as you believe that you are getting some real benefit out of a behavior you will continue to do it, and no manner of rules or discipline can stop you. You cannot stop your mind, you can only lose interest in it. The process of meditation works by spending so much time watching the images in your mind that you get bored and finally see them for what they are.

After a while, even the most ardent daydreamers among us get sick of our own thoughts. Seeing the same ideas repeat over and over again and recognizing their petty and trivial nature, we get tired of them and they lose their glamour. The trick is simply to be able to pay attention long enough and not get caught up in imaginary dramas every time they arise. The discipline and practice required is to gently and repeatedly take your attention away from a thought and return it to a present moment sensation, the way a loving parent might steer his child away from a bowl of candy.

Finding a Map

When you are fed up with your thinking mind, you might be willing to disengage from your personal drama long enough to recognize how you keep repeating the same stories over and over again. You may notice how unhappy these old stories make you, and decide that you want to get out of the repetitive thought loops that feed your anxiety and insecurity.

Getting out requires that the old way stops working for you. This is the crisis that you come to when you realize that everything you have tried has not worked, and is not going to work. It is a dead end – what they refer to in twelve-step addiction recovery programs as a "bottom."

When you reach a bottom, you can either look for a new way out, or self-destruct. If you can keep yourself from self-destruction you may discover that there are teachers and teachings available to you that offer support and guidance, such as the ones I stumbled upon in the monastery in Sri Lanka. In fact, there are guides and maps all around you once you want out so badly that you can finally see them.

While finding a map and guide is certainly miraculous, it is just the beginning of the journey. All that a map or guide can do is to show you what to look for. A good teacher can only describe the patterns of the mind so that you can more easily recognize them. Then it is up to you to learn to disengage from the content of your thoughts long enough to be able to see for yourself what is behind them.

A tool like meditation enables you to use your own awareness to see the patterns of your thinking mind and to look beyond them to consciousness itself. Recognizing that your basic consciousness is the one thing in this world that does not change finally convinces you of your real nature, just as the lion seeing his reflection finally knew who he was.

Spiritual Practice as Medicine

Meditation is a kind of medicine for breaking the trance and waking us up. The purpose of medicine is to heal us or make us more whole and alive. In Western medical science we often confuse medicine with medication that simply relieves the pain of our symptoms, but does not address or heal the actual cause.

Many of the common medications that we are used to, such as aspirin, ibuprofen, penicillin, or chemotherapy either mask the symptoms of disease so that we feel better, or attack whatever is causing the sickness. At best, these so-called "medicines" interfere with the disease-causing agent so that the body can heal itself. At worst, they merely suppress the symptoms temporarily so that we feel better. Few of them actually do the work of healing or strengthening our body.

True medicine is that which makes us stronger and more vibrant. In order to do this, the medicine must address the cause, and not simply focus on changing the symptoms. If we want to be free from suffering, the first step is to become aware of what is causing our life to feel empty, stressed, or painful. The recorded teachings of the Buddha attempt to do this quite simply in what is known as the first discourse of the four noble truths.

The Four Noble Truths

These can be summarized as:
1. The existence of suffering
2. The cause of suffering
3. The possibility of the end of suffering
4. The way to the end of suffering

The first truth is often translated as "life is suffering" and is frequently misunderstood or discounted as being overly negative and depressing. Yet all that this teaching is trying to do is make us aware of our perpetual discontent. We are famous for either denying the discomfort of life or dramatizing it. We either try to "put on a happy face" no matter what, or make ourselves out to be victims of a cruel world that is out to destroy us. In this light, the Buddha's notion that life is suffering seems quite reasonable, rational, and balanced. It neither denies the universal experience of dissatisfaction with life, nor glamorizes it, but simply states it so that we can look at it more clearly.

In the second truth, the Buddha suggests an obvious cause of our unhappiness which seems impossibly simple – that our rational mind lacks the capacity for contentment. While we have a seemingly infinite ability to digest information, memorize data, and conceive ideas, we do not know how to be content with our present-moment experience. This is the fatal flaw that motivates our endless pattern of striving for something new and better, and locks us into a self-perpetuated repetition of birth, death, and rebirth which the Buddha called the "Wheel of Life."

The third truth announces the realization that the Buddha came to that it *is* possible to end this cycle of striving and free ourselves from its depressing grip. We are not locked permanently into a perpetual existence where we lack what we most desire and there is no possibility for meaningful resolution. His teaching clarifies that death, or the ending of the life of this body, is not the way out of suffering as we so often imagine, but merely leads to another life in another form under the same unhappy conditions.

The fourth noble truth explains the way out. This is presented as different abilities that we can cultivate within ourselves which lead to becoming more conscious or awake to our circumstance - often called the eight-fold path. As we become aware of the workings of our own consciousness, we see through the illusions that our mind fabricates and realize the truth of who we are in reality. This then fulfills our expectations of life and enables a sustained sense of completion and wholeness.

Undoing the Trance

This path presented in the teachings of the Buddha is a true medicine in that it addresses the root cause and not merely the symptoms of perpetual unrest and discomfort. Instead of trying to override disappointment with some new distraction, or diminish anxiety by numbing the emotions, the way of meditation is to look directly at the workings of the mind to discover where insecurity and anxiety originate.

The teachings of the Buddha can be summed up quite simply as follows;

1. My rational mind – which I often consider to be the whole of who I am – does not have the ability to be content.

2. However, I am *not* my rational mind, and the inability of this mind to reach a state of fulfillment is simply a flawed *program* that I am using in place of my natural state of unlimited consciousness.

As I have suggested, it is my mental programming which is causing all the suffering that I experience in the world, not the mind itself. There is nothing wrong with me or my mind, but it is the way that I am *using* the mind, under the influence of this invisible programming, which is the cause of my problem.

In order to apply this teaching, I must first see the programming that defines my thoughts, then experience for myself that I am something *other* than these thoughts. To do this, I have to step away from the process of thought for a moment and *feel my existence without it*. This requires a certain discipline, courage, and faith. I am often afraid that I will cease to exist if I do not continue investing in the story that defines my life.

Facing Death

One of the ways in which many of us remain entranced by perception is not to look too closely at what we call reality. We normally avoid looking directly at suffering and blithely skip over the part where we get old, and sick, and die. A teacher of mine suggested that what we call life is like jumping off of a one-hundred story building. As we are falling past the fiftieth floor, we casually look at each other and ask, "How are you doing?" And each of us answers, "Just fine so far. How about you?"

Death is such a commonly accepted part of our existence that most of us don't give it much thought. If we do think about it, we may find the idea of ourselves or the people we love dying to be quite scary and overwhelming. We don't see anything that we can do about it, however, so we try to avoid thinking about death and do everything possible to keep it off in the future. We may minimize death and tell ourselves that it is no big deal so that we can go on with life without this shadowy end looming over us.

Not looking too closely at death keeps us stuck in our perceptual trance. We each know that death could come to any one of us at any time, and this brings a certain dread and loss of control to our lives. Nothing about death seems right or good, yet it seems that we are powerless to do anything about it. We often feel as if life is holding us hostage as we meekly wait for our time to die.

The story goes that the Buddha was born into a royal family in Northern India and was raised as a prince and prepared to inherit his father's kingdom. His father wanted to spare him the anxiety and fear associated with mortality, so he made sure that the young prince Siddhartha never saw anyone who was sick, old, or dead.

His father succeeded in shielding the prince from these frightening aspects of life until he was a young man and snuck out of his father's palace one night to explore the city with only his private attendant by his side. Prince Siddhartha was shocked when he saw someone who was sick, then someone who was old, and finally a dead person. Each time, he asked his attendant to explain to him what these unwelcome conditions were about.

As his attendant explained that everyone gets sick, grows old, and finally dies, Siddhartha was upset and outraged that his father had kept him from learning about this. He went to his father and passionately demanded to know why he had not told the prince about sickness, old age, and death. His father simply replied that he wanted the prince to be happy and not worried about life.

We tend to deal with death in Western societies as the Buddha's father did in his kingdom in India, by not looking at it. We cover it up so that we aren't constantly reminded of our vulnerability and insecurity. We put old people into nursing homes and sick people into hospitals. We whisk away dead bodies so that we do not have to face the stark reality that our lives will one day end like that.

Our ego presents itself as our defender and protector and uses the fear of death to galvanize our allegiance. We tend to defend and prolong our life in any way that we can as if we were in a contest to see who can hold off death the longest. With our elaborate medical technologies, we keep people alive at any cost, with little regard to the quality of their lives. Most of us can't stand to look at it directly because death seems to be such a final and tragic failure.

What is Death?

One of the few things that seems certain in our world is that we each are going to die. Death appears to be a dramatic and final end point, and none of us knows really what this means or what happens then. Life as we know it is similar to being in the terminal ward of a great hospital, or the death row of a gigantic prison. From the moment that we are born into a body, we begin the slow process of dying. No one makes it out of here alive.

This is the dramatic realization that stopped the Buddha in his tracks as a young prince set to inherit his fathers' kingdom in Northern India. He simply could not accept this as an absolute reality, and he determined to find a way out of this universal predicament. If we stop to really consider that one day we are going to die and our life will be finished, we recognize this as an absurd and unacceptable situation.

The Buddha did find a way out of the predicament of death as an ending to life by discovering what keeps us locked into this pattern and learning how to undo it. He realized that facing the idea of death directly was one way to break the trance of perception and to motivate people to find a way out, as he did. So one of the practices that he gave to his students was to go to their local cemetery where bodies could be seen openly decaying, and watch what happens to the body after death.

In our sanitized Western societies we have very little exposure to death and few opportunities to contemplate its meaning. Many of us live as the Buddha did when he was a prince in his father's palace, and rarely face the realities of old age, sickness, and death directly, until it is our turn to go through them.

I have still only seen a few dead human bodies in my life. When I was a boy, I saw my grandfather laid out in a coffin dressed in a suit and tie, with make-up on so that he looked like he was sleeping. The only way I knew that he was dead was when a fly landed on his face and he did not brush it away. The next dead body I saw was my father, and I was fortunate enough to be at his side while he died. I then stayed with his body for several hours, saw his skin turn white, and felt his hand grow cold.

This was one of the strangest experiences of my life. One moment my father was there breathing in his sleep, and the next moment he was gone, with only a lifeless body left behind. There was no way for my mind to make sense of this. It was as if he simply disappeared into thin air. I could not say what had happened, but I knew for certain in that moment that this body in front of me was not my father and he must be something quite apart from it.

The Illusion of the Death

If we can muster the courage to face death directly it becomes apparent that it is just a charade. I experienced this as I sat with my father's dead body and watched it turn cold and white. Whatever had animated that body and made it appear as my father just moments before was clearly gone. Yet just as clear was that such a force could not simply disappear.

Sitting beside my father as his body died allowed me to see through the illusion of perception for a moment. The idea that my father *was* that body became so plainly absurd that it made me laugh. I saw then how it is that we go around here thinking we are each these bodies that we inhabit, and how this makes us feel vulnerable and threatened by the world around us. I could better understand how frightening this world is to most of us and how we cling to what we call life, knowing that at any moment it will be ripped from our grasp.

I also realized that this story made no sense because conscious life could not suddenly appear and disappear like that. The life force energy that is in each one of us could not *go* anywhere. Where would it go? I knew from my meditation practice that consciousness had a steadiness and certainty that does not suddenly vanish into thin air. I understood at that moment that there was much more to life than there appeared to be. There was something essential and eternal about consciousness itself – something that could never die.

The trance of mortality left me for a moment and I saw beyond the story of myself as a separate personality inside this fragile body that will one day wither and decay. In the knowing that remained, beyond the limits of perception, came a settled reassurance that consciousness could never be threatened, and that all was well with the world.

Take a moment now to be with the idea of death. Close your eyes and allow the truth of the mortality of your body to become evident. Simply recognize that you will someday die, just as everyone here finally dies. Do not try to imagine what this is like or what it means. Just be with it.

If you approach this idea with dread and habitually avoid thinking about it, you remain weighed down by the heaviness and finality that awaits you at the end of our life. If you allow yourself to get past the instinctive resistance to your own mortality, you may notice a certain lightness or freedom beneath the surface of the grim reality of death.

The idea that you are here in this body for a limited amount of time, and you have no idea what happens next, puts a new spin on life. If you look at it long enough, the idea of your consciousness ceasing to exist when your body dies is rather absurd. Where would it go? Can awareness simply disappear into nothing? Does your presence depend on being in a body?

10

The Basis of Perception

As I suggested earlier, the mechanism of perception is based on polarity or duality. We set up an opposition between two competing objects or forces and the resulting tension creates definition and gives something a form that we can recognize. Perception is the result of comparing, contrasting, and evaluating one thing against another different thing. Its most basic components are the essential opposites in our vocabulary.

Ideas like up and down, large and small, good and bad, right and wrong, light and dark, or male and female, create the reference points for this paradigm of duality. We could consider this our mental binary code. We use these concepts to provide points of reference in order to generate ideas and thoughts, just as a computer program uses the numbers one and zero to produce complex images.

We can understand our physical world in great detail through this process of breaking it up into infinite parts and comparing and contrasting one part against another. Yet the knowledge that we gain from this process is relative. *We only know something in contrast to something that it is not.*

The meaning and value of everything in our world, including ourselves, is determined by comparison with something else. Nothing here has any absolute value or meaning, which means that everything is subjective. All of the knowledge that we gain through perception is basically made up of judgments and opinions which are open to interpretation and subject to change.

Everything is Relative

———————————— •◆• ————————————

Pay attention to your thoughts for a few moments right now and you will likely notice your mind involved in some form of evaluation. You may be judging this writing as good or bad, or these ideas as right or wrong. You could be assessing your physical circumstances in this moment as cold or hot, quiet or noisy, comfortable or uncomfortable.

———————————— •◆• ————————————

In each of these infinite comparisons which most of us make continuously, we are contrasting one experience or circumstance with another. That makes all of our conclusions *relative*. It means that everything that we think we know is really just a contrast or shade apart from something else.

Think of all the terms that we use to define our world such as large, small, long, short, hot, cold, up, down, light, heavy, good, bad, and so on. Most of us assume that we mean the same thing when we use these terms. We think that other people's perceptions agree with ours, and that these terms of measurement point to something that has the same meaning for all of us. We believe that there is a *right* way to perceive something, yet this is far from the truth. Most of the time we do *not* mean the same things when we use these words, because we each have a different *point of view*.

This point was made evident to me after I had set up the guest rooms at the retreat center where I live and teach. I had thoughtfully placed a mirror on the wall in each room so that people could groom themselves without having to go to the bathroom. One day a woman came to me with a complaint that she could not see herself in the mirror in her room. I was a bit baffled by this until I realized that she was about a foot shorter than I was.

I had placed each mirror carefully on the wall so that it perfectly framed my face. I felt good about my attention to this kind of detail and did not think about it again until this woman told me of her dilemma. It dawned on me then that I had not considered how much we differ in height, and what a different perspective we each have because of this.

To a person who stands six feet and six inches tall, everyone else seems to be short. To a person who stands five feet tall, everyone else seems to be tall. We think that perception enables us to understand reality. Yet the common terms that we use to define reality *only convey our personal experience*. Thinking that our perceptions are universal truth creates endless misunderstandings and conflicts between people because perception has no absolute value and is instead entirely individual.

The Urge for Universal Truth

Basing our reality on perception means that our identity is formed by comparing ourselves with other people. This requires that we constantly look to each other for recognition and validation. In relationships we often do this by comparing ideas to try to establish what is true. Listen to normal conversation and you will hear people exchanging judgments and opinions trying to agree on the way something is.

Let's say I meet a casual acquaintance in a local store. A common topic we might discuss is the weather. One of us might say, "I can't believe all that rain we have been having lately. Is it ever going to stop?" Then the other feels obliged to agree, saying something like "Yeah, I know what you mean. I can't remember what the sun looks like any more."

This conversation tends to feel good in a small way because we both have agreed with each other's perception that the rain is bad and it would be good if it stopped soon. When our opinions match those of another person, it gives us a sense of being right, which in turn appears to validate our reality. So the primary focus of our relationships with other people is to compare and match our opinions so that we can be "right" about something together.

This process of comparative evaluation has to assume some absolute value or measure in order to work. Yet in this world there *is* nothing that remains constant and does not change. Nothing is *all* hot or cold, dark or light, good or bad. Everything has to be sorted out all the time and *there is no actual fixed base line by which to measure anything.* For some of us, a rainy day is bad because we get wet or cold and miss the warmth of the sun. Yet if the ground happens to be dry and we have a garden, the rain can be a blessing.

Perception is based solely on comparative evaluation, so it tends to shift around a lot and can never be sure of anything. If you watch your mind for a moment without getting involved in any one thought you can notice that this process of sorting out and labeling never stops, and never reaches a final conclusion.

Our world of perception is like the open sea and sky was to the ancient Polynesian sailors adrift on their tiny boat in search of new lands. Everything that we know moves, and there is no final point from which to take our bearings. This is why our lives tend to feel so vulnerable and uncertain.

Grasping at Straws

The impossible situation we find ourselves in is that we require an absolute reference point for the process of perception, and we do not have one. Therefore, the mechanism of comparison has to operate continuously to assign different values to each of our experiences in order to establish a sense of relative truth on which to base our reality. Our thinking process does not stop, and cannot stop, or we immediately lose ourselves and our world. The result is that most of us are overwhelmed and exhausted by the constant chatter of our mind.

We think that this process of endlessly categorizing everything will someday lead us to a final conclusion, and that is what keeps us hooked into it. There is the promise of some grand understanding that will settle all the confusion and make everything clear in our mind. Yet that conclusion never comes. It cannot come because there is no room for it in perception.

We cannot perceive something that is whole, complete, or finite, because the process of perception itself requires duality and opposition in order to work. Perception can never fulfill the promise of a satisfying conclusion or meaningful sense of completion because it has to divide everything it encounters into opposites in order to define what each part is.

Using the process of perception, therefore, *guarantees* that our world will remain fragmented and polarized. Our way of knowing through the process of perception requires that we include all the opposing views and opinions. While this may seem to be the only honest way that we can approach the idea of truth, in the end it leaves us with a sense of being awash in a world of relativity with nothing certain in our lives.

Religions or social ideologies often look attractive to us because we long for a set of principles or beliefs that are beyond question. Fundamentalism is so prevalent because it is the only way that our rational mind can define an absolute reality and offer something fixed in the world.

When we tire of endless comparisons and are desperate for something true, we tend to turn to our conceptual mind to formulate a definitive belief. There is nothing that stands alone here, so we make up something to latch on to and identify with that has no opposition. We often just make up a story, and then believe in it as absolute truth and try to get others to believe in it. This seems to be the only way that we can achieve a sense of certainty about anything.

The problem with absolute beliefs is that they are only ideas and do not exist outside of our mind. Someone created them and then presented them as truth. Religions often make the recorded teachings of the person who inspired them into the final word about everything. For example, this is what fundamentalist Christians tend to do with the Bible. Most religions have a book based on the teachings of their founder, and these scriptures usually harden into dogma because people are so desperate for something that is fixed and unchanging to give their lives a sense of stability.

The Roots of Fundamentalism

When we think of fundamentalism we may think of dogmatic religions or right-wing political groups. Yet most of us are fundamentalist about our beliefs and think in some way that we are right and other people are wrong. This is simply the way that our minds are programmed to approach the world because comparing opposites is how perception works.

We tend to group ourselves with other people whose opinions match ours because this strengthens our sense of being right. In a world dominated by perception, this seems to be the only way to secure our sense of place. Most of us identify ourselves with other people who see things the way we do.

The problem with this approach to defining reality by consensual agreement is that perception by its nature is highly individual. While the mechanism is the same for all of us, the content is different. We each draw different conclusions from the same basic experience because each of us has a different memory of the past to measure the present against. This is where relationships get difficult and our search for validation becomes challenging.

As soon as another person disagrees with us, some part of us feels threatened because our perception is not being validated. When this happens, we often get a tight and uncomfortable feeling. We tend to argue with other people to convince them that our opinion is right, or we withdraw from them.

Having our validity depend on aligning perceptions with other people is a recipe for disaster. We draw our conclusions by comparing a common present-moment experience with our past experiences. Since no two of us have the exact same set of experiences in our past, the process of perception is bound to result in different outcomes for each of us. In the end each one of us comes away from the same situation with our own unique conclusion, and this is hard to accept when our sense of self depends on being *right*.

It is easy to see how our dependence on perception can fracture us into groups with strong opposing ideas who see each other as threatening. We are each struggling to get our view of reality to be the dominant one so that we can finally be validated. And our validity seems to be threatened if we recognize a different perspective as also valid. So we end up in fierce competition with each of us attacking the other's position in an effort to come out on top. In this way, our method of knowing something only in contrast with its opposite sets us up for fundamentalism, which divides us and leads to perpetual conflicts.

The Religion of Science

What makes our situation so difficult is that perception is the only way that we think we have to be informed about ourselves and the world around us. Most of us trust and rely on our capacity for rational evaluation to orient us in life. We have no other source of information, so we tend to place great value and importance on our judgments and conclusions, and look upon them as truth.

In Western societies, we have refined perception into the systematic rational process that we call science. The basic premise of this process is that the more people who draw the same conclusion from the same raw data, the more likely it is to be true. We have used this process successfully to predict outcomes and create technologies that have allowed us to transform our physical world. And we use our scientific process almost exclusively now to define reality.

I grew up enamored with science of all kinds. I remember when I was about eight or nine years old that I wanted more than anything to be a scientist. I pictured myself wearing a white lab coat and spending my days investigating things in a modern scientific laboratory. I never thought of it this way at the time, but for me as a boy the image of a scientist working diligently in his lab in a long white coat held the place of a high priest. It seemed to be the seat of power and wisdom in our society, and this is what attracted me to it.

Science has taken the traditional place of religion of our society, and a scientist is now the one who tells us what is real. Science is how we know anything, and it seems to be so right so much of the time that, naturally, we tend to believe in it.

Our dominant scientific theories are presented as the truth. Yet the "truths" presented by science are only approximate and relative. What science presents as reality is merely the current most popular *theory*. This is as close as we can get to some absolute knowing given that everything here has a contradiction. We can get closer and closer to something real, but we can never reduce reality to one singular thing because the process of perception cannot function without opposites and will not allow us to reach any finite conclusion about anything.

There is nothing wrong with science or the process of meticulous observation and rational conclusions. Our minds certainly have this capacity and it can be a useful tool. The problem is that we tend to believe our scientific theories are real, just as we each individually believe that our own perceptions are real. We do not tend to see them as evolving ideas or current perspectives, but as *the truth*.

In a similar way, the ideas presented by an organized church or religion are often seen as absolute truth. This is why religions are often at odds with other religions, and why these conflicts tend to escalate into war. It also explains why our new religion of science often seems to be at odds with older established religions such as Christianity.

Scientific theories change and evolve, as does everything in our world. This is the only way that our scientific process can work because it is merely a distilled version of perception. Remember that, using our collective power of observation, we once firmly believed in a flat earth that was at the center of the universe. Our common perceptions and scientific theories have been wrong many times before, and will likely be proven wrong many times to come.

Mistaking scientific theories for truth keeps us trapped in false perspectives and limits our capacity to know. We forget that scientific inquiry and discovery is an ongoing process that raises many more questions than it answers. We have been able to make use of the knowledge gained through science to control our environment to an astonishing degree. Yet, it may turn out that all our technological capacity has caused more harm than good as we realize how much we don't yet know about our world.

The Limits of Science

The process of comparing opposites to define reality is like trying to walk across a room to reach the opposite wall by moving half way with each step. It seems as though we are moving quickly and getting closer and closer to the wall, especially in the beginning. But as we get nearer to the wall, our progress slows and we become increasingly frustrated. We soon realize that by only stepping half way each time we will never fully get there. We can come very close, and get within fractions of a millimeter, but we can *never finally reach the wall.*

We can never reach any final conclusions using the process of perception because there would be nothing left to compare that conclusion with. That is why perception and our refined process of science cannot resolve our human dilemma. These processes that we have come to rely on to define reality ultimately limit us because we can never find the whole truth that we are seeking.

We like to think of our rational process as precise and accurate. We pride ourselves in our capacity for complex mathematical equations and scientific formulas, and amaze ourselves with accomplishments like sending men to walk on the moon or harnessing nuclear energy. But talk to any advanced mathematician or physicist and you will likely hear them complain about how imprecise and approximate all of our logic and reason really is.

I was discussing the process of scientific discovery once with a physics professor and he explained to me that science cannot recognize anything without first developing a theory about it. Scientific exploration can only prove or disprove an idea that already exists. It does not discover anything new that has never been conceived before.

This is the limitation of perception. We can only compare and contrast ideas that fall within the narrow scope of our experience. Our idea of what is possible, based on what we think is real, completely defines and limits our capacity to know. This is why our ancestors were once so convinced that the earth was flat and felt threatened by anyone who suggested otherwise.

People who have devoted their lives to math or science are often the most passionate about finding something certain and true that does not change. In our Western world of rationality, this seems to be the only place we are likely to find something absolute. One of our newest scientific instruments is a gigantic circular tube that spans several *countries* in Europe. This machine is designed to accelerate and smash atoms faster and harder than we ever have before, in an attempt to find what some atomic scientists are calling the "God particle."

For all the wonders of our modern science and technology, we still don't have a clue about what makes up the fabric of the universe. We keep looking for a force that holds everything together because this question is so fundamental to our existence, yet we cannot find it.

Our mechanism of perception works by eliminating possibilities. We compare two opposite things and choose one over the other. One is right and good, the other wrong and bad. We trust this process, yet it is inherently incapable of bringing us to reality. This is because in the process of comparison, evaluation, and elimination, we have to fragment our world and break it up into little pieces.

We are literally tearing apart the whole looking for the nugget of truth we so desperately seek. To find the "God particle," we are breaking matter into smaller and smaller pieces. We do not realize yet that the truth we are seeking *is* the whole – all of the infinite universe together - and by breaking it apart, we only further obscure it.

Right in Front of Our Nose

Tearing apart matter to find the glue that holds it all together is like cutting down the trees to find the forest. Perception can only see things in terms of their parts because it has to have two or more things to compare. Using this mechanism, we cannot ever see anything in its whole and complete form.

We end up destroying the integrity of everything we examine, and then we wonder why we cannot discover what is holding it all together. We cannot see the essential fabric of life, even though it is right in front of us, because we are looking at the separate pieces and not the whole that they make up together.

The truth of a round earth orbiting the sun is as plain as day if we know what to look for. Yet it took us thousands of years to recognize this fact because we simply could not see past our assumptions. We have a rare opportunity today to look back at our history and see how many times our assumptions about what is real prevented us from discovering the truth. Even when someone points directly to something true, if it does not fit into our image of reality, we simply do not see it.

We would surely be lost forever were it not for one small thing that we continually overlook. Obscured by the mind's endless attempts to reach truth by comparing one thing with another is a very simple and powerful capacity which we all have latent within us for direct awareness. Awareness touches everything directly and knows it fully, without the need to create a conceptual image or story about it.

Awareness does not need to compare or evaluate something to know it, and the process of direct awareness does not dismantle the object it is focused on. In fact, awareness *cannot* change anything. It simply knows things as they are, and not as they compare with something else or fit into our personal story. Awareness creates immediate relationships with everything and includes them as part of itself, without needing to fix or change anything.

Awareness does not look at something to evaluate its threat or benefit to us personally. It includes all things and accepts them as different, and part of a larger complete whole, at the same time. Awareness does not need to establish its own reality because it simply knows reality all the time and cannot know anything else. Indeed, it is this great simplicity and lack of ability to fix or manipulate that makes us continually overlook awareness in favor of perception.

A spiritual path is simply a way to get beyond the great complex of thoughts and images that occupy us most of the time. It offers tools to help us disengage from compulsive thinking and engage awareness instead. This does not involve learning something new, as all of us have always had the capacity for awareness. It is simply that we need to exercise and strengthen this capacity, so that we have another means of relating to the world aside from conceiving abstract ideas about it.

The Origins of Perception

Once we glimpse the patterning of our perceptual mind, begin to see its constant need to compare, label, and evaluate, and understand how much stress and anxiety this causes, we naturally might want to know how things got to be this way. A question that often arises when talking about waking up is: "How did we fall asleep? When did our ignorance and delusion about reality begin? Where did the idea of a separate self come from, and why?"

The Buddha's response to these questions went something like this:

———————— •◆• ————————

Suppose you have been shot with a poisoned arrow and you insist on finding out who shot the arrow, when they did it, and why, before you pull the arrow out. In the time that you take to investigate where the arrow came from, the poison would likely work its way into your body and you would die before you found out the answers. It would be wiser to pull out the arrow as soon as you recognize that you have been shot. Then you might live and can investigate those questions later.

———————— •◆• ————————

His point is that, knowing we are deluded, and the consequence of our delusion is suffering and death, it makes more sense to get ourselves out of this condition than it does to spend our time trying to understand how we got here. My own experience has taught me that once I am free from the delusion of perception, the questions about how perception began seem to lose their urgency.

It helps me to recognize that my mind is making this mistake each moment, rather than seeing it as something that happened in the past. I notice that the desire frequently arises to assert my judgments or try to control a situation. This usually happens when I become afraid and need a sense of security, or when there is something that I think I have to get in order to be happy. At these times, I can see my sense of a separate self arise and grow larger right in the moment.

The appeal of being an individual, separate and apart from everyone and everything else, is that I think I get to *have* things. I think I can have experiences, friends, lovers, houses, cars, children, success, accomplishment, pleasure, and love. There is a certain thrill in the struggle of getting these things and trying to hold on to them that makes it interesting. All this drama forms the basis of the story about my individual self, filled with triumphs and defeats.

The great sadness of being a separate individual, however, is that I am always left out of the picture. I get to see, feel, taste, touch, smell, and hold on to things. Yet I never get to *be* those things because I am always the one *having* the experience of them. This is a bit like being the photographer at a wedding. Everyone is having a wonderful time, and I am there witnessing it all, but I am not part of it. Ultimately, this can be frustrating and frightening, because I want to be part of the whole and not separate in my experience of it.

Perception and Isolation

Look at how we tend to crowd into cities, clog our highways with traffic jams, carry our cell phones and blackberries with us everywhere, and want to report in on everything that happens to us. Many of us have an overwhelming desire to be connected to each other and feel part of something larger than our individual selves. As much as we cling to our independence, we do not like being alone and we go to great lengths to avoid solitude.

Isolation is at the core of the suffering that the Buddha described, and it is the result of identifying myself as a separate person. The painful limitation of conditioned mind is that it always remains separate from everything around it. It is like I am going through life seeing everything through a glass wall, or handling it with gloves, instead of feeling it directly with my own hands.

The nature of perception is that I am excluded from everything that I perceive. I do not get to see what I look like or hear what I sound like, unless I carry a mirror, hear a recording of my voice, or see myself in a picture. The most common way that I get to experience myself is through other people, and this leaves me dependent on others' approval for validation. This is why getting attention from other people can seem so important.

In our Western scientific process, scientists have to be objective and exclude themselves from the subjects that they are studying. Including any part of themselves would mean contaminating the results of their experiments, and the resulting data would be flawed.

This means that we cannot fully experience ourselves. While we can observe everything around us, we are not included, and therefore we can never observe the whole. We cannot study or connect deeply with our own consciousness because perception is using consciousness as its basis. This may explain some of the sense of isolation and painful loneliness that accompanies our cherished sense of self.

Freedom through Failure

I cannot get out of isolation by trying to get more of everything or hold on tighter to what I want. I have tried this and it clearly is not working. I can never get enough to satisfy my desire because what I really want is to merge with and be part of everything, and this is the one thing that perception cannot do. The way out is to give up the one thing that keeps me apart from everything else, which is my notion of an individual self.

Of course, this sense of self is the last thing that I would think of giving up because I am so identified with it. My personality seems to offer me the only chance I have to get the things I think I need to be happy. Giving up on this means quitting altogether, and accepting failure as a human being. This is why so few of us ever find a way out. We don't recognize that the one thing standing in the way of what we really want is the thing we are holding onto the most tightly.

It takes some sort of final collapse of everything that we have strived for before most of us can see the way out. We usually have to reach a point of exhaustion, desperation, or extreme frustration before we consider letting go of the self. It can help to have a spiritual teaching in order to recognize that our own identity is what is keeping us trapped in a seemingly endless cycle of loss. Having a context for our failure as a human being can make the difference between depression and insanity or the freedom of enlightenment.

As a college student beginning my adult life with all the promises of success laid out before me, I chose to let go, drop out, and accept failure because I could not play the game any longer. I became suffocated by the restrictions, rules, and limitations and decided that it was not worth jumping through those hoops. I set out, like the Polynesian sailors may have once set out, on a journey to someplace that I could not see and was not sure even existed. I only knew that I could not stay because some essential part of me would shrivel up and die if I did.

Like the Polynesians in their tiny boat on the vast ocean, I got lucky and found my North Star. With the miraculous help of the Buddha's ancient teachings, preserved and passed down for twenty five hundred years in the culture of Southeast Asia, I came to recognize that the answer to my dilemma lay inside of me, where it had always been, waiting for me to discover it.

Living Without Shelter

I once lived for several months in a small city, caretaking a friend's apartment. I had no responsibilities for a time, and found myself getting to know some homeless people living in an abandoned box car by the train tracks. I was drawn to them because they were the only people in town who were not constantly rushing around and stressed about getting things done. They had time to hang out, and were open to having me join them.

I grew up in an affluent family where everything I needed was provided. Material wealth and achievement were the stated goals, and I was expected to make something of myself in a professional world. In this context, being homeless on the street would be the worst thing that could happen to me.

I had long ago given up the life that my family prescribed, yet I had never been completely homeless and living hand-to-mouth the way these people were. I sensed that I had something to learn from them, and pushed through my fear and discomfort at their condition to really get to know what their lives were about.

I found to my surprise that they were close to my age, in their mid-thirties, and educated about the world. It quickly became apparent as I talked with them that they were *choosing* to live this way because it was not worth it to them to pay the price of being part of society.

They had no driver's license, job, money, home, insurance, phone, car, or any of the things that many of us assume are necessary for a successful life. It wasn't because they could not have them, but because they did not want to jump through all the hoops required in order to get them. They had come to the conclusion that it was simpler and easier to think only about where to get food or how to stay warm and dry at night.

Freedom and Vulnerability

I gradually came to see my homeless friends in a different light. I had unconsciously been assuming that they had failed and could not make it in society because this is what I had been taught. It had never dawned on me that they did not *want* to strive to secure a place in our competitive society. They were opting out and were willing to live with the consequences.

I came to respect them for this and gained a new appreciation for people who I thought could not handle being responsible. I recognized that their experience was similar to mine. I also saw that they were living in a much more vulnerable way than I was. Being without a home, car, or money meant that they were outside much of the time with no buffers between them and the world around them. They were constantly exposed to the weather and other people, and had little personal privacy or protection.

We were once all walking together on the paved bike path that led from the city down to the railroad tracks and eventually to the beach where they hung out at night. They had their dog and an old grocery cart which served as a kind of wagon to carry cast-off things they picked up along the way. All of a sudden one of them said with a bit of alarm, "Here comes a roller-blader!"

I looked up and saw something barreling down upon us. Hidden behind a helmet, padding, and dark sun glasses, the robotic figure flying at us with breakneck speed held an eerie resemblance to Darth Vader, the ultra-villain in the classic *Star Wars* movies. Our tranquil scene exploded as we scattered like leaves in the wind to keep from getting run over. It felt as if a freight train had just swished us off the tracks in its powerful wake.

I thought of how many times I had ridden my bicycle on that path, and even roller-bladed there before. I was humbled to experience this seemingly ordinary scene from the vantage point of people who lived here and walked this path daily to get basic necessities such as food, water, or clothing. I was able to see how bikers and skaters could appear callous and menacing as they roared past, barely noticing the people who called this path home. To the box car people, the world around them was moving at this frantic pace and all they could do sometimes was to get out of the way.

This experience helped me to understand how a car, home, or job offers a kind of protection from the world by insulating us from other people. At the same time, these comforts can isolate us and undermine our basic need for companionship and belonging. My new friends living in the box car had little to protect them, yet they enjoyed a sense of community that my life seemed to be painfully lacking at times.

11

Beyond Time and Space

It is natural to assume that a spiritual path involves a movement toward some other place and future time. The very concept of a path implies going from one place to another over a span of time. Space and time form the essential matrix for the paradigm of perception, and we orient ourselves by them constantly. Most of us depend on concepts like past and future, here and there, up and down, near and far, to locate ourselves.

Yet, as with everything in our perceptual world, these are relative measurements with no absolute basis in reality. Our rational mind constructs them to give us a context for our sense of self, but they have no inherent meaning. Past is only meaningful in relation to the present or the future. The definition of near depends on far, and what we call small depends on what we consider large.

Perspective

I remember going back to visit my elementary school as an adult and having to use the bathroom. I was surprised and disoriented when I saw how small the toilet, sink, and urinal were. I distinctly remembered how large they had been when I was a child going to school there. This really disturbed me and I was scratching my head in confusion trying to figure out why someone had remodeled the school and made all the fixtures half-sized.

Then, in a flash, it dawned on me what was really going on. I realized that the bathroom fixtures were made for children and that is why they were half the size of regular ones. I was certain that the bathroom fixtures had become smaller, but *they* had not changed – I had. The last time I had seen them, my body was half the size that it is now, and of course to me then they seemed large. When I first saw them again, I assumed that something had changed external to me, when it was only my *perspective* that had shifted.

This story illustrates how I often experience the world from my own limited and self-centered viewpoint, relating everything to myself and assuming that things really are the way *I* see them. When I visited my old elementary school, I knew that something had changed. Even though it made no sense, my first assumption was that the bathroom had been redesigned.

In this same way, most of us color the world around us with our own perception, and thus obscure the truth. The main problem with this is that it keeps us ignorant and limits our capacity to know what is real.

Questioning the Basis of Perception

In the past few years I have gained a new understanding of how time and space do not exist on their own and we have to *make* them part of our reality. In home-schooling my three children, I came to see that measurements of all kinds have to be taught and learned, and are not a natural part of our experience. Things that I take for granted, like the time, day, month, and year, all have no meaning to children. Neither does the concept of towns, cities, countries or continents make any sense to them at first. So it was with the idea of temperature, speed, distance, or weight.

Our world is not inherently broken into these segments or boundaries that allow us to measure and keep track of things. We made them up, and have to teach people what they are and how to use them. And, as I found out, making these concepts feel real takes a lot of effort.

I had to go over each one again and again, and practice with the children a bit each day, until finally they began to understand and were able to make sense of the time of day or days of the week. Even then I was surprised at how long it took before they would look at a clock or a calendar on their own. In this process, I realized how little relevance these common measurements have to our basic existence, and how arbitrary and artificial they all are.

Using time and space to order our lives may be necessary to live in society as we know it, as is learning how to talk, write, handle money, use a computer, make a telephone call, or drive a car. The problem is that we easily mistake all of these for *reality*. We forget that some people before us made them up, they are not inherent or permanent, and we all had to learn them at one time. Soon we cannot see beyond them, and then they limit us because we don't believe there is anything outside of these artificial constructs.

The Limits of Space and Time

Space and time are an inseparable part of perception. Perception creates them, and they in turn support the process of perceiving things. However, they also limit us, and create a world that can feel uncomfortably restricted and confining.

Time often seems to go too fast or slow and I struggle against it constantly. I either have too much time, or not enough, and this creates emotional tension and anxiety. Space is often too expanded or too contracted as well. I either feel cramped and claustrophobic because there is not enough space around me, or overwhelmed and exhausted by the vastness of the distance that I have to traverse to get where I want to go.

As limiting as space and time are, they have become so familiar and comfortable that I would be terrified to find myself suddenly without them. Imagine going beyond the bounds of time and space for a moment and you will see what I mean. Without space I could be anywhere or nowhere, and without time I would have no past or future. This experience can be disorienting and disturbing at first because I have become so used to these familiar references. However I can experience reality perfectly well without them, and when I do, the sense of freedom is exhilarating.

The only parts of the paradigm of space and time that are *actual* are "here" and "now," and I can only experience these directly without interpreting them through language. "There" only exists as a concept as does "then" or "when." In order to find reality therefore, I can only refer to the experience that I am having in this moment, without thinking about it or trying to relate it to some other experience.

———————— •◆• ————————

Close your eyes and pay attention to what is happening in this moment. Notice the small things that you might normally overlook, such as the way this book feels in your hands, the position your body is in right now, or how you are feeling emotionally. Let go of everything else.

In these direct experiences, is it important to know the time of day, day of the week, month or year? Does it matter what country, city, building, room, or place you are in?

———————— •◆• ————————

Nowhere to Go and Nothing to Do

If I embark on a spiritual path believing that the end is off in the future, I will never reach that end. It will always be off in the future. This seems paradoxical at first, yet it is an essential step in understanding the process of awakening. Consider the example from the previous chapter about trying to reach the far wall by crossing half of the distance with each step. Although it may seem as though I am making progress with each step, the way in which I am crossing the room means that I cannot ever reach the far wall.

I can't help but see myself on a journey with distance and time involved to get to where I am heading. However, the only time that I can have an experience of reality is now. That is because reality does not exist anywhere else.

The spiritual awakening that I am describing is not an accomplishment, nor does it require any learning or the perfection of any skill. It is not something that you can work toward, get better at, and finally master. It does not involve adding anything, embellishing yourself, or becoming any different than you are now. There are no levels to it and no measures of your progress toward it. It is completely unlike any other endeavor that you are likely to undertake, as it does not involve creating something new. It involves merely cultivating your capacity to be aware of what has always been here.

This at once makes a spiritual path simple and difficult. There really is nothing for you to *do*. The work of waking up is letting go, not acquiring more. Instead of trying to gain more knowledge, it helps to let go of everything that you think you know and allow yourself to *not know* anything for a moment.

This is not because there is anything wrong with knowing. It is because what you think you know is based on a false premise, and is not true in an absolute sense. Knowing something based on comparison with what it is not is an incomplete way of knowing. You end up knowing what it isn't, but have no way of knowing what it is as a complete whole.

With the mechanism of perception you can only get a sense of the many fragments, but never the whole. This is simply because *there is nothing to compare the whole of reality with.* When you use comparative evaluation as a tool for understanding, the whole will always remain invisible. All you can see are the fragmented pieces of something and imagine the whole they might add up to.

The process of becoming more conscious is about being willing to see something very familiar, that you think you know all about, from an entirely new perspective. It is a shift in the way that you *see*, not a change in the way that you *are*. Most of us are convinced that this world is a certain way based on how our perception interprets all the sensory information we take in. And, as I have suggested, a spiritual experience is simply seeing the world the way it is, not the way we *think* it is. This is what happened when our ancestors began to recognize that the earth is round.

You don't need to become something better to be fully conscious. You already *are* fully conscious and simply need to become aware of that. Waking up from the dream that you call life is just like waking up from a nighttime dream. One moment you are caught up in a story and the next moment you open your eyes and see that you have been asleep in your bed, and the story was a dream. Nothing changed. You simply became aware that you were sleeping and what you mistook for reality was just your imagination.

Seeing Things as They Are

A teacher of mine named Byron Katie once told a story to illustrate how we mistake our thoughts for reality.

———————————— •◆• ————————————

Imagine that you are walking on a dark road at night and you see a large snake stretched out in the road directly in front of you. Chances are that you would startle and become afraid. You may begin to think of all the ways this snake could attack you, the pain of being bitten, and the possibility of being poisoned.

We depend on this rational process for our safety. When we are threatened, the mind automatically begins to sort out the situation, assess the danger, and make a plan of action. In this situation you might consider running the opposite way, crossing to the other side of the road, or trying to chase away the snake.

Once convinced of a threat, the mind cannot stop thinking about how to deal with it. There you are, frozen for a moment on that dark road, staring hard at the snake directly in front of you. Your body is flooded with adrenaline and tensed with stress, and your mind is racing trying to figure out what to do. All this may be reasonable and perhaps even necessary to be able to respond to real dangers and look out for your own safety. However, the problem with relying on perception in this way is that you often go into an emergency response mode before you know for certain what the danger actually is.

As you look a bit longer and see that the snake is not moving, you feel a bit more courage and take a few steps closer for a better look. You pick up a large stick and slowly edge forward, heart racing, keeping your eyes fixed on the snake. Then, as you get a clearer view of the snake, you suddenly realize that it is not a snake at all but is really just a piece of rope. In a moment all your fear and anxiety evaporate. You shake off the adrenaline, chuckle at your folly, and continue walking without giving the rope another thought.

———————————— •◆• ————————————

A dramatic shift just occurred in your whole being. You went from being very afraid to a state of complete calm instantly with no change in your physical environment. The shift happened because you stayed present long enough to see what was actually happening, and you finally saw the reality of the situation.

If someone had tried to convince you that the snake was a rope, you either would believe them or not, but your fear would likely still be present because the thought of a snake would still be with you. You could try hard to overcome your fear, put the thought of the snake out of your mind, and gear up your courage to just keep walking. However, your fear would still remain and part of you would still be thinking about a snake.

Once you see for yourself that the snake is just a rope, however, all of the fear disappears instantly. No one needs to convince you, there is no belief involved, and you can never again see it as a snake. This is the nature of a paradigm shift or radical change in perspective. And this is how spiritual awakening works.

Letting It Be

Becoming conscious does not change anything outside of us. It is our inner perspective that shifts and we see ordinary parts of our world from a whole new angle. This direct seeing then changes our relationship to ourselves and our world.

Much of the frantic thinking going on in my mind is based on things that I cannot know nor do anything about. I cannot change my past, no matter how hard I try. And I can never know what will happen in the future, or how I will feel about it. *Most of the time my thoughts are focused on things that I have no control over.* I waste an enormous amount of time and energy in this way, only to end up feeling frustrated and hopeless as none of my efforts seem to make any difference.

My mind is programmed to evaluate my past, looking for meaning and trying to understand what happened or why. This programming also drives me to plan and rehearse the future, trying to conceive of as many possible scenarios as I can in order to be prepared. I think that this is the way to have some control and make myself safe. However, the result is that I often imagine things that are not true and then respond to them as though they are real. This is what happened in the previous story about the rope that looked like a snake.

I never achieve any peace or real sense of security this way, because the process is endless. I am never able to fully understand my past and I can never know the future, so all of my efforts leave me still feeling vulnerable and uncertain. I end up making "mountains out of mole hills" and the process itself tends to exhaust and overwhelm me until the mind drives me crazy and I just want to get away from it all.

Becoming more awake and conscious means simply that I do not follow the mind every time it sounds an alarm or tries to figure out what something means. Instead of merely reacting to my interpretations, I learn to set aside these thoughts and come back to a present moment experience in order to give myself a chance to see things as they are. I question my assumptions and hold my perceptions lightly, knowing that I might be wrong.

This takes courage, faith, and wisdom, and often requires practice. Meditation is a simple and direct way that I can learn to unhook from my perceptual mind and experience things as they are. By letting go of thoughts and coming back to a present moment experience, I learn to sense the difference between an actual experience and my interpretation, and I am not so easily fooled by my perceptions.

Interrupting the Process of Becoming

My perceptual mind, as discussed above, can only see fragments of the whole because its capacity to "see" depends on contrasting one thing against another. I know light because it is not dark, and small because it is not large. This means that I can only perceive myself in terms of what I am *not*. I therefore define myself by what I lack, because this is the only way that I can experience myself through perception. A natural result of this process is that someone else always appears to have something that I don't have.

This is why I am always trying to have or become something else. I am always reaching out for something that I want to get or be. My life story is that I am not complete, and that something outside of me will make me so. I am constantly searching for some knowledge, skill, possession, or person that will finally make me whole. Inherent in the process of perception is that the notion of wholeness, completion, or just being enough, remains an abstract ideal to be achieved sometime in the future.

Having enough or being enough is the purpose of all of our striving. It is what most of us are wishing for and working toward in some way. And the very nature of perception, that we can only know ourselves in relation to what we are not, means that *we cannot get there from here.*

In comparing myself with everyone else, I usually come out feeling as though something is missing. This explains the sinking feeling of desperation and sense of futility that often underscores my experiences. It is why I feel so trapped and confined here, and why life can seem hopeless and depressing.

Our rational response to this predicament is to try harder to become something more. We set up a complex educational system, for example, with steps and measures and degrees of completion. We see learning as something with a beginning and an end, and knowledge as something to accumulate and hold on to. Yet there never seems to be an end that we can easily identify, and we never have enough knowledge or information to feel complete.

A spiritual path does not work this way. It is not a linear progression toward a conceivable end point. What we have acquired in the past, and our future plans, have no meaning or benefit because we have no control over them. The only thing that is relevant to awakening is this present moment.

Our part in being conscious or awake is simply to interrupt the pattern of trying to become something else. Giving up ambition or striving is like cutting off our arms and legs and will feel like quitting to most of us. It doesn't make any sense within our familiar context, and is usually the last thing we are willing to do.

A true spiritual teaching will not force you into giving up. A coerced surrender is not a real surrender, and the mind will simply hide its strategy below the level of awareness. A teaching that is effective can merely show you how your strategy is not working, and in fact is causing us more suffering than it relieves. The goal is simply to get you to see for yourself that the process of becoming is an endless treadmill that is exhausting your vital energy and has no conclusion.

Once you see what your mind is doing and the endless cycle in which you are caught up, you automatically become willing to let go. It is like seeing the rope that you thought was a snake. After you see the rope, there is no difficulty letting go of the idea of a snake is there? Yet if you don't see this for yourself, the possibility that the rope might really be a snake will forever haunt you.

12

Exposing the Program

If there is any skill involved in waking up it is in simply knowing how to interrupt the patterns of perception so that you are not continuously fooled into believing that your thoughts represent reality. An effective spiritual teaching merely highlights the common patterns of your conditioned mind so that you can see them for yourself. Once you see the patterns and can predict what the mind will do next, you have a chance to interrupt them and see the illusion for what it is.

A Good Coach

In high school I played on the ice hockey team. One day our coach was talking to us about another school's team that we were going to play against that week. The team had a star player, and the coach had been to several of their games to watch him play. He told us that this player was fast and good at skating around his opponents with the puck, and as a result he scored a lot of goals. He said that we had to deal with this player effectively if we wanted to beat that team.

My coach then told us that he noticed how this player always did the same move. He showed us the move. It went something like faking to the right, then left, then skating hard to the right. He told us to watch for that move if this player was coming towards us with the puck. Then we would know what he was going to do next and be able to interrupt his maneuver to get the puck away from him.

It turned out to be very helpful for our coach to observe this about the other player and give us this information before the game. Just as my coach told us the predictable moves of this opposing player, an effective spiritual teaching describes the predictable patterns of the rational mind. A coach cannot go out onto the ice and confront the player himself, as a teacher cannot enter our mind and free us from our obsession with our thoughts. All he can do is tell us what he has seen and encourage us to see it for ourselves.

Like that star hockey player on the other team, the conceptual mind repeats the same patterns over and over again. By watching for these patterns we can learn to interrupt them and break the mesmerizing hold that our thoughts have over us. The essence of meditation practice is to reveal how our mind creates the illusion of reality, so that we can interrupt it and experience reality directly for ourselves.

If my coach had not gone to watch the other team's player, none of us would have been able to see that his move had a set pattern to it. We would assume that he was making it up each time, and would not have been able to interrupt him because we would constantly be trying to guess what he was going to do next. However, once we knew to look for a pattern, we could see it and realize for ourselves that he was simply repeating the same move.

Focus on the Pattern

Most of us never suspect that our thought process is limited and controlled by a predetermined program. We are usually so entranced by the complexity of the thoughts and images in our mind that we don't ever notice how they all stem from a few repeating patterns. Therefore, just the notion that there *is* a pattern to our thought process offers enough guidance in the beginning. Hopefully this will encourage you to use your awareness to look a bit closer at the way stories are framed in your mind.

Just as my hockey coach pointed out the other player's pattern, I will name some common mental patterns that most of us share so that you can look for them specifically in your own thought process. These programmed patterns are so familiar that you usually cannot see them at first. The hardest part of breaking out of your patterned thinking is simply to bring it to your awareness. Once you see that you are repeating the same patterns over and over again, and recognize the struggle and pain that this causes, your natural response will be to stop and try something different.

Until you recognize your primary thought patterns as the source of your struggles in life, you are limited to merely addressing the *symptoms* of your discontent. Just as it seems impossible that the tiny grain of sand in your shoe is the cause of your fatigue, it is difficult for most of us to understand just how much our thoughts control our experience. A spiritual teaching attempts to demonstrate *how* our thoughts define our experience so that we can see for ourselves where the obstacles in our life originate.

In this chapter and the ones following, I will suggest some of the patterns that I find most prevalent in my own thought process and hear about most frequently from other people. While the content of our seemingly individual minds may be quite different, and the conclusions we draw from our experiences vary widely, the basic template of perceptual mind is the same, and most of us utilize a similar set of pre-determined patterns.

Is the Grass Really Greener?

The "grass is greener" pattern centers around the belief that there is something better that is not here. We often use the expression "the grass is always greener on the other side of the fence" when someone is longing for something that they do not have. It comes from the way grazing animals like sheep and cows respond to the grass on the other side of their pasture fence. No matter how good the grass is where they are, the animals always seem to want to get through the fence to the grass on the other side.

———————— •◆• ————————

Watch your mind right now and you will likely be able to see this pattern in action. You may be thinking that this writing could be better, there is a better book to read, there is a better place to read it, or there is something better that you could be doing with your time.

Notice how focusing on what you don't have keeps you restless and uneasy. Pay attention to any tightness or discomfort in your body that you might be feeling now.

———————— •◆• ————————

The way this pattern holds my attention is to keep me focused on some alternative which is more desirable and not readily available. I often get hooked by the idea of something better than this, and keep my focus there instead of seeing the programmed pattern that generates this idea repeatedly, regardless of my current circumstances.

I can often sense this pattern at the beginning as a vague discomfort with my current situation. Something is not right, but I can't say exactly what it is yet. This causes me to reject my present circumstance and project a future situation that is better. Then I focus on the difference between the two and see only what my current situation is lacking.

This simple and predictable thought pattern is responsible for much of my discontent and unrest in life. It keeps me from appreciating my present circumstances and eliminates the possibility of contentment with *anything* that I have in this moment. It propels me to move from one situation to another, always with an eye on what could be, and never fully experiencing what I have now.

This pattern tends to perpetuate itself and guarantees that I remain stuck in a hopelessly irresolvable dilemma. As soon as I manage to get to the "other side of the fence" where the grass seems so much greener, I immediately become disillusioned, and begin looking for another place with even *greener* grass. Usually, the very grass that I just left on the other side of the fence instantly looks better once it is out of reach.

When we look at it objectively in this way, the insanity of this pattern is obvious. We can see how it leads to frantically chasing rainbows and results in perpetual discontent. Yet, most of us remain stuck in this pattern and it undermines any chance of fulfillment. This is because we never see the thought pattern itself, but are distracted by the object of our desire which is always located off in the distance instead of here where we are now.

Fooled Again

The mind is very good at this pattern and tricks us over and over again into believing that there *really is* a better situation somewhere else. This reminds me of one of Charles Shulz's *Peanuts* cartoons that I read as a child. In it, Lucy entices Charlie Brown one more time to come and kick the football that she is holding, promising that this time she will not yank it away at the last minute, as she has always done before.

Charlie Brown heaves a big sigh, looks at her skeptically, then decides to go for it, thinking that this time she means it. You can tell that he really wants to kick that ball and is just hoping that Lucy will keep her word.

Charlie starts running faster and faster toward the football. As he gets closer to the ball he checks to see that Lucy is still there holding it for him, and he feels more trust and confidence that she is indeed going to stay. He runs harder and puts everything he has into this kick.

Then, just at the last moment, Lucy pulls the ball away and Charlie Brown does this huge kick into thin air. The force of his kick flips him over and lands him hard on his back on the ground. We see Lucy in the background with a look of mischievous guilt, while Charlie Brown sighs in desperation.

Maybe This Time...

The perceptual mind is just like Lucy, always promising a better situation but never delivering on that promise. This pattern keeps me reaching toward the future, and never content with the present moment. I put everything I have into getting this *one thing*, just as Charlie Brown puts everything he has into this kick, because this is *the one*. And I inevitably end up humiliated and flat on my back in pain, as the object of my desire is ripped away at the last minute over and over again.

The problem is that this present moment is all that I ever really have. Keeping my focus on the future guarantees that I *miss* the present, and as a result I end up feeling desperate and hopeless much of the time. My life often has a hollow emptiness to it because I cannot ever fully enjoy what I have now, and this feeds the idea that something better *is* around the next corner.

The grass is greener cycle keeps me focused on what I am lacking and wish were happening. Just like Charlie Brown, I keep myself interested in playing this futile game by the hope that *this time it will work*. In a similar way the wizard of Oz, from the movie mentioned earlier, keeps Dorothy and her companions focused on the commanding image of a face in the middle of the room. As long as they keep focused on the image, they never see the man in the booth in the corner of the room who is projecting it, and believe that the ominous face surrounded by smoke and flame is really an all-powerful wizard.

If I stay focused on what I don't have, I never see the pattern that is responsible for these images, and believe there really *is* something better somewhere else. This sense of incompletion then fuels my desire to look for something better, and on it goes, until I get smart and look instead at the pattern itself.

When Will it be Enough?

Those of us fortunate enough to live in affluent societies, where there is an abundance of everything that we need, have a unique opportunity to see this mental patterning that is responsible for our chronic lack. We don't have to spend our days concerned about how to get enough food, for example. Food is so inexpensive and readily available that most of us spend little time thinking about this basic need. Yet, many of us approach food with a fear that there will not be enough.

We buy more food than we can eat and eat more food than we need. When we eat to relieve ourselves of this fear, we can never seem to get enough to make the fear go away. Our bodies then grow larger and we become ill from being overweight. The abundance of food that was supposed to relieve us of our fear of starving and make life easier turns out, in fact, to be killing us.

This common paradox can be seen throughout our developed world. We are in the midst of more material wealth and comfort than people have ever known on earth before, yet there still is never enough. Despite the abundance all around us, many of us feel hollow and empty inside. We do everything with a sense of desperation, and even the most wealthy among us often feel deprived.

It seems that as soon as we are about to get something we want or need – just as we are going to finally grasp it in our hands – it suddenly vanishes into thin air just as Charlie Brown's football vanished at the last minute. This experience is very real for most of us and completely frustrating. It is no wonder that we often feel a sense of despair and depression and struggle even harder to get more.

Yet getting more is not going to solve our problem. There will never be enough, because what we lack is simply the *capacity to experience fully what we already have*. Our perceptual mind can only know things by taking them apart and comparing them with something else. The very mechanism of conceptual thought makes it impossible for anything that we experience to be enough by itself. Everything has to be compared to something else in order for perception to understand it, and this means that nothing can ever be whole and complete.

In this way, we are programmed for perpetual lack. The process of perception itself guarantees that we remain unsettled, never able to rest in the present moment. We cannot enjoy what we have now because our habit is to constantly compare and evaluate it against what we once had, or what we imagine we could have.

The consequences of trying to satisfy our perpetual sense of lack is that we are systematically destroying ourselves, each other, and all of the natural systems upon which our lives depend. Our habit of over-consuming is depleting the basic resources of our planet, and making many of us overweight, lethargic, and isolated. And we find ourselves mired in conflicts with each other as we compete for limited resources in our desperate attempt to feed our endless desires.

There is no lack here. The resources that we depend on would naturally maintain an abundance of everything we need if we used them simply to fulfill our basic needs instead of to drown out our fear. We are not looking at the source of our problem and have been fooled into thinking that the sense of deprivation that we all feel is based on actual lack. Many of us think that we are starving, when really we are destroying ourselves by over-consuming.

The Thrill of Anticipation

One simple shift can turn this desperate situation around. We can look at the basis of this idea of lack. We may then see that the problem is not outside of us as we have always imagined.

It is not that we don't yet have what we need to be happy. It is that *perception merely lacks the capacity for present-moment awareness*. In other words, we cannot experience what we have now through the mental filter that we use to understand the world.

This explains why the things we most desire seem to melt away just as we reach them, and we are perpetually disappointed. It explains why we feel deprived, even when we are surrounded by wealth and affluence. We are not lacking for anything. We simply do not know how to fully experience and appreciate what we already have.

For most of us, the most thrilling moments of our lives are when we are anticipating getting something that we want. The satisfaction of having it lasts only a short time, and very soon we are thinking of something else that would make us happier. Consider the way children often compete for a toy. They usually want the toy that another child has and often make a huge fuss about getting it. As soon as they get the toy, however, they begin to lose interest, and soon they don't want it anymore.

We can often see this pattern play out at a typical family Christmas celebration in an affluent country like the United States. In my family growing up, the focus of Christmas was opening the mountain of beautifully-wrapped gifts under the tree. As children, we could not wait for the moment to tear into our presents. Often, the scene would turn into a frenzied ripping of paper and squeals of joy as present after present was revealed.

The excitement lasted as long as there were more presents to open, then it suddenly all faded away. It felt like the whole thing was over just moments after it started. None of the gifts seemed to have the same glow once they were opened and became ours. Recognizing this, my family bought more and more presents each year, just to prolong those exciting moments.

As a young man, I became disillusioned with Christmas because it began to feel empty and hollow. It seemed to only feed the illusion that something new and better would appear in the next present. In the end all this gift-opening did was to promote over-consumption, and make us less and less happy. We were not learning how to be content with what we had, enjoy each other's company, nor to be more conscious people. Most everything about Christmas seemed to be taking us in the opposite direction of what Jesus was trying to teach.

Desire

In order to interrupt this pattern of always wanting what we don't have and make it visible, it can help to relinquish the object of our desire for a moment. We can take our attention away from the greener grass on the other side of the fence in order to step back and see the cyclical pattern that is making us constantly look to the future for our fulfillment.

This feels like a sacrifice to many of us, and in spiritual teachings is often misunderstood as living a life of material austerity. Both the Buddha and Jesus taught that giving up worldly desires and possessions plays an important part in becoming conscious. Our perceptual mind then concludes that to be spiritual means that we have to give up what we most want in the world.

Most of us either reject this idea and turn away from spirituality, or embrace it and become identified as the one who is making sacrifices in order to be more holy. However, both responses keep us locked into the mental pattern of wanting what we do not have. One way involves simply giving in to it, and the other way resisting it.

Both approaches assume that the desires that burn within us have a basis in reality, and there really *is* something better over there. Whether we ignore them or indulge them, we still think that our desires are real, and this gives them power over us. The only way to be free of this cycle is to see it for what it is. Once we see that our restless desiring is caused by the limitations of our programmed thought pattern, and not by a real lack in our lives, these thoughts cannot control us as they once did.

Hiding our Desire

The most basic desire that we have is for self-preservation. This urge to maintain our own existence is so primal that most of us rarely question it. All other habits of wanting and clinging are based on this one. We tend to justify our impulse for self-preservation as a simple fact of life. Most of us believe that if we do not look out for our own basic interests, we will perish, and there is rarely a time when our mind is not occupied with securing our place in the world.

The rational mind tries to contain our inherently self-centered nature through morality. We create religious beliefs that frame selfishness as a sin and attempt to control it through judgment and condemnation. This approach leads to rules and laws that involve sacrificing our desires for the sake of being good or holy. We then measure our holiness or goodness by how much we can deny ourselves and give to others.

But this approach causes endless struggle, and rarely reaches a conclusion. Most of us do not succeed in fully relinquishing our self-interest and instead harbor a perennial tension between what we want and what we are *supposed* to want. We use morality as a weapon to judge and condemn each other, and rely on guilt to contain the damage done by our restless urge to gratify our desires.

Clamping down on our desires prompts us to create elaborate facades of being good and right in order to hide our guilt and shame. The only way that we can be good is to appear to be without desires or personal needs. Using morality in this way perpetuates denial and furthers our ignorance by rewarding us for pretense and encouraging hypocrisy.

Giving Up Guilt and Denial

The idea of giving up wanting things will always appear as a sacrifice to perceptual mind. If I force myself to relinquish my desire, I immediately create another nucleus for the idea of self to formulate around. I become the one making this noble sacrifice. There is effort involved and the ego has a role to play. I can measure myself by how much I can give up, and compare myself with other people who are not giving up as much, or perhaps are giving up more.

The teachings of the Buddha and Christ were never to deny ourselves what we most want in order to be holy. These teachers taught instead how to address our desires at their root and see that they are not based in reality but are merely an illusion of lack created by perception. The essence of their teaching is that the self that we are trying so hard to preserve *is not real*, and that our efforts to cater to the endless needs of our individual personality can only lead to exhaustion and despair.

The idea that our self does not exist in reality is inconceivable to most of us. The self I refer to here is your *image of yourself*, not your essence. In other words, you certainly do exist, but not as you perceive yourself. We are simply talking about a mistake in perception.

I think that I have a self which I need to protect and enhance or I will not exist. Yet the simple truth is that I exist apart from this idea of being a person. And, it is the image of a person whom I call "me," that is actually creating the endless desire and the resultant suffering that I experience.

My sense of self constantly needs to get more things in order to keep building up and maintaining its image. This process is never ending because the self has no basis in reality and is therefore totally dependent on the drama in my life to establish its identity.

This false idea of self is *based on lack and fear* and only exists in relation to things that it can possess, or things that it needs to protect itself from. Therefore, as long as I identify myself as my personality, I will be compelled to grasp for more, and it will never be enough. It *can't* ever be enough or my cherished sense of self would disappear.

The Illusion of Sacrifice

Most of us have a hard time realizing how to truly let go. Our mental programming only allows for:

"I like this and want to get it," "I don't like this and want to get rid of it," or "I don't know."

This conditioned mind does not understand:

"I like this and want to get rid of it," or "I don't like this and don't want to get rid of it."

The closest that we get to valuing hardship on a spiritual path may be something like:

"I like spiritual awakening and will endure this so that I can get that."

Then our giving up becomes a kind of exchange. It is simply the price that we have to pay for enlightenment.

This approach creates a chronic struggle within myself, however. I try to calculate just how much I have to give up in order to get enlightened, and think of it like negotiating a financial deal. I always want to get a bargain in a financial deal, so I start playing this game to see how little I can give up and still get into heaven or become enlightened. Conceptual mind can only frame a situation like this in terms of what is in it for the self, and this is how spiritual teachings become religions.

Religions often create another context for the individual ego by offering rewards and punishments in return for good or bad behaviors. They make spiritual advancement like a board game with winners and losers by attaching some kind of price that we have to pay or sacrifice that we have to make.

This isn't anybody's fault, nor is it a conspiracy to manipulate and control the people. It is a natural outcome of the way the mind is programmed. Perception is a mechanical means of measuring things based on the labels good or bad. Naturally, perceptual mind would take a spiritual teaching that is pointing to a goal like enlightenment or heaven, and devise a formula to follow in order to get there.

The problem with religion is that it usually diminishes the teachings of the person who inspired it by presenting them solely within the context of perception. We think that the purpose of religion is to help us assign labels of good or bad, and to create measured achievements through which we can access God, heaven, or Nirvana. Yet, all this does is to strengthen the ego and separate us further from the present moment.

We do not advance spiritually by giving up pleasure and enduring pain. The perceptual mind will turn a spiritual path into a struggle against desire or endurance of sacrifice because this gives our ego something to identify with and hold on to. There is a nobility in fighting our desires and a self-righteousness in sacrifice. The ego loves to be a martyr and endure pain so that good can triumph over evil.

In the end, this approach tends to further our sense of self by giving us something new to struggle against. It merely takes us back into the unconscious pattern of becoming the noble one who is fighting against the dark forces. Instead of freeing us, this idea of spiritual sacrifice feeds the illusion of a separate self.

The reason that fighting against desire does not work is because we are struggling against ourselves and there is no possibility of winning. It is like having a contest between your two hands to see which one will dominate the other. It is pointless because you cannot defeat yourself. And this is what we do when we try to approach spirituality from a place of morality. We do not understand that limiting desire is only a means to allow us to see the pattern that is causing the desire. Then we make the elimination of desire an end in itself.

The need to let go of desire for a moment is not because desire is wrong or the things that I want are bad. It is merely a skillful means of taking my focus off of the object I want so that I can look instead at the pattern *behind* my wanting. Without some pause in this cycle of wanting and getting, I don't have a chance to see the program that is causing it to repeat itself over and over again. So a spiritual path requires the discipline to look away from the object of desire long enough to see what is really happening.

Letting Go

Letting go is simpler, less dramatic, and takes less effort than sacrifice. There is usually some discomfort and fear involved, and we often need to exercise faith that we will be alright in the end. But true letting go is not a heroic act of good triumphing over evil, a contest to win or lose, or another test to pass or fail. Real surrender is an ordinary common sense response when we see that our plan for achieving permanence for our ego is not working and is based on a fundamental error.

Letting go becomes simple and relatively easy once we recognize that holding on to the idea of a self, or lunging after the objects of our desire, causes us pain. The Buddha said that the human condition is like grasping onto a burning hot coal with our bare hand. The first step in resolving the situation is to become aware enough to realize that we are in pain.

This is a challenge for many of us because we have learned to ignore pain, medicate it, or distract ourselves from it. It is difficult to simply recognize that we feel pain, especially when it is emotional and we cannot see an immediate cause. To become more conscious, therefore, we can simply be with ourselves, without distracting or numbing, long enough to feel the chronic pain that underlies our existence.

The next step is to find the source of the pain. Many of us who *do* recognize the pain are looking anywhere but in our own mind for the cause. We blame our pain on other people, make them responsible for it, and either try to change them or get away from them. Or we try to change ourselves, thinking that we have to *be* better or *do* something better in order to make the pain go away. We also may think that it is our life circumstance, and so we get a new job, house, relationship, or car, thinking that this will solve our problem.

Yet, none of these efforts succeed because we have not located the real cause. Many of us never do find the real cause of our pain and live our lives merely trying the old ways harder, or finding new and different ways to distract and numb ourselves. Our lives then are underscored by a sense of failure and futility. It is when we give up these efforts, admit that we are failing, and just stand still for a moment, that we finally see the hot coal in our hand. This is what meditation practice and a spiritual teaching can help us do.

To let go of our thoughts and trust in our present moment experience requires a leap of faith. This spiritual kind of faith is about letting go into the unknown and is completely different from religious faith. Religious faith usually means believing in an ideal that is "right." Spiritual faith means giving up all ideas of right or wrong and admitting that we cannot tell the difference. It means allowing ourselves to free fall, trusting that we will be alright without the comfort of these familiar reference points, and accepting that we don't know what will happen next.

Once we see that we are grasping onto a hot coal, and realize that it is the source of our pain, letting go becomes quite obvious and natural. There is no great striving, courage, or struggle involved. It is not some heroic act or great achievement. It is an utterly simple and common sense act of opening our hand and letting the coal fall out.

The hot coal that is burning us is a concept so seemingly central to our fundamental existence that most of us cannot conceive of questioning it. It is our idea of a separate self. This is what we need to let go of, not things or events or other people. It is the way our mind *uses* things, events, and people *to formulate a concept of self* that causes us pain. Keeping a distance from life and giving up possessions or relationships is not the solution.

Life will bring us a steady stream of experiences, and we can fully participate in and enjoy them. As soon as we try to possess or repel an experience however, it becomes painful. This is the moment when we create the self over and over again. Instead of letting an experience be what it is, our habit is to identify with it and make it ours. We think, "this is *my* food," or "this is *my* pain."

Practicing direct awareness breaks this habit, and cultivates your capacity to be fully part of an experience without taking ownership of it. Becoming aware means interrupting your impulse to personalize each experience and give it meaning within the story of your life. With awareness the story fades away, and along with it goes your struggle and discomfort, leaving just the experience itself.

The Limits of Perception

The cause of the pattern of always wanting what we do not have lies in an inherent limitation of perception. Remember that perception is a process of comparing one thing with another thing in order to create an abstract image of what that thing is. Perception cannot know something directly but only indirectly through the creation of a concept or image which represents it. This is similar to the way a photograph represents the objects that are in the picture. The photo may look exactly like something, but it is *not* that thing.

What this means is that the perceptual mind cannot ever have a direct experience of reality. It is only able to "see" through the images it creates. And these images are always a memory of the past or imagination of the future. While perception can generate infinite images that are varied, complex, and realistic, it cannot ever have a *direct* experience of the present moment. In a similar way, a television can display fantastic and realistic images, but these images cannot interact with us here and now.

The process of perception is like always looking at the world around us through its reflection in a mirror. We can only perceive something that we can compare with something else. We cannot compare the present moment with anything because there is only one – this one. So perception deals exclusively with the past and future. We constantly compare past moments with imagined future ones to try to figure out what is real or right.

This process happens so quickly and repetitively that we rarely notice it. In a similar way, we don't notice the individual frames in a film, but only see the motion picture that results. This habit of comparing past experiences and projecting the future keeps our attention by continually promising something new and better than what we have now.

Having your experience translated by the process of perception is like being locked in a room in a house and experiencing life only through photographs and stories that people share with you. After a while, these stories and pictures are all that you know and they appear very real. If someone told you that the images in the pictures represented real things outside the house, you may not believe them. For you, the images and stories have become reality, and you cannot conceive of anything else being real.

This is the condition that you create by using perceptual mind to translate reality for you. It is as if you are always inside and have a servant who goes outside every day and comes back to tell you all about what he experienced. This can be interesting and give you some idea of what the real world is like, but it cannot compare with the experience that you would have if you walked out into the world yourself.

The Roots of Desire

The root cause of my perpetual desire and discontent is that I cannot recognize the present moment through perception, so I can never fully appreciate what I have right now. I can only appreciate and value concepts and images with my perceptual mind, not direct sensory experiences.

I can savor the memory of how ice cream tastes, or imagine myself eating some right now. Indeed these images can be so vivid that my mouth waters as if I were actually eating the ice cream. Yet if I were to go get some right now and eat it, my perceptual mind would not be able to taste it. It is my *awareness* that tastes and feels and senses.

Only through awareness can I be content with what I have right now and not be longing for the past or anticipating the future. That is why awareness practice can bring immediate joy and contentment.

By becoming more aware of my immediate experience, I allow myself to appreciate and savor what I have right now. This simple enjoyment of the present moment is the point of spiritual practice. Waking up is about finding the simple pleasure in being conscious, and has nothing to do with sacrifice.

It does not work to relinquish desire by forcing yourself to do without the things that you want. If you have things taken from you while you still want them, you simply continue to hunger after them, and no real peace is possible in your life. That is what happens when you force myself to give up a habit or push away something that you truly desire. And this is why the kind of sacrifice portrayed as holy by most religions often does not work.

A Gradual Surrender

If you pay attention, you can see that your mind always returns to where you received some sense of pleasure or satisfaction. When you have an experience that feels good, you tend to remember what you did and do it again. The problem is that it often does not feel as good the second time. And when you have done it over and over again, it barely registers as pleasure at all. Still, you may keep doing it, hoping for the experience that you had in the beginning. This is the fundamental nature of addiction.

As you wake up and become more present in your life, the unsatisfactory nature of these repeated habits becomes obvious and you may try something different. A simple practice of awareness can gently lead you away from your tendency toward addictive habits that do not really make you happy or serve your best interests. Instead of forcing them to go away, you merely become conscious of them and it gradually becomes clear that the level of satisfaction which you receive is not worth all the effort and struggle that they cost you.

We all had toys as children that we thought we could never part with. Some were lost, taken, or fell apart in a way that may have been upsetting, but many of our toys simply lost their appeal. That is not because there was anything wrong with them, but because our interests changed and we outgrew them.

It is not a sacrifice to give up something that you no longer want. This is what real spiritual growth is like. The Buddha is simply pointing out to us that struggling to maintain a separate self-identity brings us more pain than pleasure. He is suggesting that there is something else that we want more which is truly nourishing and satisfying. As we become more conscious, wanting what we don't have becomes less interesting because we can feel the constrictions, and we naturally prefer the freedom of living in the present moment.

———————— •◆• ————————

Pay attention to your impulse for wanting what you do not have right now. Notice any resistance in your body to what is happening in this moment. What does this resistance feel like? Can you locate the source of it?

You may be choosing to read this, yet it is likely that some part of you believes there is something better that you could be doing or something else that you want that you don't have. See if you can feel that sense of dissatisfaction and notice how it constricts your body and darkens your thoughts.

What happens to this resistance if you accept exactly what you have right now and give up trying to change anything about this moment?

———————— •◆• ————————

13

The Myth of Personal Pleasure

Many of us feel dissatisfied with life. Sometimes this appears as a low-level anxiety or sense of mild discomfort. Other times it may be tremendous physical or emotional pain. We may feel it as a chronic sense that something important is missing and our lives are incomplete. Our attempts to fill this emptiness do not seem to work, so we often try to numb or distract ourselves from these uneasy feelings, hoping they will just go away if we don't pay too much attention to them.

Yet ignoring our pain in this way just makes it go underground. We become privately obsessed with our misfortunes and our thoughts focus on what we lack instead of what we have. We may not admit this to anyone else, but most of us are secretly consumed with self-pity, hoping that someday we will finally get what we deserve, then our lives will be complete.

The Attraction of More

When the Buddha described the human condition as suffering, he was not meaning to be morose or fatalistic, but rather he wanted to help us pay attention to our situation so that we can do something about it. The Buddha described the cause of our suffering as our chronic sense of lack and perpetual craving for something to fill that lack. He suggests that the very mechanism which we have been using to remedy our situation is actually the cause of our problem. And this is where his message may become confusing.

Most of us are operating under the assumption that our problem is that we lack something we need to be happy, and our task is to acquire that. Our efforts are naturally focused on getting things that we think we need. The Buddha is simply pointing out that it is this *basic sense of lack* which is the problem. We are mistaken when we think we are incomplete and need something else to be happy. Yet, instead of looking at the sense of lack itself, we tend to put our energy into getting more things to fill the void that we feel within.

Our endless desire is causing our suffering, not because desire is wrong or selfish, but because *it does not work*. We never can fully quell our craving by acquiring things because it is not *things* that we lack. No matter how much we have or control, it is never enough, and we always seem to need more. Our way of trying to be happy leads instead to more frustration and anxiety and perpetuates this pattern, and we often end up stuck in a perennial loop of dissatisfaction and longing.

A simple way to describe this deep universal longing is that we each feel incomplete and want to reach a state of wholeness. Seen in this light, our cravings make sense. We naturally assume that the way to become complete is to get more. Yet we can never seem to get enough, and those of us who live in the affluent societies of the twenty-first century are in a unique position to recognize this. Look around at the people you know of who seem to have wealth, power, and fame. Do they seem to be happy? Do their lives seem complete and filled with contentment?

In fact, when we look at the lives of other people who seem to have it all, it becomes painfully obvious that, instead of leading to contentment, getting more seems to only make us *more restless and unhappy*. It is astonishing to see how many wealthy, famous, or powerful people end up addicted to drugs or alcohol and have failed marriages or dysfunctional families.

The Buddha is not trying to scold or chastise us, but is merely pointing out that we are hurting ourselves by allowing desire to control our lives. He is acting as a loving parent would to help and protect his child out of compassion and deep love for us. His message is meant to show us what he learned by breaking free of his own mental conditioning, so that we may do the same.

The Mistake of Morality

It is tempting to over-simplify the Buddha's message into some platitude like "don't worry, be happy." While this may be a true expression of his teaching, it encourages us to pretend to be happy in order to look spiritually advanced, and leaves many of us feeling privately frustrated and inadequate. The Buddha was not asking us not to have desire or to simply ignore our discomfort. He was encouraging us simply to look at the *cause* of our desire instead of denying it or trying to satisfy it by getting more.

A spiritual teaching always contains a seeming paradox, and that is why it can be so difficult to decipher. Most of us *do* feel a genuine sense of being incomplete, and giving up our efforts to do something about it seems to be a sure way to fall into despair and depression. We cannot understand how giving up trying to find something satisfying in life could possibly make us happy. We are convinced that just the opposite is true.

A teaching like the Buddha's cannot be understood or followed with our rational mind. We only end up with a morality that tells us that it is holy not to want things. We then use this moral code to measure ourselves and each other in order to compare our spiritual progress. We think that we are getting somewhere because we have learned to control our desires more than someone else, yet nothing has really changed because the premise that led to our cravings has not been revealed.

This is how spiritual teachings become formulated into religions, and it explains why religion does not work to transform us. We tend to approach a spiritual teaching with our rational mind because this is the only way that we can. Yet, this approach means that the teaching becomes translated into the relative terms of perception where things only have meaning when measured or compared with something else. Once we do this, we lose the essence of the teaching, which is pointing to something beyond perception.

The Experience of Unity

Another way to describe our longing for completion is that we want unity. Our anxiety often comes from a sense that our lives are too complex and fragmented. While our Western civilization has progressed rapidly in the past several centuries toward greater personal independence and individual freedom, our lives have become increasingly separate and we feel more isolated than ever before.

The Buddha taught us about our capacity to know through direct contact that does not involve conceptual thought. Most of us need to develop our ability for direct knowing because we have invested ourselves in our rational mind and allowed our direct experience to be overshadowed by our thoughts.

This is where the practice of meditation comes in. Every time I bring my attention back to a present moment sensation like the body breathing, I strengthen my capacity for pure awareness. Being aware of something is how I know it directly, without comparison with something else.

By trusting my capacity for direct awareness, and referencing my life to this instead of to my conceptual thoughts, I solve the problem of fragmentation. In awareness, everything is already unified, because there is nothing except my direct experience of this moment. When I am simply aware, each moment is whole and complete in itself. I do not need to compare this moment with another moment. I simply know it directly as it is.

In a moment of pure awareness, desire and craving do not exist. By letting go of the past and future, I have nothing to compare my present experience with. All degrees of good or bad disappear outside of perception, and everything exists only in this one moment. There is nothing to gain or lose and nothing to crave or grieve. There is just this one experience now. And I discover to my astonishment that, whatever else this moment may contain, it is filled with an indescribable joy and contentment.

The discomfort of desire resolves itself the moment that I experience my full presence. It becomes apparent in the light of my expanded consciousness that something *was* missing from my life, yet the very mechanism that I was using to find the missing piece was preventing me from seeing it. My cravings were based on the assumption that I was not enough just as I was, and I needed something more to complete me. Meanwhile, it was merely my own full *presence* that was lacking.

All the time and effort I invested in the calculated and laborious process of reflection and comparison simply served to obscure my capacity for awareness. I assumed that perception was much more powerful and capable than simple attention, and I cast aside the very thing that I needed most because it appeared so insignificant.

Personal Pleasure

To the ego, or false sense of self, unity means becoming a whole complete personality. My perceptual mind is programmed to solidify the ego as a means to achieve the unification I long for. Yet, as the ego tries to solidify itself by enhancing the personality or sense of individual "me," it separates itself from the world. In the end the only way that the ego's plan for unity can work is for there to be only "me" in the world, and nothing else.

The limitations of the ego's plan for unification become apparent each time I get what I think I need to be happy. When my calculated efforts finally succeed and I get to enjoy what I have been craving, the sense of pleasure and satisfaction is often tainted by loneliness and isolation. In a world of separate people and individual needs, if I get more, it means that someone else gets less.

A glimpse of this came to me when I became intimate with my first partner. We had been in love for over a year before we decided to be sexual, and we chose to open ourselves to each other physically with a lot of preparation and awareness of what we were doing. One time after we made love, we each felt disturbed because we had been focused so much on ourselves and our own pleasure that we lost the connection with each other.

The kind of pleasure desired by the ego is purely personal and cannot be shared. This leaves us alone in our moment of getting what we want, and this feeling of being alone often casts a shadow on our sense of satisfaction. Anyone who has had a dream come true and received something that they longed for discovers finally that the momentary high is short lived. In the end the sense of individual satisfaction is drowned out by our desire for belonging and connection with others.

Many people in affluent societies today struggle with the sense of disappointment that inevitably follows getting what we want. We don't expect getting our way to feel like this, and it leaves us disturbed and confused. We have no context for why our successes feel so hollow, and we often blindly rush into our next achievement thinking that the answer must lie in getting something else.

This is how we continuously over-achieve and over-consume, and end up hurting ourselves and damaging our environment. None of us are bad people. We are merely mistaken about what makes us happy. It is not our personal pleasure but our *sense of unity with all things* that fulfills our deepest desires and makes us truly content. And to experience this we have to question our individual cravings and suspend our wanting for a moment so that we can see how blinded we are by the impulses of our ego.

Our Mistaken Notion of Progress

In the history of Western civilization, progress has been defined primarily as the capacity to accumulate personal wealth, resources, knowledge, or property. Most of us take it for granted that the more of these that we have or control, the more security and happiness we will have. This assumption is what led the monarchs of Europe to invade, colonize, and plunder the natural resources of so many less-developed nations in the past millennium. And it is what drives today's huge corporations with their bottom-line profit motive to expand and dominate at any cost.

Instead of looking at anyone's behavior as right or wrong, let's consider for a moment our notion of progress and see if we have achieved anything worthwhile from it. We assume that the answer to life's problems is in having *more* education, money, food, housing, machines, or new possessions. We seem convinced that these are the essential ingredients of a good life and that getting more of them will always make our lives better.

Many of us are actively engaged in getting more of these for ourselves, and believe that this is the purpose of life. We in the West have built a culture around the accumulation of wealth and power. The single aim of a capitalist corporation, as it is for many individuals, is to make more profit. We tend to esteem people who are able to get more, measure each other by our capacity to compete, and determine success by how much money we earn compared to others.

These standards are so ingrained in us that we may have to look twice to see that we have actually glorified greed, aggression, and selfishness. We often value people by their monetary worth, assuming that this is a reflection of their character or an outcome of their heroic effort. While financial success can be the result of hard work or personal sacrifice, it is more likely the product of deceit or aggression and comes at someone else's expense. When we reward or esteem people for their ability to win, we feed the worst part of our human nature and encourage the tyranny of the ego.

Some of us may reject this unseemly part of our culture, rather than glorifying it, and turn our attention to the poor and disadvantaged people in the world. We are interested in more than merely the accumulation of personal wealth, and consider it our responsibility to help the needy. We derive a sense of purpose in our life from helping others gain access to more of what we have, and assume that as they realize the benefits of progress, their lives will naturally improve.

We may help build schools, homes, or roads, grow businesses, provide jobs, or give food or money to people who do not have these. And these acts of generosity certainly may benefit other people in some way and give our lives a sense of purpose. Yet, all this assumes that this kind of progress really does make people happier and more satisfied with life.

I grew up believing that having more meant a better life because everyone around me believed it. I only began to question this assumption as a young adult when it did not add up. I was surrounded by people who had a lot, yet were *not* happy or content. And when I lived outside the U.S. for a while in what we would call a "poor" undeveloped country, I saw for myself that it was not true. In Sri Lanka I met the happiest, most content, generous, and loving people I had ever known. These people were also living under the most basic and simple conditions I had ever seen.

I understood then why I felt so unsettled and disturbed as I reached adulthood and was being prompted to make something out of my life. It became clear to me after living in Asia for six months that our Western idea of progress was not making us happier or fulfilling our deeper longings. And now, with the specter of full planetary catastrophe at our doorstep, it is painfully apparent where our idea of progress has led us.

There has probably never before been a civilization on earth whose people are as educated, affluent, and abundant in food and material possessions as many of us in developed parts of the world are today. Yet we find ourselves posed on the brink of an unthinkable calamity caused by our own ignorance, greed, and delusion.

How Do We Know When It Is Enough?

It is time to recognize that our notion of progress is fatally flawed. We in the West are in a unique position to understand that *more does not make us happier.* Education does not make us wiser, power and control do not make us more secure, wealth does not make us more content, and competition does not make us better people. If we can just get this one idea, we have a chance to switch gears and try something new before it is too late.

The essential problem with our current paradigm of progress and success is that there is no way to tell when we have enough. The mandate of a capitalist "free market" system is that business has to grow in order to succeed. We have to build more, consume more, use more resources, create more waste, and continually "develop" more. There is never an end point to all this frantic "progress." And it is becoming ever more clear that in our headlong rush toward material growth and development we are destroying or depleting the basic natural resources upon which we all depend.

Our economic model of growth requires that we take as much as we can from the resources of the earth as quickly as possible. It does not account for depletion of these resources because either they appear to be unlimited, or we consider the basic elements of the earth the rightful property of whomever can lay claim to them and extract them first.

We have been acting like children with no adult supervision at a dessert buffet. Our frenzy to take more resources before anyone else has blinded us to the waste and devastation that we are causing to the one common source we all depend upon. If it does not become apparent to a critical mass of us soon, it will be painfully obvious to whoever survives our callous disregard for the balance of nature that competing to see who can get the most is a formula for self-annihilation. When we see the earth as merely a resource for our own unrestrained consumption, we ignore the fact that our planet is a self-contained living ecosystem, which we are intrinsically a part of, and utterly dependent upon.

Rethinking Progress

A simple way to reframe our situation is to redefine the meaning of progress. We now think of growth primarily in terms of the unrestricted use of natural resources in order to accumulate wealth or achieve dominance. Another way to consider growth and progress is in terms of our emotional or spiritual development.

We have an innate longing for fundamental change and an undeniable urge to grow and develop. Western civilization has mistaken this urge for a need to have greater control over our natural environment and to expand our physical capacity. While some degree of material comfort and security is necessary for us to feel safe and stable, this is not what nourishes us the most.

We are highly sensitive and intelligent beings who require purpose and meaning for our lives to feel fulfilled. Merely increasing our technological capacities or accumulating more wealth can never meet these deeper needs. We find our deepest sense of nourishment and answer our need for growth and development by expanding our consciousness, not controlling our environment or competing for resources.

We each have the potential to become fully conscious and we will not be satisfied until we have done so. This is why we are here. Our true contentment and satisfaction in life comes from growing emotionally and increasing our awareness and understanding of the fundamental meaning of life. We each have a deep urge for cohesion and connection with others that no degree of personal wealth or power can satisfy.

Gradually, some of us are discovering that we are not happy and our plan for getting more is not working. We realize that we are over-fed, over-educated, and over-developed, and we are losing interest in competing or winning. We feel stuffed, gorged, lethargic, and exhausted by this endless treadmill. And we are turning our attention to our own inner development and looking for ways to cultivate emotional and mental health and well-being.

This is the meaning of the crises we face now. All the centuries of hard-won "progress" and personal struggles that we have been through have been to get us to this point of realizing that things are not working out as we planned. Pain and suffering are not enemies to vanquish by increasing our means or numbing ourselves. The discontent that we feel with life is a vital signal to get us to turn inward. The purpose of suffering is to make us recognize the innate capacity that we have for sustained contentment which requires only our attention to become activated.

Knowledge and Wisdom

Some of you will argue that we do not define progress only in terms of our capacity for greater consumption, or material comfort. You may believe that Western civilization emphasizes education as a primary measure of success, and values knowledge and scientific discovery above the accumulation of wealth. Yet, just as our extraordinary level of personal affluence has not translated into contentment with life, so our high degree of education has not made us happier or more intelligent.

As we assume that progress means obtaining more wealth, we also believe that education is about obtaining more information. Our current model of learning is based primarily on the process of rational comparison and logical deduction that we call science. We develop conceptual ideas or theories about how things are and then attempt to distill these into some absolute truth by a meticulous process of observation and comparison.

While this process of obtaining knowledge works to some degree and has enabled Western civilization to dominate the earth through our superior technologies, it has not made us wiser or increased our capacity for happiness. Establishing reality through our process of perception is painstakingly slow and inefficient and leaves us with more questions than answers about our place in the world. And, as my experience in college proved to me, education does not satisfy our deeper longing to find the meaning or purpose of life.

We might think of someone as smarter or more educated if they can remember and articulate more information, because we believe that a complete and final understanding will come from putting all the pieces of the puzzle of life into one whole story. Yet we only gain relative understanding and approximate truth through such a process. Remember that perception precludes a whole complete and final answer because it requires everything to have an opposite.

The overwhelming situation that humanity faces today demonstrates that we are now reaching the limits of perception. More education or knowledge is not going to resolve our dilemma, and we in the West are in a unique position to see this. Our high level of education is not helping us to understand our predicament. Using our current methods, we simply cannot learn fast enough to get ahead of our looming crises.

Education

As part of redefining progress, we also can redefine education, learning, and what it means to be intelligent. I am noticing as I help my daughters with their elementary school work that many of the things I learned forty years ago are irrelevant today. Computers can do basic math, spelling, grammar, and access any kind of information more efficiently than I can with all my years of education. It is no longer necessary for us to memorize information because technology can do that more efficiently and accurately.

Using our current measure of intelligence, computers now rival our human capacity for storing and organizing information. We have entered an age where our technologies are smarter and can do many things better than we can. This may accent our sense of futility with life and highlight our lack of meaning or purpose. Yet, it also can be just the catalyst that we need to discover what it is we can do that is uniquely ours.

Remember the story from an earlier chapter about the woman who held up the keyboard of her new computer to the monitor and complained that the computer still could not "find" it. This is a simple example of the limitations of mechanical intelligence. One way to describe this limitation is to say that the computer cannot *be present* with an event that is happening now.

A computer can only access past information stored in its memory, and use that information to project future scenarios. This is similar to the way most of us are using our mental capacity. As I pointed out earlier, science can only attempt to prove or disprove a theory that *already exists*. In other words, we are confined by our notions of what is possible, which is based on our past experiences.

As our mental capabilities become superseded by computers, a sensible response is to develop our own unique capacity – the ability to simply be conscious and aware. We can redefine intelligence as the ability to be *fully present in this moment*. Instead of relying on our ability to store and access information, we can cultivate the one strength that we are uniquely suited for, which is our ability to pay attention.

We have ignored and undervalued our capacity for presence because it seems so insignificant in contrast with conceptual thought, memory, and imagination. Yet all of the effort and faith that we have placed in the process of perception has not resulted in us being more content, and instead seems to be causing us to be chronically restless and unsatisfied. The challenge offered by the teachings of the Buddha is to explore the possibility that our capacity to simply *be with* the experience of this moment will lead to a sense of fulfillment.

Natural Intelligence

True intelligence is the ability to be fully present and see what is really happening without the filter of perception. It requires a great trust on our part that we can see for ourselves what is true and respond accordingly. Remember the story in a previous chapter about walking at night, seeing a rope in the road, and thinking it was a snake. When we trusted our perception and believed that it was a snake, we set off a whole sequence of events which included physical tension, release of adrenaline, increased heart rate, and chaotic thought patterns that we could not stop.

These automatic fear-based responses consume our energy and wear us out for no reason. They often block our awareness of what is real and instead of making us more intelligent, they make us more ignorant and prejudiced. Once we see for ourselves that the "snake" is really just a rope, all the fear responses vanish, leaving us clear-headed and calm. Intelligence in this case is the courage to challenge our pre-judgments and investigate the situation at hand in order to be more aware of what is really taking place.

Our current system of education assumes that our greatest capacity is to use our intellect for storing and organizing information and drawing rational conclusions, much like a computer. Under this paradigm, becoming more educated means increasing our ability to process data. However, this approach tends to discount or ignore our direct experience in favor of our abstract mental conclusions. As such, it does not make us more wise, intelligent, or capable of responding to our immediate circumstances.

We can rationally understand that oil and other fossil fuels are a finite resource which we are depleting and it does not make sense to further our dependence on them. In a similar way, we may be able to recognize that if we eat foods which are high in sugar and fat, we are going to gain weight and have health problems later on. Or, it may be logically evident that smoking tobacco can cause lung disease and cancer and shorten a person's life span. Yet, despite these commonly understood realities, many of us continue to depend on oil, eat junk food, or smoke cigarettes.

Logical conclusions by themselves do not usually motivate us to change our behavior or inspire us to solve a problem. This is because they exist only in our mind in the abstract form of thoughts. It is easy to use our capacity for abstract thought to gain some understanding of our situation, yet this understanding does not actually change anything. This is why we cannot usually resolve our dilemmas by thinking our way out.

The inadequacy of the abstract thought process can be witnessed clearly in meditation. By being more aware of my thoughts, I can see that my rational mind is not as intelligent and precise as I often believe. I notice how my thoughts are often random and contradict each other, with no linear progression leading toward a concrete conclusion.

As I notice the simplistic patterns that confine my thinking, it becomes obvious why perception is so approximate and unreliable. My mind is limited by its basic programming, and like a computer, lacks the capacity to simply be present. This realization encourages me to turn away from my obsession with thought and instead learn to rely on the natural intelligence of direct awareness.

———————— •◆• ————————

Watch your thoughts for a moment and consider what your rational mind is trying to accomplish right now. Are you trying to figure something out or draw a conclusion?

Now let go of the process of thought and put your attention on a present experience such as a sound, sensation, or sight. Breathe deeply and let the thoughts simply dissolve.

———————— •◆• ————————

14

The Lure of Opposition

Another predictable pattern programmed into perceptual mind is that there is always something outside of us which is threatening us or causing us to suffer. Having an outside enemy who appears to oppose us is one of the basic ways that our ego finds definition. Most of us need something to compare ourselves with that is not what we are, in order to perceive ourselves. And, because our judgments of good and evil provide the basis for this mechanism of comparison, our opposite is necessarily evil in order for us to appear good.

———————— •◆• ————————

Take a moment now to check this out in your own thought process. Close your eyes and bring to mind someone who you regard as threatening in your life right now. It may be a large threat that is easily recognized, or it may be just a slight sense of unease with another person.

———————— •◆• ————————

No matter how innocent, peaceful, or loving I see myself, I often find myself facing some antagonist who seems to be keeping me from getting what I want. In a world defined by perception, I can only know something in contrast to what it is not. Therefore, my sense of goodness or innocence depends on there being evil or bad people in the world who I can measure myself against. The more ugly and evil I make my opponent out to be, the more I highlight my own rightness and goodness.

As with the pattern of desiring what I do not have, this pattern of needing to always have an opponent automatically focuses my attention on something outside of me. As soon as I have an antagonist, I begin to create strategies for overcoming that person. In this way, seeing myself as an innocent victim struggling against an evil aggressor gives my life definition and purpose.

This pattern of opposition is responsible for much of the perpetual conflict, hatred, violence, and war in our world. It ensures that we always have an enemy, and that there is always a struggle for survival against someone who intends to do us harm. Because our minds are programmed alike, each side in a conflict has the same perception of the other as an evil antagonist, and ourselves as the innocent victim or heroic martyr. This is why power struggles, conflict, and war are so common. Both sides feel justified in doing violence to the other from a place of moral superiority and righteous innocence.

This also explains the violence in our world that is done in the name of religion or morality. Each side believes that the other represents a threat to their god or belief system. To the extent that religion and morality define who we are, a threat to our belief system seems to be a direct assault on our existence. We can easily convince ourselves that it is necessary to destroy any opposition in order to ensure our own survival.

Responses to Opposition

A common response to feeling threatened by an outside force is to try to overpower and dominate that force for the sake of our own security. Many of us do this to some degree in our personal lives, and between nations this is the cause of war. Some of us believe that this is the most direct and effective way to achieve peace and stability in our world. This thinking is what justifies aggression and violence, and it is why war is still the main way that we try to resolve conflicts.

We have seen what happens when we attack. It creates an escalating cycle of violence that causes enormous pain and destruction and rarely results in lasting peace or stability. We cannot overcome opposition once and for all by forcing our enemy to surrender. A defeated enemy does not willingly or completely assimilate into the culture or beliefs of the victor, and so there is always division and opposition simmering beneath the surface.

Another common response to opposition is to surrender or simply withdraw and avoid our opponent. While this approach may result in less conflict and violence, it does not resolve the situation because we remain unconscious of our programmed need for opposition. We still see other people as a threat and believe that *they* are our problem.

Seeing the Source of Opposition

I cannot break free from opposition by force, submission, or avoidance. The only way to eliminate opposition is to reveal the unconscious conditioning that causes me to create it over and over again. I have to see that *my mind is programmed to require opposition in order to establish its own identity.* As long as this remains an unconscious habit, I will continue to have enemies, conflict, and war.

The way to free myself from opposition is to take my attention off of the enemy for a moment and look at the pattern that is causing me to *need* an enemy. The challenge is to let go of my survival strategy long enough to become conscious of my own thought process. It can be useful to stop defending myself for a moment, and risk being overwhelmed by my enemy, so that I can free my attention to look for the real source of the conflict.

This is why the Buddha teaches us to be without defenses, and Christ invites us to "turn the other cheek" when a perceived enemy strikes us. It is simply that if we follow our survival instincts and either defend ourselves or run away when we think that we are being attacked, we never get a chance to see the unconscious pattern which causes this situation to keep repeating itself in our lives. When we respond to an imagined enemy with the conviction that they are the cause of our problem, we become mired in a cycle of attack and defense that has no resolution.

Mistaking Means for End

Perceptual mind will predictably take a teaching like this and turn it into a moral code. We usually take a suggestion like "do not harm another living being," or "love your enemy," and make it into an ideal. We mistake the means for an end when we make defenselessness an ideal to be attained in the name of being right or holy, or use non-violence as a standard of behavior to measure ourselves and other people against. This approach does not eliminate the cycle of opposition. It merely buries it under a moral cover that ensures that it will stay alive, hiding below the level of our awareness.

I cannot eliminate the pattern of opposition by forcing myself to be inclusive or non-competitive in the name of some higher ideal, just as I cannot eliminate opposition by defeating or dominating my imagined enemy. The only way out is to undo the programmed pattern at its source, and this is simply a matter of bringing it into the light of awareness. Once I see this pattern and understand that my mind is conditioned to need opposition, this cycle begins to lose its power over me.

Many of us are so familiar with having some opposition to our happiness that we assume this is just the way life is. We often try to accept this situation and make the best of it, ignoring our opposition as long as we can. However, minimizing its effects like this only creates an apathy that keeps us from investigating the real cause of the threat. We may also become aggressive and lash out at our perceived enemy, which often ends up hurting our relationships and leaving us isolated.

Another option is to face our opposition directly *without defending ourselves* for a moment. Interrupting our instinctual response to a threat gives us a chance to see the reality of the situation for ourselves. Often when we do this, we recognize that we have made the situation up or blown it out of proportion in our mind.

Neutralizing Conflict

In the earlier story about the "snake" in the road, it appeared to be a threat and we approached it as something out to hurt us. The resolution to this conflict was not defeating the snake, running away from it, or trying to ignore it. The situation resolved itself completely and effortlessly when we saw it for what it was. We realized that our mind had made an enemy out of an old piece of rope. Conflicts finally resolve when we allow our *perception* about the other to change.

My habit is to believe that other people who appear threatening are *trying* to hurt me. I then focus on them and how to deal with them so that they cannot harm me. Yet, if I stop and look at what is really going on in most conflicts, it becomes obvious that other people are not focused on defeating me, but are merely trying to ensure their own security. In these situations, other people may perceive *me* as *their* enemy, and convince themselves that attacking me is necessary for their own safety.

If I can see that other people believe that *I* am a threat to *them*, it changes the picture. They no longer appear as an evil force out to defeat me, but rather as wounded children who may be lashing out at me because they think this is how to protect themselves. This opens up a possibility to resolve the situation by finding out more about what is threatening the other person. Perhaps then we can find a way to work together to neutralize the situation so that neither one of us feels threatened by the other.

Behind most conflicts in our world is merely the conditioned habit of seeing opposition and responding to it by either avoidance or attack. When I respond to a perceived attack by attacking the other back, I only serve to galvanize the perception the other person has of me as an enemy. And when I distance myself from another in the name of my own safety, I reinforce my own belief that they are out to get me.

However, once I see that other people are simply trying to get their needs met in the only way they know how, it is easier not to take the attack as a personal assault. I can recognize it as the ineffective attempt at self-preservation that it is, and not a deliberate attempt to harm or destroy me. I can then step back a moment from the conflict and respond with more clarity and wisdom.

If you are being physically or emotionally hurt by someone, it may be wise to get some distance from that person or put up a clear boundary. You do not have to close your heart to them, however. Closing your heart hurts *you* because it shuts a part of yourself off. You can maintain a strong boundary or a safe distance in order to protect yourself, without thinking of the other person as an enemy.

The Arbitrary Nature of Enemies

I was born in the decade following World War II. It was a conflict on such a large scale, impacting so many lives that it was constantly talked about and referred to throughout my childhood. We all knew about Hitler and the brutal aggression of Germany, and how the Japanese launched an unprovoked attack on the United States at Pearl Harbor. We also knew that both of these nations suffered a resounding defeat which ended the war.

If there ever was a clear case for good and evil on a massive scale, this was it. It was a story full of morality and hope, as the innocent, victimized nations of Europe and the United States defeated the evil, aggressive enemies of Germany and Japan. Yet the story does not end there, neatly concluded with right triumphing over wrong.

I was reading recently about the amazing technological and economic success of both Germany and Japan fifty years after the war. This caught my attention as I had noticed this myself and wondered about how these two countries had become so advanced after being crushed so definitively. I then read the most astonishing account of how the United States and its European allies had agreed to rebuild and provide economic support to Germany and Japan after the war.

The story described how, in the world-wide reshuffling of territory that came with signing treaties and forging alliances at the end of the war, it was understood that both Japan and Germany could not simply be cast out or left to ruin. The powers involved in these negotiations agreed that regardless of how much devastation and death these two nations had caused just a few years earlier, they needed to be included as major nations in our world and given a new life.

The story went on to describe how both nations were given the resources to rebuild, and because they had to start over, they were able to build industrial infrastructures based on the latest technologies. In this way, both Germany and Japan got a head start in the global technological revolution that escalated in the decades to follow.

This story reminded me of a day when I was looking after two young boys who lived in a community with me for several years. At one point, they got into a fight which quickly escalated into yelling and hitting each other. I became alarmed and intervened when they grew louder and more violent and started to hurt one another. I physically separated them and told them each to go home right away. I was so upset that I was shaking and had to go for a walk to cool myself off.

I ended up about fifteen minutes later at the home of one of the boys, and went in to see how he was doing. Much to my amazement, both boys were there playing peacefully and happily together. I was still shaken by the ferocity of their violence toward each other, and could not believe what I was seeing. Both boys simply looked up at me and smiled as if to say "what's bothering you?" I went away, shaking my head in confusion and disbelief.

Both of these stories illustrate how it is that we arbitrarily designate someone as an enemy one moment, and call them a friend the next. Of course not all conflicts turn out this way, but if we look honestly at how we fight with each other, we can see that on some level the business of designating enemies is simply a charade. We hear of attorneys who bitterly fight in the courtroom, or legislators who angrily call each other names on the floor of the chamber, and then go out for a drink together at the end of the day. As a divorce mediator I noticed how many couples seemed to want to prolong their conflicts with each other as a way of staying connected after their separation.

There is more than meets the eye to our habit of opposition. In the end, the lines separating good from evil are not so clear, and an enemy one minute can be an ally the next. The stability and security that we seek from making these arbitrary divisions is simply not real. And whatever purpose or definition it seems to offer for the moment, the devastating results of conflict are surely not a worthy exchange.

The Healing Power of Awareness

I had a dramatic demonstration of undoing opposition while I was going through a painful divorce from my first marriage. Just before our second wedding anniversary, my wife left suddenly without much explanation or discussion. Several months later she hired a lawyer and sued me for half the value of the home, land, and retreat center where we lived, all of which had belonged to me before we were married.

Nothing could have frightened or hurt me more. I was overwhelmed with pain, confusion, and loneliness at her sudden departure, and now she seemed to be threatening to take away my home and fledgling business. I had no savings or other assets besides the property where I had lived for ten years. I had put all of my resources into making this a long-term homestead and retreat. The idea of going to court to let a judge decide the fate of this property was more than I could bear, so I asked a relative to lend me a sizable amount of money to offer her a settlement. I sent her the offer hoping that she would take it, but heard nothing back from her for many months.

Almost a year after she left I was still reeling with emotional pain. In an effort to take care of myself, I attended a ten-day meditation retreat at a center where I had done a lot of sitting. The teacher of this retreat helped me open to the hurt places inside me and create some space around the pain. Half way into the retreat, my mind was settling and I was feeling some peace and clarity in my heart for the first time since all this happened.

One day during this retreat I found myself standing at the tea counter next to a rather frantic woman who was trying to make several cups of tea at once and was making a mess all over. I had seen her before and had felt a strong aversion to her energy. As I stood next to her I noticed my mind beginning to judge her harshly for being so restless and unstable. Then something switched suddenly and I was able to see the pain that she was in. I recognized that she was having a difficult time being with herself on retreat, and this is why she was so agitated. Realizing this, I felt a deep wave of compassion arise toward her.

Then, in a flash, I remembered that my former wife had acted this way in our home on numerous occasions. I recalled how harshly I had judged her at times, and for the first time since she left, I could feel her pain and have compassion for the struggles that she went through during our time together. I went back to my room at the retreat center and wept for her.

I imagined myself holding her in my arms to sooth her pain and anxiety. My entire feeling toward her changed and I no longer saw her as an enemy who was trying to take my home away. Instead, I could see that she was in pain and trying to take care of herself in the only way that she knew how. Nothing changed in our situation, however, I no longer was taking her hostility as a personal attack on me.

Opening to her pain in this way seemed to widen my capacity to feel, and the next thing I knew I was feeling my own pain in a similar way. I could sense how betrayed and lost the little boy in me felt about her leaving me and turning against me so fiercely in such a short time. I imagined myself holding this boy and soothing his pain, just as I had done for her before. And I spent some time just being with myself, feeling empathy for my own trauma for the first time since all this occurred.

In these instances, I was not trying to heal anything, and did not think about responding with empathy toward her or myself. These responses arose organically from within me once I had cleared my mind and allowed my heart to open to what was happening in the moment. They were genuine and spontaneous movements of caring and compassion that I never could have organized myself. It was simple awareness that brought about such a beautiful healing.

Stepping Out of Time

These events seemed to prepare the way for an even greater miracle to occur. For the past six months, I had heard nothing from my former wife in response to my settlement offer. I knew that if we could not settle, our case would come before a judge in a contested hearing. And, if I wanted to keep the property, I would have to defend myself and try to prove that she was wrong.

This kind of attack and defense was the last thing that I wanted to happen. I could not imagine dragging her or myself through such a traumatic public hearing, yet there did not seem to be any alternative. As I sat with an open heart and mind, it became clear to me that I would do anything to avoid hurting each other more in such a way. I then had another realization that shifted my perspective once again.

I had been making a childlike prayer repeatedly to myself since she left a year earlier. I wanted more than anything to be given a chance to go back in time and do our relationship over from the start. This was one of those fantasies that the mind resorts to in extreme trauma when the present situation is impossible to accept. It was like wishing for someone who just died to come back to life. I knew it would never happen, but could not help asking.

One of the things that often happens on a longer retreat like this is to lose a sense of time. Sometimes I cannot tell if I have been meditating for minutes or hours, and often lose track of what day it is. This kind of disorientation was happening for me on this retreat and I suddenly realized that it was possible to make my impossible wish come true. I could sense that time was relative and fluid and knew that I was not stuck a linear progression of past and future.

As I opened to the realization that time was not fixed, and felt the intensity of my desire to be given another chance to do this relationship over again, I realized that I was right back in the same dilemma that had caused so much power struggle and trauma in our marriage. The times when we had our worst fights were when she wanted something from me that I was deeply attached to. Her requests felt like unreasonable demands as she always seemed to want something that I was not willing to let go of. And the harder she pushed, the harder I resisted.

When she left our marriage suddenly, I looked back at those difficult times and realized that if I had known that the relationship was at stake, I would have surrendered. I recognized that the things she wanted from me that I was holding on to so desperately did not mean as much to me as my relationship with her. I would have gladly given her all those things if it meant saving our marriage. And now, on this retreat, it became clear to me that we were once again locked in the same struggle, and I did indeed have another chance to do it differently.

We were again in the same pattern where she wanted me to give her the most precious thing that I had, except that now the stakes were much higher. She was demanding half of the monetary value of the home and retreat center. She knew that I had no savings to pay her with so this would mean selling the property and dividing the money. And the last thing on earth that I wanted to let go of at that moment was this place.

It had been my dream for twenty years to build a homestead and retreat center in a rural setting where I could live, grow my own food, host retreats, and teach. I had purchased the land ten years earlier as a broken-down old farm, and paid it off before I met her. I had spent much of those years building it into a beautiful homestead and sanctuary, and we continued to develop it together, using mostly my financial resources and labor. This place felt like my child and was the culmination of my life's work and vision.

I realized that I had a chance now to handle a similar conflict between us in a new way, and it gradually became obvious what I had to do. I went back to my room and drafted a letter to her saying that instead of selling the place I would prefer that she and her new partner have it, if that is what they wanted. I told her that I would take my things and leave the entire property to her. As soon as I wrote this, a great weight lifted off my shoulders, and I felt light pouring through me for the first time in almost a year.

A Miracle

As I left the retreat to drive home I recognized that my mind was quite open and flexible and it would likely not stay this way for more than a few days. I knew that I could do anything in this state and it would be alright. So I sent a prayer to whoever was looking after me that I be shown clearly and quickly if I was supposed to give away the retreat and homestead. And I made a promise that I would do whatever I was told to do.

On the drive home, it grew dark and a light, freezing rain started. All of a sudden my truck lost its traction on the highway and began to spin in circles. I was going fifty miles an hour and I remember looking out my windows and seeing the scenery going around and around. Because of my heightened state of awareness I stayed relaxed and did not tense up or become scared. I looked around and noticed that there were no other cars on the road and the landscape did not pose immediate dangers.

In a few moments my truck came to a stop right in the middle of the highway. I realized in amazement that I was fine and the truck had not even been scratched. My heart was not racing and I was still relaxed as I calmly put the truck in gear and drove home. This experience showed me what an extraordinary state of grace and presence I was in from the meditation retreat. I knew something big had happened for me there, and that I had released a lot of fear and pain in the process.

When I arrived home, there was a pile of mail waiting for me, and in it was a letter from my former wife's lawyer, from whom I had not heard in over half a year. I opened the letter and read that she had accepted the offer which I had made six months earlier. I put down the letter and wept for relief, gratitude, and joy. I had received the clear message that I requested as quickly as I had asked for it. I was being told that I could stay at my home and retreat and continue building my vision, and there would be no court battle. After surrendering the most precious thing I had, I was graciously given it back.

15

The Power of Thought

It appears that reality exists independently from me, and my life is about interacting with a world in which I have little control. I tend to respond to what life deals me, and often bemoan my plight because it seems that I have so little say in what happens. I normally am not aware of how the programmed thought patterns described in the previous chapters create my experience of reality.

The Limits of our Paradigm

Based on the unconscious patterns of wanting what I do not have, and needing opposition to define myself, I tend to approach objects in the world as either a threat or an opportunity. Everything that I interact with here is seen for its potential to satisfy my desire or to harm me.

Perception sets me up to be separate from the world and to objectify and evaluate everything in it to see how it relates to *me*. This self-centered approach means that I never get to experience anything simply *as it is*. I take in information from the world around me and analyze it to see how it relates to my fears and desires. I am constantly observing the world and filtering my observations as a way to protect myself and get what I want.

In this paradigm I can only see a world that is there for me to use, or that I need to protect myself from. I use the mechanism of perception to define how the world relates to me, and then my limited expectations determine what I see and experience. In this way I am actually making what I call reality, and this "reality" does not exist apart from my own ideas.

The problem with this paradigm of perception is that it limits me to a reality narrowly defined by the innate fear and insecurity of my imaginary self. I often experience this as a painful constriction or a gnawing sense of isolation that I tend to blame on the conditions or people around me. I rarely glimpse that it is my own thoughts that are suffocating me.

Seeing the Invisible

Not so long ago in the history of Western civilization, our ancestors knew nothing about microscopic organisms like parasites and viruses that can cause illness and death once they get inside our body. They had all sorts of theories about what made people sick, such as evil spirits, a curse from the gods, or divine punishment for their sins. And they employed all kinds of magical remedies to address them. However, many of these remedies were largely ineffective because they did not know what was actually causing the sickness.

They could not know, given their level of perception at the time, that tiny organisms called parasites and viruses were causing the disease. It required the development of a microscope to enable us to see these organisms and begin to understand the part they play in human illness.

Up until this time, human waste and dirty conditions were regarded as a nuisance, but not a threat to health. Once this knowledge of microscopic organisms began to be accepted, more people understood the dangers of bacteria on rotten food and viruses in human feces, and the importance of hygiene became clearer. Our personal habits of cleanliness and sanitation began to change and we were thus able to greatly reduce human disease and death.

We face a similar challenge now in the form of our own personal thoughts. The pattern of our thoughts is determined by pre-determined assumptions. These pre-judgments or prejudices determine our reactions, shape our conclusions, and tend to perpetuate themselves. This is what I mean when I say that the mind is programmed, and this is what the Buddha referred to as conditioned mind.

Once I have identified enemies for example, I usually react to defend myself or attack those people. Their response is often to defend themselves, which then threatens me more. As my designated enemies appear more threatening, this confirms my judgment that they are trying to harm me and compels me to further defend or attack in order to protect myself.

In a similar way, once I have identified something I want that I do not have, I tend to orient my life around getting that thing. If I do succeed in getting it, I genuinely feel a momentary sense of satisfaction and gain. This reinforces the idea that there is always something more that I need to be happy, and perpetuates this unconscious assumption of lack.

Getting What We Want

My mental programming follows set patterns and limits the possibilities that I can conceive. I am programmed to continually want what I do not have, and to require opposition for my own definition. This is the only way perception can work, because this is the way it is formatted.

Therefore, my thoughts are continually creating a world in which I focus on what I do not have and blame this on an opposing force that is trying to hurt me. This naturally then is the world I experience as reality. And when my perception confirms this story of lack and oppression, I take it as proof that this is how the world truly is.

This limiting framework is responsible for much of the stress and disappointment in my life. Yet, I tend to perpetuate it because it keeps my world predictable. Staying within these set patterns of thought guarantees a familiar outcome and gives me some sense of control, even if it means that I do not get what I need to be happy.

If I can predict lack and opposition, and see these predictions come true time and again, I gain a small measure of reassurance that I *do* have some power here. Of course, this habit is entirely dysfunctional as it guarantees that I stay stuck in suffering. However, most of us prefer our familiar pain to the uncomfortable sense of losing control that accompanies a completely new experience. And we tend to accept the limitations of our conditioning because we don't know any other way.

The Paradox of Control

The paradox of awakening is that I have to give up trying to have control in order to see that I have always been in charge of my reality. This is simply because the means that I am using now to exert control in the world are based on a false premise and cannot work. I am trying to gain control over my world by manipulating other people and objects to be the way I want them. Most of us do this with varying degrees of success. And at some point, we are likely to feel thwarted in our attempts to control our surroundings and end up feeling frustrated, confused, and powerless.

We have already considered how thoughts create a matrix or story which explains our world and our place in it. This is not just a whimsical fantasy, but rather, this tapestry of thought manifests as the world that I experience. That is why I cannot control it by acting on the forms around me. The way that I perceive everything is determined by the framework I am using to define reality. Therefore, changing the framework is the only way that I can change my world.

When I wish for something in my life, or pray for it to come true, I am attempting to override the mind's programming of loss and opposition. This is similar to what occurs when I use a positive affirmation that I repeat to myself again and again. These strategies can work some of the time because they are finally approaching the true source of reality, which is my own thoughts. However, they are limited and unpredictable in their effectiveness because they do not address the patterns that govern my thoughts where the very notion of struggle and loss originates.

In order to realize that I am creating the world I experience, it can help to stop trying to control things with my will for a moment. I can give up my wish for things to be different and relinquish my desire to change reality. If I stop trying to change other people or circumstances, I may get a glimpse of how my experience is determined by pre-scripted patterns of thought that I was not even aware of.

A New Approach

A spiritual path, such as the one presented by the Buddha, uses the mind's own capacity for awareness to expose the patterns that dictate our process of thought. Exposing the programming behind our thoughts begins to disengage us from them. Once we see the conditions that our mind is bound by, they naturally begin to fall away and we are left with our true nature and the mind's unlimited creative potential.

If I am willing to be without a familiar frame of reference for a moment, my natural state of wholeness can become apparent. This requires that I allow myself to not know anything, not even what I want. Or rather, I can admit to myself that I have never been able to know anything with certainty, even what I want.

As we have already considered, admitting this is hard. It often feels like utter and complete failure, and is usually the last thing that I am willing try. That is why the spiritual path is so elusive. It does not take great will or brain power to figure it out. It does require an extraordinary degree of surrender, which most of us are simply not willing or able to do until we have no other choice.

When I do surrender my cherished capacity for perception for a moment, it begins to dissolve because it was only my belief in it and continuous use of it that kept it alive and made it appear real. Consciousness does not add or manipulate anything in reality. It simply stands still in full awareness, and allows what is not real to fall away.

Seeing the Program

By cultivating awareness through a practice like meditation, it is possible to recognize that things do not just happen to you as it appears, but that your experience is determined by habitual thought patterns in your mind. You begin to see how the continuous thought stream that you hardly pay attention to materializes into your experience of reality. This is freedom, because you now have choices that you could not see before. You can choose simply to let go of a thought or idea, and undo the impact that it is having on your experience.

The Buddha explained that each of our thoughts carries a weight which we rarely recognize. We tend to ignore what our mind is doing much of the time because it is so constantly evaluating and commenting on everything. Most of us learn to tune out our thoughts just as we might tune out a radio or television that is constantly on. After a while, we barely notice the content of our mind, and often view it as merely background noise that we have to put up with.

It is difficult at first to recognize how this ordinary mind chatter could be responsible for my experience. I normally think that my experience is dictated by circumstances. Either I get what I want and am happy, or I do not get what I want and am unhappy. I tend to assume that this simplistic formula is how life works, and orient myself accordingly.

Yet, it is not the objects or people in my life that determine my experience, but my *response* to them. And, as I have pointed out, my response is dictated by my expectations and assumptions, which are entirely contained within the limited world of perception. The nature of perception is that it cannot recognize the present moment. My programmed mind can only create an image of the present moment through comparison with a remembered past moment or an imagined future one.

Using perceptual mind, I cannot relate to things in my world as they are, but only as I think they are. My entire experience is filtered through the framework of the ego, which, as I have suggested, separates all things into either threats or opportunities.

This means that all of my responses are confined within the limits of this program which is based on never having enough, and always having an enemy who is threatening me. Things, events, and people either enhance or threaten my ego, and I respond either by grasping on to them or pushing them away, depending on which category my mind puts them into.

Karma

The Buddha used the idea of Karma to explain how this repeating thought pattern perpetuates our false sense of self. He suggested that each time we try to change our experience of reality by exercising our will, we create a momentum that keeps us stuck in the world of perception. By believing in our thoughts and acting on them, we continuously re-create a world of illusion in which we exist as a separate and vulnerable person struggling for our own survival.

Karma is simply the popular Western physics principle of cause and effect applied to the process of perception. Just as every action has an equal and opposite reaction, so every thought has an impact. We tend to be so occupied with our thoughts that we rarely see how they shape our reality. All that we are normally aware of is the seemingly random and chaotic nature of life which often makes us feel helpless and confused.

Most of us remain caught up in this endless cycle of conflict and loss until the hopelessness and confusion of life finally outweighs our fear of losing control. This is the point where we may stop trying to get things to be different than they are, and give up entirely. It can feel like a moment of collapse and failure because the surrender is so complete. The Buddha described this as the end of karma.

The way to free yourself from this limiting program is to stop generating new karma or to cease acting out of your own volition, and withdraw your support from the illusory world of perception. Of course this can be the most difficult thing to do because your will seems to be the only hope that you have of getting your way in the world, and without it you may feel totally out of control.

The Buddha suggests that the way to wake up from your dream state into reality is to simply stop trying to make things different than they are. He suggests that you cannot do anything about your accumulated past karma, and old judgments and reactions will continue to arise within you until they are exhausted. He suggests allowing the fires of this accumulated karma to burn themselves out within you, without reacting to them. And this is what the practice of meditation enables you to do.

Developing Insight

Just as we had to develop technologies that allowed us to see micro-organisms before we could effectively protect ourselves from harmful bacteria and viruses, we also have to develop tools to help us disengage from our thoughts and stop reinforcing our mental programming. Unlike most of our previous technologies, the tools required for this inner work have to be developed by each one of us individually. No one else can witness your consciousness or interrupt your thought patterns for you.

The kind of support helpful for this process often begins with a teaching that points you inward instead of outward and gives you some idea of what to look for in your inner landscape. It helps to have a technology such as meditation that enables you to focus on the process of consciousness itself so that you see clearly what is happening.

This process begins with learning how to take your attention away from a thought and place it instead on a physical sensation that is happening in this moment. This is the essence of meditation. It usually takes time and repeated effort because we have become so entranced by and invested in our thoughts. Once you have learned to interrupt a thought and refocus on a present moment experience, you can begin to see how your thoughts construct a story that you often mistake for reality.

The Arbitrary Nature of Conclusions

The idea that our thoughts create reality is easier to see if we become aware of how our mind is constantly judging and evaluating. We continuously sort all things according to pre-designated reference points that we arbitrarily assign. If each of us were looking at one person in the room, our physical sight may give us all a similar picture of that person. We see roughly the same shape, color, size, and so on. However, each one of us has a different opinion or set of judgments about that person. And these personal judgments or conclusions seem so final and certain that we mistake them for reality. We think this person really *is* the way that we perceive them to be.

Practicing direct awareness gives me a chance to witness my mind doing this. I can see how I formulate judgments about every experience without being conscious that I am doing so. In a similar way, the individual pictures on a film strip move so fast across the light of the projector that all I see is the illusion of characters in living motion. Until I see for myself the individual pictures lined up one after another on the film strip, it is difficult to convince me that the moving picture on the screen is not alive or real.

Just so, until I see for myself how quickly and continuously my mind assesses each experience and assigns a value to it, I cannot imagine how my thoughts could construct such a seamless image of the world around me. Once I see conception at work, it becomes obvious how my pre-conceived values instantly color each sensory experience. I can observe how quickly the mind draws conclusions in each moment of consciousness, and how each small evaluation combines immediately with the next one to form the illusion of a whole story.

It is my *idea* of the world around me that I respond to, not my direct experience. I react to images that I have made of things, and not to the things themselves. While we all may see the same street, tree, cat, or house, each of us has a different story that we tell ourselves about them. And it is the *story* that we consider most real, not the image that we take in with our senses.

Meditation is simply the practice of refocusing on your immediate sensory experiences, instead of your story. In this way you begin to see that the story is always made up of arbitrary conclusions that you draw in your thoughts. You discover how much investment you have in your thoughts about how things are, and how little you actually know of the things themselves.

As you learn to rely more on awareness than perception, you can experience the reality that exists outside of your story. You can then feel the difference between what is happening and what you *think* is happening, and see how the tension generated between these two causes so much stress and confusion in your life.

———————— •◆• ————————

Be still and notice a story that you are telling yourself in this moment. It may be about this book or the ideas you just read, the physical environment you are in right now, or something going on in your life. Pay attention to your thoughts and see how your mind is evaluating your experience by passing judgments and drawing conclusions. What are some of your conclusions about your current situation or the ideas in this book?

Are these conclusions true? How do you know that they are true? What happens if you let go of your conclusions and simply allow yourself not to know for a moment?

———————— •◆• ————————

16

The Need for a Story

One way to see behind the veil of perception and glimpse how your thoughts create reality is to notice how most of us need a story which defines our place in the world. My mind is habitually weaving the fabric of the story of myself with every thought. I endlessly review my past, combing every detail in my memory for meaning, and then project myself into the future, planning and rehearsing each step again and again. The sum of all this thought is a seamless storyline supporting the notion of my existence as an individual personality. Some of the defining themes that run throughout this story are the patterns of desire and opposition that we have already discussed.

The outline of the story is made up of these predictable programmed thought patterns filled in with an endless variety of contents. As the particular details of my life story are continually changing, I believe that *I* am changing, growing, and discovering new territory. I tend to get caught up in the content and focus on the specific dramas that unfold with different characters and events, and rarely glimpse the patterns that are behind them. I often don't notice that I am repeating the same scripted formula over and over again, and that nothing is really changing at all.

This is why life can feel so constricted, repetitive, and dull. I am blindly following these pre-set patterns of thought that keep my reality limited to a small range of possibilities. I tend to assume that it is some outside power that is restricting my movement, yet it is really the invisible template programmed into my own thought system. This explains why I often struggle against the conditions around me, trying with all my might to change other people or the circumstances in which I find myself, yet nothing seems to move. I often then feel hopeless and depressed, believing that change is impossible.

Our Cultural Womb

We can see this habit of story making throughout human history if we look at the bigger cultural myths or stories told by civilizations to define our place in the world. Not only does our mind weave a continuous story about our personal existence, but as groups, we create cultures that tell the story of us as a people. Every organized human society tells a story about its origins that define a place for that group of people in the world. Each one contains an explanation of where the people came from, and in some way defines how things work.

These stories make up a culture, which provides a basic context or container for the lives of the people within it. A culture defines a community of people, just as a personality defines an individual, and we tend to be proud of and revel in our culture just as we do with our personality. Many of us see our culture as a foundation for our identity in the world, and turn to it for a sense of comfort and security. However, we rarely see how it is limiting us. And even if we do see this, it often seems impossible to escape our ingrained cultural beliefs.

I was once traveling through the southwestern United States and stopped by the side of the road to view some beautiful red rock canyons. Sitting on the edge of the canyon rim were two young Navajo men of the local Native American tribe. My friend and I sat and talked with them for a while and they began to tell us about their lives.

They seemed particularly unhappy and expressed to us how confined they felt by their traditional culture. They were drinking beer, and each time they finished a bottle they would carelessly toss it into the canyon with an expression of anger and disdain. Their anguish was articulated by the sound of glass smashing into pieces against the hard rock far below.

They pointed across the canyon to some large caves in the opposite wall and explained that while *we* could freely go into and explore those caves, *they* could not. They had been raised to believe that there were evil spirits in those caves who would harm them if they went inside. These young men knew that this was only a story, and they told us that they did not believe in the reality of it. Yet they were quite distressed because they could not get past it.

They said that they had once tried to enter the caves and immediately became terrified and had to leave. For them, their culture was no longer a source of comfort and security, and had become a source of fear and limitation that they could not escape.

Getting Out of the Box

A similar shift happened for me when I was in college and lost faith in the society in which I had been raised. I began to see the program of formal education leading to a profession in the world as a small, tight box that did not allow for the full expression of who I was. I felt constricted by my culture and compelled to escape it any way that I could.

When I went off to live in Sri Lanka, no one in my life could understand my urgency to get out of my cultural context and experience something completely different. People felt afraid for me because I was leaving the familiar cultural womb that was intended to keep us safe and secure. For me however, the cultural womb had become a prison, and all I wanted to do was get out. I was so hungry to experience something different that I jumped into this new culture with both my feet.

The men in Sri Lanka wore a simple cloth tube around their waist that looked like a tight long skirt. The younger men were also physically affectionate with each other. They would constantly put their arms around each other and even hold hands while they walked. Both of these customs would be considered taboo for a man in my culture at the time. No man would ever wear a skirt or be seen touching another man in this way for fear of being labeled as homosexual.

The young men that I hung out with in Sri Lanka were not gay, they simply had no cultural taboos forbidding them to be affectionate toward each other. For them, expressing their caring and support for one another in this way was natural. It provided them with a sense of connection and companionship and they saw it as entirely good. It took me some time, but gradually I came to feel relaxed holding my friends' hand while we walked and putting our arms around each other when we talked. I learned to love the freedom of the cloth sarong or long skirt and I also stopped wearing shoes, as none of my village friends wore them.

I experienced a freedom in Sri Lanka from some of the restrictions of my culture that had been suffocating me. Yet, it was only by immersing myself in a different society that I was able to see my own cultural limitations clearly. I was not aware of how isolated I had felt as a man always having to compete with other men and looking only to women for deeper companionship or affection.

When we grow up in a culture, it becomes a complete paradigm for us, and its restrictions and taboos are largely invisible. Living in Sri Lanka taught me that there is nothing inherently evil about eating with my hands, or men wearing skirts and touching each other affectionately. I realized for the first time that these were only forbidden by my culture's social code, not by some universal law.

Seeing the Cult in Culture

In the decades following the sixties in the United States, we began to hear a lot about cults. These were religious groups often with a charismatic leader who convinced young people to become members. Often membership was a total commitment that involved giving the group all of one's money, agreeing to certain limitations on behavior, and adopting a prescribed belief system. Young people at that time were attracted to these organizations because they offered a sense of certainty and belonging that was difficult to find in our fragmented, individualized world.

These cults often presented a complete world view or spiritual formula that gave life a new meaning and context. They derived their power and strength from requiring unquestioned allegiance to a central belief system, and often to the leader as well. For people who were lost and searching for something to give their lives meaning and purpose, these cults seemed to be an oasis in the desert. They offered a certainty in a world where everything seemed turned upside down and there was nothing to cling to for stability.

The problem with these cults is that they created an absolute division between those in the cult and those outside, and they tended to strip each member of the capacity to be responsible for their own well-being. In the end they were often exposed as not caring about their individual members and instead serving only the leaders in their accumulation of wealth and power.

We tend to use the word "cult" to describe an overly controlling organization that usurps our individuality and often uses people to accumulate wealth and power. Yet "cult" is merely the basis of the word "culture." If we look more closely we can see that most religions and cultures have many of the same characteristics of these cults. The Catholic Church is an example of an established and accepted religion in the West that has often controlled people in a similar way for its own accumulation of wealth and power. In our current Western culture of corporate dominance, it is clear how large business interests manipulate and control people for their own profit by investing huge amounts of money in advertising and lobbying.

Many of us tend to look to our specific culture or religion to define us and our place in the world. Cultures and religions require an allegiance to certain beliefs which in turn offer us clear values to use as reference points for perception. We usually receive a sense of righteousness and belonging from our culture or religion that helps us to cope with the inherent insecurity of life. Many of us feel lost without a group that believes in the same things we do and shares a similar sense of right and wrong.

A culture is a largely invisible set of beliefs and assumptions about the way things ought to be. We become so familiar with our own cultural values that we often do not notice them until they are broken or we are without them. This is what happened for me living in Sri Lanka. Suddenly, I could see all the unspoken rules that had defined my world as a boy. I had assumed that these norms were universal and beyond question, yet they clearly were not that way. I saw that different people did things in very different ways, and the way I grew up doing things was just *one way*, not *the* way.

This cross-cultural experience opened my eyes and exposed the conditions of the culture that I grew up in. I wanted out so desperately that I gladly tried out the beliefs and values of another people. Because it was all so new to me and different from the way I was raised, I could try on the Sri Lankan culture without any of the heaviness or baggage that normally accompanies traditional rules and restrictions. It all felt like freedom to me.

However, the longer I stayed with the people there, the more I began to see that they also had an oppressive set of rules which they were following. The teachings of the Buddha had predictably been formulated into rigid social norms, religious morality, and superstition. Kindness and generosity bought merits which one could cash in during a future life, and there were endless rituals that Buddhist monks performed at different times and places to bring good luck, or keep away evil. Had I been raised in this culture, I would likely have found it just as restrictive as I did my own.

The point of looking closely at these programmed mental patterns and cultural rules is to see that we are not free. This mind can only operate within a structured format that the mechanism of perception can recognize. That is its limitation. Our imagination can create such elaborate and realistic images and stories that it keeps us mesmerized and distracted most of the time, and we don't see the limitations. Similarly, a computer program enables the computer to create such an amazing variety of images and do an enormous number of functions that at first we are not aware of its limits.

Many of us can feel this sense of being limited and constricted by *something* in our lives. We simply never think to examine our values or beliefs or observe our thought patterns to find the cause. Once we do recognize how we are limited by our cultural or personal beliefs, a natural response is to get beyond these in order to be free.

Creation Myths

An essential part of every culture's story is a creation myth that explains how the people came to be. This common practice demonstrates the basic need that perceptual mind has to create a context for itself in time and space. Creation stories, like other aspects of culture and religion, seem to give our lives legitimacy and purpose. Yet, in the end they profoundly restrict us by ensuring that we remain within a limited and artificial paradigm.

The story of how we got here forms the foundation of our paradigm and defines the lens through which we perceive the world. As such, it is largely invisible to us. Most of us assume the truth of our own creation story and hardly notice it because it is so familiar. Remember that a paradigm has to remain beyond question in order for it to provide a basis for reality. Therefore we normally become aware of our underlying assumptions about the world only when they are interrupted somehow.

My own cultural context was significantly interrupted when my life began to lose meaning and purpose during my early college years. I began to reject aspects of our commonly shared reality that seemed beyond question to most of the people. I no longer believed, for example, that education or money would lead to security or happiness. And when I allowed myself to integrate with the vastly different culture of Sri Lanka, I was finally able to see my own cultural conditioning clearly in contrast to the social norms there.

Western civilization is in the midst of a major shift in its dominant creation myth which has interrupted our story and rendered it visible for a time. For much of our history the story written in the Old Testament of the Judeo-Christian Bible defined where we came from. This story features a being called God with super-human abilities who created the heavens, earth, and all life forms, ending with the creation of man which he molded from clay, and woman which he made from a rib of the man. As with many other cultures, the story of how we came to be has been the domain of religion and kept by the church.

Like so many other cultural myths, our story was remarkably simplistic and involved imagination, fantasy, and superstition more than rational observation. Creation stories have often been based on fantasy simply because none of us ever has known for sure where we come from. Our limited and vulnerable sense of self requires a story in order to explain our existence, so we make something up.

Western society has changed in the past few centuries to utilize logic and reason more than belief or superstition to explain the world around us. The mechanical use of perceptual observation that we call science has gradually taken the place of religion. As part of this shift, a new story with a different explanation of our creation was proposed a little over a century ago.

This story was based on systematic observation and recorded data, and utilized new technologies such as a microscope rather than merely imagination. In this story we grew to become the way we are now as a gradual process of minute genetic changes that that took millions of years. Just as the size of the earth and scope of the universe had been beyond comprehension to us before the advent of science, so the immense span of linear time that it took for life on earth to evolve into what it is today made it impossible for us to witness the process of gradual evolution within our normal means of perception.

Without the tools of science to put into perspective the vast amount of incremental changes life forms have undergone to become what they are today, we were left to assume that things had always been the way we see them now. In a similar way, we could not know that the earth was round because the size of our planet made it impossible to see the curvature of it with our eyes. With no other way to explain our existence, we naturally made up stories of God simply creating the earth and life upon it as a man would create a sculpture or build a city.

Once this new theory of evolution was presented, it came into conflict with the church, which saw itself as the keeper of the creation story. This conflict is still going on today in some places, with each side claiming that the other is telling the wrong story. That there is still such a passionate struggle between two different creation stories tells us the importance that these stories play in our existence.

Between Two Creation Myths

A creation myth only works to define our place in the universe if we believe in it without question. In Western civilization today we find ourselves in a most interesting time of transition between two stories, which enables us to see and question both of them. We might describe our society as having just passed the threshold from one creation myth to another. The biblical story of Genesis has largely been superseded by Darwin's theory of evolution. Yet, the scientific explanation of our existence is still relatively new in the context of human history, and some of us are still unsure about it.

We tend to think of science as hard truth, and very different from mythical stories like an all- powerful God creating humans out of clay and bones. However, if we look objectively at the theory of evolution and modern science's story of the creation of the earth, these can seem every bit as imaginary and fantastic as the biblical creation story.

Our new creation myth begins with the "big bang" theory of the origins of the universe, which proposes that life as we know it began when all matter and energy was compressed into an infinitely small point. This theory suggests that in a mysterious gigantic explosion matter and energy were flung out into space, which led to the beginning of our planet as a ball of molten minerals and gas. The idea of evolution is that life forms began to spontaneously evolve as the ball cooled and the basic elements for living organisms materialized. And these life forms have been going through incremental genetic changes over millions of years as a result of a process of natural selection. The result is the multitude of different plants and animals that inhabit the earth today, including ourselves.

This unique time of transition between two opposing creation stories allows us to see that each of them is only a *guess*. We still do not know much about our origins with certainty. The theories about genetic coding in DNA and the vast time scale of the formation of the earth come from the careful observations of our scientific process. To many of us, the idea of evolution seems to make more sense than a single god who created all of this in a week. Yet we still do not have a good explanation for where all of the materials that form our world came from or how conscious life manifested out of inert matter.

If our Western scientific process has taught us anything, it is how much we *don't know* about our reality. Understanding how much of the world around us remains shrouded in mystery is an essential step in the process of becoming more conscious. We have to admit that we don't know before our minds can open to a new way of seeing.

It seems likely that the theory of evolution will become our dominant myth, and in time the story of Genesis will be nothing more than a primitive superstition. Yet, let this not distract us from the more significant observation that *we still think we need a story to define where we came from.*

Our dependency on a story to explain our existence is a result of relying on perception to understand reality. Perception cannot know anything for certain but can only approximate something in the way a photograph approximates a real scene. Relying on a story to explain our creation is not the same as knowing where we come from or who we are. In this way perception always leaves us with an element of doubt and uncertainty.

Getting into Heaven

While creation stories like the theory of evolution may offer us some clues as to how humans came into existence, they give us little information about *why* we are here. The Biblical story of Genesis suggests that we are here to rule over all the other life forms on earth, while the theory of evolution suggests that our function may be merely to survive in order to continue our species. However, neither of these begins to answer our innate hunger for the deeper *purpose* of life.

Religion is a common way that we try to explain life's meaning. Yet, religion often reduces the meaning of life to beliefs and moral measurements that frame our purpose in terms of an exchange or accomplishment. These are the ego's terms. They tell us what we need to do in order to be good, or how to make up for our sins in order for our vulnerable sense of self to be accepted and validated. These pursuits may hold our attention for a while, yet do not satisfy our need to know what life is really for.

In the modern Christian religion that I grew up with, the aim of life is to be good enough to get into heaven when we die. Heaven is portrayed as a place without any suffering where we abide in the afterlife if we have cleansed ourselves of all sin. In contrast, Hell is described as a place of eternal discomfort that we are condemned to if we are not good enough.

While this simplistic view of life may provide some motivation and sense of purpose, the story of heaven and hell merely keeps us locked into our world of perception. Our programmed mind uses the stark contrast between these two opposing fates as a way to measure our spiritual progress, yet the definitions are so murky that most of us have no idea what they mean or where we fit in.

Religions tend to make a complex maze out of the quest for heaven that can only be interpreted by some higher authority and leaves most of us confused about our place in the world. How do we know when we are good enough? Who makes this monumental judgment that could impact our experience for eternity? The only way to answer this is to conceive of an ultimate authority figure called God, who knows everything including our private thoughts, and makes a final judgment about us once we die.

Perception can only make a future goal out of heaven, which keeps us trapped on the treadmill always trying to reach an elusive end. The whole story of heaven, hell, and the final judgment is constructed by our ego in order to provide a place for itself. The conditions for getting into heaven are vague enough to keep us striving endlessly, while the outcome always lies in the future after we die. This leaves us focused on something that we can never achieve in this lifetime which depends on factors beyond our control.

With a story like this as our basis for meaning, some of us play the game to our fullest, trying to outdo everyone else and be good enough to get into heaven. Or we become cynical and jaded, rejecting the whole notion of an afterlife and merely trying to get what we can for ourselves now. Some of us end up feeling hopelessly depressed and withdraw from life because the rules of the game seem so obscure and impossible to follow.

Our Need for Meaning and Purpose

These questions about life's ultimate meaning come from somewhere deep in our consciousness and cannot be answered within the narrow confines of religion, culture, or creation stories. The urge to discover our life's purpose is a fundamental part of what makes us human. It is the seed that we all carry latent within us, and this impulse to understand life on a more profound level creates the deep unrest which many of us feel.

We sometimes find this inner turmoil tortuous, and try to get rid of it by numbing or distracting ourselves. We struggle to ignore and deny our need for deeper meaning, try to satisfy it through adherence to some religious or cultural formula, or bury our longing under momentary sensual pleasures and distractions. Yet we cannot resolve our discomfort until we discover directly for ourselves why we are here.

It could be said that the quest for meaning *is* the purpose of life. Certainly the most meaningful way we can use our time here is to try to understand what it is all *for*. If you observe your mind you will notice that it is continuously trying to assign meaning to every detail of your experience. However, it is not possible to find meaning through perception, and that is our dilemma.

It is not that meaning is so obscure or difficult to discover. It is that the means we are using to find it are precisely what is keeping us from seeing it. Perception itself creates a distance between us and our immediate experience, which is fully and completely meaningful if we allow it to be what it is.

Creation stories, religions, and cultures of any kind end up confining us because they merely provide a context for an imagined self to exist in a world of perception. This world is a facsimile of reality represented through images conceived by our thoughts. It can never satisfy us *because it is not real*. That is why our lives can seem so pointless and we are starving for something actual that we can base our existence on, instead of mere stories.

———————— •◆• ————————

Take a moment to recognize your beliefs about where you came from and why you are here. It may be a mix of common religious or scientific ideas and your own conclusions. Don't be concerned with painting a whole picture. Just call to mind whatever pieces of the puzzle that you can.

Notice that these are only ideas, and you may not know for sure. Relax your urge to find an answer to this fundamental question, and consider that perhaps no one has the real story. Try to simply be with the question, and let go of needing to have a final answer right now.

———————— •◆• ————————

17

Back to the Garden

Stories that define where we come from and where we are going tend to confine us within the world of perception and foster superstition. The Christian idea of heaven paints a picture of a perfect world that we can only reach after we die, *if* we prove ourselves worthy. This effectively puts heaven out of reach for most of us because it is either too distant and nebulous, or we cannot get past our own sense of unworthiness.

We create elaborate rituals and rites that appear to offer a way to cleanse ourselves of guilt and shame through conscious suffering, such as in the Catholic idea of being a martyr. Or we make deals with God that if we do certain things God will allow us into heaven or grant our wish here on earth. Sometimes these exchanges become incorporated into institutions like the church, and we pay a priest to have our sins removed or accumulate merits to buy us a better afterlife by doing good deeds. More recently, corporate advertising convinces us that in order to be accepted or good enough we need to buy a certain product.

Cultural myths often reduce life to some sort of divine board game, however, they may also contain coded information that can help us find a way out. In the history of Western civilization, there is one story that is perhaps the simplest and most well-known. It is part of our traditional creation myth from the Old Testament of the Bible. The story is of Adam and Eve in the Garden of Eden, and it presents us with a remarkably clear explanation of why we are here.

In this story, God created the earth as a bountiful garden and made a man and a woman to inhabit the garden. The biblical Garden of Eden contained all that Adam and Eve needed, with no dangers or threats to their safety. There is a sense of them being connected to each other and to all the other animals and plants in the garden, without conflict or opposition and in constant joy and abundance.

According to the story, Adam and Eve lived in continuous and unlimited happiness in the garden. The only condition that God gave them is that they could not eat the fruit of the tree of the knowledge of good and evil. However, after some time, they were tempted to eat the fruit from the forbidden tree. And from the moment that they ate this fruit, their world transformed into something like what we know today.

Losing Innocence

Instead of being inherently connected to everything in the garden, Adam and Eve suddenly found themselves separate and apart from their world and each other. While before they were simply part of each other and their surroundings, they now saw everything around them as different from themselves.

They covered their bodies to hide their differences, began naming each separate thing in the garden, and used their new knowledge of good and evil to distinguish between things that were good and useful to them, and things that were evil and harmful. There was now danger and fear where before it had not existed. The garden was no longer a paradise for them, and they were cast out of it to fend for themselves.

The Christian Church has tended to focus on the sin that Adam and Eve committed of disobeying God, and portrays them being thrown out of Eden as a punishment. It uses this story to suggest that we are all somehow tainted by this sin and thus our lives are full of hardship and suffering. The church tells us that we have to make up for our disobedience to God now by trying to be good in the hope that when we die God may forgive us and allow us into heaven.

The established church has lost the power and control it once had, and this story of sin, punishment, and redemption is too heavy for many of us to bear. We may see the Bible as a fiction that has no real bearing on our lives, and reject stories like Adam and Eve and the Garden of Eden as pure myth. Yet some of us still wonder about the idea of Eden and why life seems to be so fraught with fear, pain, and loss.

We may refer to this story when we imagine what we most want the world to be like. We wish that we could recreate this garden or somehow find our way back there, but we cannot see how. The idea of a world of abundance without suffering, loss, fear, or pain haunts us even as we shrug it off as merely a fantasy. Yet there is a clear message here if we remove the church's interpretation of this ancient story, and focus not on the sin of disobedience but instead look at what Adam and Eve actually did.

The Beginning of Perception

The story of Adam and Eve in the Garden of Eden simply describes our condition before we entered the world of perception. In the garden we knew no opposites, and did not require the mechanism of comparing things to measure reality. We functioned perfectly without having to separate out and weigh everything in order to decide what things were.

Everything was part of one whole and there was no need to take it apart in pieces to try to understand it. We were part of the garden, as the garden was part of us, and there was no separation, so we did not need comparative evaluation or judgment. We were at peace and all of our needs were met. In this world all that we had, and all that we needed, was conscious awareness.

Eating the fruit of the forbidden tree gave us the *knowledge of good and evil*. Before this we could not tell the difference, and did not need to know the difference between what was good and what was bad. Suddenly, we entered the world of opposites where everything is measured against everything else, and nothing is whole or complete in itself.

The knowledge of good and evil split our world into fragments with each thing having another side. In order to have good we had to have bad, right required wrong, dark needed light, up needed down. Everything became neatly divided, and Adam and Eve began the process which we are still in today of categorizing and naming everything in order to understand its place in the world.

Before human beings had the capacity to distinguish between good and evil, all was well in the world and there was no conflict, struggle, pain, sickness, or death. Once we acquired this ability, we lost all this. In the biblical story of Eden, *nothing external to Adam and Eve changed*. It was the same garden and was only their *perception* of it that was different.

Taking on the capacity to distinguish good from evil did not suddenly create harmful things in the garden that they had to protect themselves from. All that it did was to change the way they *looked* at everything. Instead of being connected to all of life, they now saw themselves as separate. Instead of simply knowing everything through awareness, they now had to formulate labels and concepts in order to make sense of their world.

Eating the forbidden fruit programmed their minds for perception and gave them the capacity for comparative evaluation, which they did not have before. And as soon as they added this filter to their minds, they saw duality, opposition, and danger, where it *did not actually exist*. This story is describing the beginning of perception and illustrates how fear originates with our paradigm of duality. Now there was life and death, sickness and health, pain and pleasure, and all things were relative, temporal, and mortal.

Surrendering the Knowledge of Good and Evil

The message here seems perfectly clear if we can bring ourselves to accept it. We are being taught in this story that the way back to the garden is simply to give up our knowledge of good and evil. We are being invited by this ancient myth to surrender the paradigm of duality that underlies our process of perception. The story suggests that if we let it go, we will find ourselves back in Eden, where all of our needs are met and there is no opposition. Evil and danger do not inherently exist in the world, and if we pause our mechanism of comparison for a moment, the threats that we perceive will simply disappear.

The difficulty is that we now cherish this capacity to tell right from wrong beyond any other ability that we possess, and utilize it continuously to assess danger and provide us with a sense of certainty and security. Judging right from wrong is the very core of what defines us as individuals and validates our concept of self. We are sure to feel lost, helpless, and naked without it.

We have made such an icon out of rational thought that the mere suggestion of detaching from perception is heresy. Surrendering our capacity for logical discernment is unthinkable and amounts to self-annihilation. It seems like a massive denial that could only lead us into a dark hole of ignorance and stupidity. We have come to value this ability to tell right from wrong, that we acquired in disobedience with God's wishes, more than the Garden of Eden itself.

Yet, for all the importance that we place on distinguishing good from bad, we have not yet found a reliable way to do this. To finally determine right from wrong, we need something fixed to compare all things against. And, in all of human history, we have never discovered an absolute reference point from which to measure good and evil for certain.

In order to create the *illusion* of an actual right and wrong in our world, we tend to make judgments about people or things and then assume that these are true. Not only does this fragment our world, but it *maintains our ignorance*. We blind ourselves to what is actually going on by clinging to our beliefs about things. Instead of seeing what is true, we only see *what we want to believe is true*.

We do not mean to do harm, and we are not bad people because we do this. Most of us form prejudices about the world around us in order to maintain the kind of oppositional duality that is necessary for perception. The limitations of our mental programming *require* that we make these arbitrary judgments in order to provide a basis for our rational thought process. The consequence of our continuous use of evaluative judgment, however, is that we live in a world that is more make-believe than real, and our lives are permeated with a sense of being hollow or superficial.

Our Obsession with Sorting Out

I have three daughters in their pre-teenage years who often seem obsessed with making value judgments about everything. When I spend time with one of them alone, and there is a chance for deeper or more intimate conversation, they inevitably begin asking me questions like "what is your favorite book (food, movie, place, animal, plant, color, song, or person)?" I am always a bit surprised and befuddled by these questions, as I was hoping that we would discuss the meaning of life or something more profound. And I usually leave them frustrated by telling them that I don't know.

These constant questions about what I like or dislike were unsettling to me at first. I had been gradually shedding my opinions and prejudices for decades, and was not interested in making such crisp divisions in my life any more. I finally came to understand that the children were so focused on discussing opinions because they were formulating and crystallizing their personality. We form our ego, or sense of self, by trying to sort everything out from everything else, and assigning labels of good or bad.

When I am talking about a person whom she has not met, one of my daughters will often ask, "are they a good person or a bad person?" Each time she says this, I find myself trying to explain that people don't fit into neat categories like good and bad, and it is not helpful to label them as such. The vacant look on her face often tells me that she doesn't understand exactly what I mean, and I let it go at that.

When we become adults, we learn that it is not proper to talk openly about people being good or bad. However, most of us continue to do this sorting out process in our private thoughts, just as Adam and Eve did in the garden after they ate the forbidden fruit. This is why our thinking mind is so busy, requires so much of our energy, and constantly distracts us from our present moment experience. We think that we have to sort through all of our experiences in order to categorize them so that our world can have order and meaning. If you want to see proof of this, just spend time with children who are just formulating their egos and find out what is important to them.

True education or learning that leads to real growth and development stretches us to expand our mental framework beyond our judgments of good and bad and see things as they inherently exist, not merely as we perceive them from our point of view. This is something which we undertake as adults when we realize that we have come up against the confining walls of our own thinking and we want to be free and know the truth. It requires that we venture outside of our comfortable ideas and risk not knowing for a moment.

———————— •◆• ————————

Think about a person in your life whom you would consider to be bad or wrong and see if you can think of something good about them.

Think of someone whom you consider to be right or good and try to see something bad about them.

———————— •◆• ————————

We can all do this if we give it some thought, because no one is all good or all bad even though we tend to assign these labels to people in our lives and assume that they are true. The people you think of as bad probably do not see themselves that way. Some of them may think of *you* as bad and *themselves* as good. Things that you consider bad today might once have appeared good to you, or might someday seem that way. All of our judgments turn out to be arbitrary and temporary in the end and fail to provide any real certainty.

I used to think that computers were bad, and now I am writing this book using my favorite laptop. I once loved to eat meat more than anything, and now I don't believe in killing or eating animals. I once thought it was wrong to ever cut down a tree, and now I use my chainsaw to make our winter fire wood from live trees on our land.

I could list many more of these internal value shifts, and so could you if you think about it. The lesson here is simply that, while our habit is to make judgments about our world because this is how our mind is programmed to operate, we do not have to take them so seriously or use them to define who we are. In fact we will ultimately be frustrated if we do this because, while our judgments may seem so absolute and final now, *they eventually change.*

A New Story of Eden

For me, the story of the Garden of Eden holds a great promise. I have a sense of God being all of our awareness put together – a whole consciousness that contains all of our seemingly individual minds as one. Adam and Eve were one with this consciousness and knew themselves to be inseparably part of God. Everything in the garden was part of them and they experienced no lack or separation. When God asked them not to eat of the tree of the knowledge of good and evil, it was simply a caution not to use perception to divide and separate things but to leave them as one whole.

Adam and Eve could not resist the temptation to use perception, and so they ate the fruit. This was an understandable mistake, and one which most of us are still making today. Of course it is tempting to try out perception and put ourselves in the position of being the judge. The result, however, is a world where nothing is certain and everything keeps shifting and changing. And the instability of this world makes us feel anxious, insecure, and afraid much of the time.

The story offers us a clear way back to Eden. We have to question our cherished capacity of perception and ask ourselves honestly if our ability to judge and evaluate is making our lives more peaceful and content, or if it is creating more anxiety, stress and confusion. If we can see that we have never found a way to judge good from bad conclusively, and that most of the evaluations that we make are arbitrary and erratic, then it will not be such a sacrifice to let this habit go.

In Search of Security

Ever since we left the Garden of Eden, we have been in search of the security and sense of completion that we had there. We traded the comfort of the Garden for our ability to divide the world into good and evil, and now we rely on our capacity for distinguishing right from wrong for our sense of safety and self-identity.

The problem is that, instead of unifying our world, dividing things into opposite categories only further isolates us. We approach the world with a complex set of beliefs about what is good and what is bad that *creates* separation. We mistakenly believe that by exercising our capacity for judgment we can make our world whole again, yet this process requires that we exclude whatever we think is bad, and so it guarantees that we remain divided.

We are stuck in an endless cycle where the harder we try to attain unity by gathering together all the good and excluding all the bad, the more we reinforce our division. There *is* no inherent good or evil in the world as we assume. These are arbitrary distinctions that we think we have to make to keep ourselves safe. Yet it is this very habit, which we value so much, that makes our lives feel so unstable and insecure.

It is our allegiance to judgments of good and evil that justifies the violence, hatred, and war in the world. Once we label others as evil, we can convince ourselves that it is alright to attack or kill them. In fact, we believe that until we disable or destroy them, our world cannot be whole and complete. This is how we find ourselves involved in wars which cause enormous suffering over and over again.

This kind of violent conflict is embedded in our thought system. As much as we might dislike the idea of war, many of us rationalize that it is the only way to achieve unity. We believe that we have to eliminate the bad in order to have a world that is good. We talk about a "just war" and see it in terms of right triumphing over wrong.

Shattering our Wholeness

I was recently at a retreat center where there was a group of combat veterans attending a retreat. I met some of them, heard their stories of war, and learned about the impact that being a part of organized violent conflict has had upon their lives. If you hear honestly from anyone who has been to war and seen the violence of it first hand, it is obvious how much it has challenged their integrity and left scars in their hearts and minds.

We tend to focus only on the physical impacts of war and assume that if a soldier returns home with life and limb intact then they are well. But if you spend time with any combat veteran you may see that this is not so. Most soldiers who go to war come home damaged emotionally, and some never recover. This is because making someone else an enemy, casting them out of our heart, and seeing them as the villain and us as the victim destroys the integrity of the world that we belong to. It is inevitable that we hurt ourselves by doing this as much as we hurt our imagined enemy.

One man in the retreat described how he had carried a handgun around with him for a while in his life, looking for a reason to shoot someone. Another talked about how he had nightmares about the faceless people that he had killed. And a third veteran talked about how difficult it was now for him to feel safe or trust anyone. In 2007, CBS reported that in 2005, at the height of the Iraq war, an average of

17 suicides were committed *daily* among United States combat veterans.

Even if we win the war, and "good" does triumph over "evil," the consequences are devastating. While there may be the pretense of unity in the world once an enemy is defeated, the individuals who fought against each other are emotionally fragmented. In this way, violent conflict destroys the winner as much as it does the loser.

The Empty Boat

This Zen Buddhist story that I heard offers some wisdom about our habit of creating enemies:

———————— •◆• ————————

A man was rowing a boat across a river to get to the other side. Suddenly, he heard a loud bang and his boat shook violently as another rowboat crashed into the front of his. The man was understandably upset and indignant that another rower would crash into him carelessly like that, damaging his boat and impeding his progress across the river. He felt overcome by rage and stopped rowing to address the idiot who had hit him.

As he turned to face the other rower and was about to express his anger, the man saw to his surprise that the other boat was empty. It had lost its mooring and was simply drifting on its own down the river. When the man saw that the other boat was empty, his rage disappeared instantly and he resumed his endeavor to get to the other side, leaving the empty boat to drift away on its own.

———————— •◆• ————————

This story illustrates how we look for someone to blame when we are hurt or our path is blocked, and automatically make that person into an enemy. In the case of the man in the rowboat, there was no one to blame. It was an empty boat that hit him, and as soon as he saw this, his anger disappeared.

Just as in the story from a previous chapter about the rope that looked like a snake, the circumstances did not change - the person's *perspective* on the situation did. As soon as we see that the "snake" is actually a rope, or our "attacker" is an empty boat, we drop our story because it is no longer relevant. And, in dropping the story about something threatening us, we lose all the fear and stress that accompanies it.

It is our *interpretation* of each seeming threat in our lives that we are reacting to and defending ourselves from, not the actual person or situation. It is the way we perceive a situation that causes our insecurity and fear. These teaching stories demonstrate the instant and miraculous change that occurs as soon as we let go of our conclusion and simply be aware of what is.

When someone hurts us, it is as if their boat has come loose from its dock and drifted away on its own. No matter how hostile other people's actions seem to be, no one usually has the *intention* to hurt us. We are each simply trying to make ourselves safe in the only way we can think of in the moment. Often we respond to a situation out of habit, or we are doing what someone else did to us.

When someone else crashes into our life in a painful or disturbing way, they are not in control of their boat. There is no one there who is conscious and focusing with intention. Their fear is running them and the boat of their life has been cast adrift with no one rowing it. They are acting unconsciously, unaware of what they are doing.

Remember the famous words of Jesus as he hung painfully from the wooden cross, nails through his hands and feet, while the Roman soldiers and people in the crowd taunted and tortured him: "Forgive them, Father, for they know not what they do."

As much as someone's aggression or carelessness might cause *us* pain, it often hurts *them* more because it effectively fragments their world and disrupts their integrity. Being forceful and violating someone else does not work to get our needs met and only makes our situation worse by isolating us or giving cause for retaliation. In reality there are no true villains or victims.

18

Personal Integrity and Morality

If we look at how people have struggled with defining their values through the ages, we find that determinations of right and wrong tend to boil down to arbitrary perceptions based on personal comparisons. This is why values conflicts such as the issue of abortion or same-sex marriages in the United States can be so volatile and can go unresolved for so long. We each tend to see reality from our own personal perspective, and none of us can see the whole. It seems that once we entered this world of opposites we gave up our capacity to know anything at all with absolute certainty.

The Distortions of Perception

The introduction of the concepts of good and evil that gave birth to our process of perception made everything in our world relative and subject to change. Our struggle ever since has been to determine some absolute right and wrong and to know for certain the difference. The best that we can do is to follow an abstract morality or religious code, but we really don't know for sure and have no good way of telling.

Instead of creating clarity for us, the use of these polar opposites to measure ourselves and the world with has caused nothing but confusion and conflict. We each hold on to our own personal or cultural beliefs about what is good and what is evil, and we are compelled to struggle against any people or culture that disagrees with us. This sets up our world for endless struggles as one side battles the other to see who is right and who is wrong.

As I suggested earlier, both sides in a conflict see themselves as right and the other side as wrong. So this fundamental need to divide the world into opposites tends to feed conflict and cause wars that have no conclusion. We have no way to finally distinguish good from evil, so we end up killing each other in order to prove that we are right.

We are caught in a barbaric situation where the only method that we have to determine right from wrong is through violent conflict. In the end this knowledge that we yearned for in the Garden of Eden, and cannot think of parting with now, has only undermined our integrity and caused immense suffering.

Letting go of our need to determine right from wrong may become easier if we recognize how much difficulty it creates for us. Giving up our need to make this fundamental distinction is how we reclaim our original innocence. We admit that we do not know, and cannot know, the difference between these two polarities. And we allow the whole question to simply fall away, unanswered.

This is essentially what happened for me in the monastery. I thought that I had to sort out right from wrong in order to make sense of the world, and my struggle to do this became impossibly heavy. Yet, as soon as I learned to focus on my awareness instead of my thoughts, the world made absolute sense and the struggle to understand it through my thinking mind was resolved. I found a new way to be in the world that did not require separating everything out and placing a value judgment upon it.

Our Inner Compass

An obvious question that arises with the idea of letting go of our moral compass is how we can function in the world without it. I have suggested so far that this compass is not working, and has never worked to give us a clear heading in life. Dividing life into good and bad is the *cause* of our suffering, and letting it go is not the loss or sacrifice that it seems to be. However, it still remains for us to discover how we can navigate life without these familiar references, as dysfunctional as they are.

The answer to this is that each of us already has a perfect compass built into our consciousness. There is a way that we can know for certain which way to go and how to be in the world. It requires only that we listen to a quiet voice inside and trust what it tells us. I use the word "voice" symbolically as it may come to us in the form of words, or simply a gut feeling or sense. We each hear our own inner guidance a bit differently, but it is there for all of us if we learn to listen to it.

It helps to relax the process of perception in order to hear this voice, as the din of thoughts will always drown it out. As I learn to pay attention, this inner knowing becomes louder and clearer and I am able to trust it more. Sometimes I refer to this as intuition or a hunch. I often do not know how to explain it in a world that puts so much faith in the rational mind. Yet, my internal guidance system is very real and can direct me with a precision and clarity that perception can only approximate.

A key to finding this inner knowing is to be in integrity with myself. This means essentially doing what I sense is right for me in this moment, and trusting this sense above all else. This may take practice because I have been trained to rely on a moral code dictated by some outside authority, and taught specifically *not* to trust my own feelings.

Is Morality Working?

Many of us believe that if we let go of our religious or culturally established morality, we will degenerate into reckless savages bent on destroying each other for our personal gain. However, if we look honestly at our world today we see that it is filled with aggression, violence, and hatred that no laws or moral codes have been able to effectively control.

It may be hard to let go of the idea that without some authority telling us right from wrong, our society will fracture into anarchy and chaos. It is an appealing thought that one universal code of behavior could unify all of us here on earth and create lasting peace. Given that we know of no other way to keep ourselves or our society together, this could be seen as a reasonable experiment.

However, it must be clear by now that this approach is failing us miserably, and has only served to divide us. We use morality primarily to judge and condemn one another, and it encourages us merely to deny and hide our own immoral thoughts and actions, even from ourselves.

The most destructive side effect of universal morality is that it teaches us not to trust the only real means that we have of being honest and true in the world. Religious or cultural morality is based on the assumption that as individuals we cannot tell right from wrong and we need an institutional authority to tell us. Many of us grow up believing this and never learn to use the perfect system of guidance that is built into our conscious awareness.

Personal Integration

I believe that we *do* need effective principles and boundaries to guide us, but these are personal and situational, not universal and permanent. These principles are not meant to judge ourselves or another person against. They simply provide a means to maintain our personal integrity. In contrast to a universal morality, a personal code of ethics serves well to unite each of us within ourselves, which is where we must begin if we want unity in our world.

Integrity means that I am whole within myself and am not using denial or rationalization to divide me internally. It means that my values are not static ideas which I measure myself and others by. Instead, my values are what I know is true in this moment, as expressed in my behavior. This can only happen when I listen to and follow my inner knowing. Personal boundaries that I establish for myself simply help me to see when I am out of integrity, so that I can be aware of it and come back into wholeness again.

Personal integrity is my only chance of becoming whole. I cannot complete myself by following the rules, being good enough, or winning the approval or recognition of other people. Ask anyone who has become a cultural celebrity if the attention or admiration of large numbers of people makes their lives feel fulfilled. It is easy to assume that this would fill the emptiness inside, but it usually does not work. That is why so many celebrated people become alcohol and drug addicts and end up destroying their lives. When even fame and wealth do not satisfy their hunger, they naturally become depressed and discouraged and lose hope that there is any way to fill the hole inside them.

The way out of this is to allow that hollow place inside me to be filled from inside instead of outside. I can learn to listen to my inner knowing and establish a relationship with the still place within me that is my source. This begins with learning to trust myself and find a sense of unwavering certainty that comes from being fully present in this moment without relying on abstract judgments about what is right or wrong.

Meditation is simply a vehicle for establishing this relationship with myself. It allows me to drop below the level of thought and begin to feel my direct experience in each moment. This in turn grows into field of awareness or ground of being that I can lean into and stand on. Setting personal boundaries for myself, and establishing a personal code of ethics, is merely a way to clear away distractions in order to create the stillness within that allows me to hear my own guidance.

———————— •◆• ————————

Notice any doubts that you may have about yourself, or an impulse to refer to someone else's ideas to validate the choices that you are making. Feel the uneasy pull of wanting to conform or get it right.

You may be judging yourself as lazy because you are reading instead of "getting the job done." Or, you may be thinking that you should be doing something else, perhaps something more productive.

Set all these thoughts aside and allow the basic rhythm of your life to reveal itself from within you. Feel your own integrity, and realize that only you know what is right and wrong for yourself.

Give yourself permission to be right where you are now. Trust that you are doing exactly what you are supposed to do, and that you will know when it is time to do something different. Relax and let go of any uncertainty about this moment.

————————— •◆• —————————

The Shadow of Morality

Morality is a set of pre-determined rules for all situations that we measure and evaluate ourselves against. It has a fixed rigidity that tends to feel stagnant and suffocating. Even those of us most zealous about morality often despise its deadening heaviness and secretly derive a sense of glee from evading it.

Personal integrity on the other hand is simply a commitment to be present with myself and feel in each moment how I am responding to what is happening. My own emotional response can tell me what is good for me and what is not good for me in this moment if I allow myself to feel it. I feel positive emotions when I am thinking or doing something that is healing or nourishing, and negative emotions when I am engaged in an activity that is hurting me. This signal sent by my internal emotions is much more precise and immediate than comparative judgments can ever be.

Many of us reject out of hand the idea that we each can decide for ourselves in the moment what is right. We claim that this gives the ego free reign to do whatever it wants with no consequence. Yet the real reason that we reject personal integrity as an alternative to morality is more likely that the kind of sensitivity required to respond to our own feelings requires a much higher degree of awareness. We have to be present, pay attention, and cannot know ahead of time what is right or wrong. We have to feel it out, be flexible, and stay constantly tuned in to our own feelings This is a commitment that few of us have been willing to make, and so we rely on an abstract set of rules because it seems easier to follow a formula than it is to be fully present.

In fact, it is the abstract judgments of morality that are removed from reality and easy to manipulate or deny. My parents used to smoke cigarettes and at the same time they impressed upon us that smoking was wrong and bad and told us not to do it. As a child, this made no sense to me. I could see that they believed it was right and good, *because they did it.*

We can easily say that we believe smoking cigarettes is wrong and then continue to smoke. To do this, however, we have to divide ourselves internally and keep one part of ourselves hidden from the other. If we smoke cigarettes, of course we believe it is right. If we say it is wrong, while we are still doing it, we split ourselves and weaken our integrity.

The Charade of Perception

Using perception as our only guide, we are capable of enormous hypocrisy because it is easy to believe one thing and then do the opposite. Through perception we can make things look any way that we want them to look because there is no absolute basis for judgment. We can easily fool each other and ourselves into believing that what we are doing is good and right under any circumstance.

Using denial and rationalization we can make one thing look like something entirely different. We try to sharpen our power of perception so we can see the truth; however, using comparative evaluation, the closest that we can ever get is an approximation. The knowing that we achieve in this way is simply judgment or opinion, which means that perception can never know what is real.

It is our reliance on perception rather than awareness that gives our egos enormous freedom and flexibility to do whatever we want and then make it look right and good in our mind. That is how Catholic priests can abuse the children entrusted to their care for so long with no one doing anything about it. It is how political leaders can arrange for their own private companies to get government contracts or evade regulation. It explains why we go to war again and again in the name of peace, and how we can kill people and destroy their culture while we say that we are helping them.

Fooling ourselves and others in order to appear to conform with some law or moral code has become standard behavior for many of us. Look at how giant corporations do enormous damage to the environment or deplete our natural resources and then portray themselves as "green" and convince us that they are caring about the earth. Cigarette companies once convinced people that tobacco was good for their health, just as the United States government once convinced us that nuclear energy was cheap and entirely safe for the environment. There are politicians and corporations today who deny that our burning of fossil fuels is creating global climate change.

If we rely on perception to determine the truth, we make it easy to trick each other and be tricked, because *there is no actual basis to perception.* All knowledge is relative and anyone can convince us of anything using some sort of logic. So we end up with an endless assortment of conflicting beliefs with no way to effectively sort through or verify any of it.

Our most hallowed sanctuary for truth in Western civilization is science, and we see today how easy it is to interpret scientific theories to support different perspectives. A corporation, government, or political party can take scientific data and present it in a way that affirms entirely conflicting conclusions. With the pervasive nature of our modern media and the dependency that corporate interests and politicians have developed on advertising, we have set up a perfect storm of virtual realities. We have become masters at convincing ourselves and each other to believe anything that we want to be true, *regardless of its inherent reality.*

The problem is not that some villain is trying to manipulate us. It is that perception lends itself so easily to manipulation because it has no fixed basis. The terms of perception can be altered on a whim. It depends on what we consider good and bad in this moment, and as much as we don't want to believe it, these reference points are in constant flux.

Of course, this situation leaves many of us feeling vulnerable and confused. While intellectual debates and wide varieties of opinion can be stimulating, they offer nothing solid to stand on and tend to undermine our sense of security or stability in the world. And with the dramatic crises facing us today, now knowing how to tell what is real and true is deeply unsettling. Morality and fundamentalism then seem to be the only way to gain a sense of certainty.

Free Falling

Most of us believe that some sort of morality or law is necessary to maintain order. We naturally assume that personal integrity would only result in people acting selfishly and disregarding everyone else. We think that each person looking out for themselves would translate into the disintegration of society. This assumption is what motivates us to create and cling to moral codes and human laws. We see no other way to limit the destructive effects of human greed and hatred.

First, let us admit that our current experiment with moral codes and human laws has done little to stem the tide of greed, hatred, or violence in our world. In fact, if we look at it more closely, we can see that it is *responsible* for causing much of the violence that we do to each other. Consider all the killing and destruction in our world that has been justified by some religious belief or sense of righteous purpose.

In one recent example, the United States invaded Iraq in 2003, resulting in the violent death over the ensuing years of over one hundred thousand Iraqis, and almost five thousand U.S. soldiers or allies. This invasion was justified by the idea of destroying an evil dictator who could use his power to hurt the United States, and liberating his brutally oppressed people. In addition to the direct casualties of the invasion, the result nine years later is a skeleton of a country plagued by violent insurgency, a hopelessly broken infrastructure, and warring tribal lords.

We may honestly say that we don't know any other way, but we cannot say that basing our actions on self-determined moral authority appears to be working. All that we accomplish when we act out of a sense of righteousness is to further divide ourselves and weaken our own integrity by fragmenting the whole that we belong to.

Next, let us consider what personal integrity actually means. It is not based in perception as morality is, and does not involve arbitrary judgments of right or wrong. These can all be distorted and manipulated to mean anything that anyone wants them to mean, as we see in our world today. Rational judgments of good and evil merely enable us to point the finger of blame at another person and judge them for being immoral, while we ourselves are doing the same behavior and justifying it in our own minds as good and right.

Personal integrity does not rely on such an erratic basis as opinion and judgment. It references itself to a much more basic and simple foundation, which is our emotions. While we can manipulate and design our perceptions to fit our ideals, we can do no such thing with our feelings. They are what they are, and cannot be manipulated or controlled easily by our rational mind the way ideas can. So, we can trust our emotions to tell us what is actually happening in our direct experience.

We can look to our emotional response to let us know if we are in integrity with ourselves or not. If we genuinely feel good about something that we are thinking or doing, then we are in integrity. If we feel uneasy, tight, or uncomfortable inside, then we are out of integrity. This simple signal system is always accurate and never fails to indicate the way that is right for us in this moment. It is with us all the time and we cannot get rid of it even if we try. It comes with our consciousness, and our only choice is to pay attention to it, or ignore it.

Undermining Our Own Integrity

Another word for personal integrity is conscience, and many of us have systematically tried to diminish it. We often see our consciousness as a problem because it forces us to maintain our integrity, at the expense of the ego. The ego does not trust consciousness and portrays it as weak, incompetent, and evil, convincing us that we will turn into a selfish monster if we trust our own integrity to guide us.

In fact, this is a perfect description of our ego, or the image of a self that is created and maintained by the process of perception. The ego is *using* our consciousness and is what most of us think that we *are*. It is no wonder then that we believe we need a strong moral code and rigid social rules to contain such a potentially destructive force. With a strong self-centered survival impulse driving us and masquerading as our true self, it becomes clear why we trust ourselves so little and think that we need an outside authority to keep us from hurting ourselves and others.

This also makes it clear why so many of us dull our minds and choose to be less conscious in our daily lives. We may turn to alcohol, drugs, sex, sugar, television, or any number of ways to escape our mind and cloud our consciousness so that we don't have to be subjected to the ego's constant judgments and commentaries. However, all that we accomplish when we do this is to further damage our own integrity. By numbing our feelings, we make it much harder to hear the signal that is telling us what is right for us in this moment.

This is an understandable approach, given that we can see no other way to escape the weight of our internal judgments. Yet, in the long run, it is self-defeating. Dulling our thoughts and emotions so that we are not overcome by them is like the Western medical practice of attacking cancer with radiation. The hope is that the deadly radiation will kill the cancer cells before it kills our vital life force. Sometimes this works, but often with the price to be paid of a long recovery from the debilitating effects of the radiation. And sometimes the radiation is what kills us, just as sometimes our addictions and self-medications end up destroying us.

A greater problem with the substances that I take to dull my judging mind, and the moralities which I impose on myself and others to try to control the ego, is that they weaken and erode my inherent strength. I become dependent on these forces outside of myself to limit and control the damage that my habit of judgment inevitably causes. And my natural capacity for internal awareness becomes diminished to the point where I do not trust my own ability to know what is good for me in this moment.

A True Medicine

This situation can be reversed and I can restore my original integrity. To fill the emptiness inside and enable the sense of completion that I seek, I can reconnect with my natural goodness. Each one of us is capable of awakening our own personal conscience and learning to strengthen and rely on it for safety and direction, giving us a reliable compass to navigate the uncertainties of life.

A spiritual practice like meditation is medicine for restoring integrity. In meditation I look at my judgments instead of trying to escape from them. This is what makes the practice so difficult at first. To directly confront my judging mind instead of trying to hide from it goes against all of my impulses. Yet, in the end, this is how I can move past my mental formatting and free myself from its grip.

When I become aware of my judging mind, I can see that it constantly divides my world. I see how my mind is continually trying to figure out what is good and bad and is often scheming about how to get the good stuff and defend myself from the bad. I begin to notice how this process wears me down and will not let me rest. And I may recognize how it distracts and fragments me internally and weakens my integrity.

Once I see how arbitrary my judgments are and how much confusion and complexity they cause, I am more willing to simply let them go. As I relax my judging mind, I also undo my ego which relies on judgments for its foundation. And, as I undo my ego, my selfish and destructive impulses fall away. Without the ego, I am not a danger to myself or other people.

Allowing my self-centered impulses to relax and fall away is much more effective than morality to make my world safer and allow me to be compassionate toward others. It is merely the fears of my ego that motivate me toward greed, hatred, or aggression. When I try to contain these harmful behaviors with social rules or religious morality, while still maintaining my individual sense of self, I put myself in a bind. I am split internally between fighting for my own survival, and trying to be good and kind to others.

However, if I am simply present in this moment without a personal story accompanying each experience, I don't feel threatened by others and fear has no place to take root. I don't need to work hard to be good or force myself to override my selfish impulses with kindness toward others. These efforts have never worked anyway. I simply need to pay attention and see that my fragile and easily threatened ego is not who I am.

No Place to Hide

A man once came to the retreat center where I teach asking if he could help. I agreed to let him stay for a while to see how things worked out. We were having a silent intensive meditation retreat in a few days and I asked him to participate so that he could understand what the retreat center was about.

On the second day of the retreat, he came to interview with me and described how he had been unable to focus on anything because his mind was full of restless agitation. He told me that he had come here on false pretenses, had not been honest with me, and his deceit was eating him alive from the inside.

It seems that there was a warrant out for his arrest for evading child support in another state, and he had come here thinking that he could hide from the law. He went on to say that while facing himself in the silence of meditation the pain of his dishonesty was too great for him to bear, and he knew that he needed to talk to me before he could find any sense of peace or rest.

I asked him what he wanted to do and he told me that he needed to go back and face the consequences of his actions, and reconcile the situation. I listened without comment and simply nodded in understanding and agreement with what he had to say. I was awestruck at the power of simple awareness to bring to the surface the truth that he had tried so hard to hide.

Activating our awareness in this way is something we often avoid because we are afraid to see what we are hiding. Most of us prefer to fool ourselves rather than face the truth. We think that if we admit we are doing something which is not honest or caring, we will drown in guilt or shame. However, all that happens when we allow the truth of a situation to surface is that we recognize how we are weakening ourselves and see what we need to do to bring ourselves back into our own integrity.

This is how practicing awareness can gently but firmly bring us back into alignment with ourselves. Restrictions imposed on us from an outside authority encourage us to deny and hide our hurtful behaviors, while the practice of awareness brings them to the surface and requires us to respond to them directly and honestly. Maintaining our personal integrity in this way is more effective and efficient than any amount of moral codes, rules, or public laws.

19

From Isolation to Integration

As a child, I was taught not to trust my inner knowing and to rely instead on my capacity for rational thought. I have access to this inner vision all the time, but I tend to minimize and ignore it, judging it as insubstantial. I am aware of these signals from within, and even follow them much of the time, calling it intuition or having a hunch. Yet, I don't know how to explain this way of knowing so I often think of it as invalid.

To awaken and strengthen my inner vision it helps to set aside everything that I think I know. I can admit that I have no way to be sure, and that all of my accumulated knowledge is only theory or ideas about how things are, with no absolute reference points. It us useful to humble myself for a moment so I can recognize that there is another way to know which is more dependable and certain.

This is the leap of faith required in the spiritual journey to wholeness. There is a moment when I let go of the entire thought process that has taken me to this point, and I have nothing to replace it with. It seems that I am suspended with no way of knowing anything, and my fear tells me that I will cease to exist if I don't immediately return to my rational judgments. Yet, if I remain here in this place of suspended judgment for a moment, a clarity begins to appear that is free of all the relative comparisons and is not subject to the whims of opinion.

Knowing Without Reference

It is primarily our fear of this singular clarity that keeps most of us from taking the leap. We have a taboo against personal inner knowing and tell ourselves that it is somehow corrupt. We practice a fierce allegiance to our rational mind, and anything that threatens to supersede that is automatically suspect. In this world of relative perception, where everything is but a fragment of the whole, we do not allow for someone to simply *know* something without reference to something else.

When I sent my first book to a professional editor for review, one of the comments that he made was that I made too many assertions without referencing to other books or sources of information. That book, like this one, was largely based on my personal experience and insights. I was not trying to compile data from other people to prove a point, nor was I presenting my conclusions as the truth. I simply wanted to voice as clearly as I could some ideas that have revealed themselves to me which I have found useful.

As suggested in the forward, I refer to a teacher like the Buddha or Christ primarily to recognize their teaching as a source of inspiration for my own exploration. I present this book as a possible source of inspiration for you to discover your own truth. I have come to understand that this is how truth actually works. As much as we might wish it were so at times, there is no final authority that can tell us what is real.

Reality is not revealed either by compiling as many different sources as possible and comparing them. All that we can achieve through this method of comparison is *approximate* truth. Our process of science is based on this model, and while it can lead us to discover aspects of reality, it is painfully slow and leaves us with much more that we do not know.

Comparing our ideas to sift out the ones that most of us can agree on seems to be the best way to access truth in a world of relative perceptions. We do not value personal insights because we assume that truth is some universal knowledge that is static and final. We may insist on using the process of rational evaluation because we think of truth as a fixed concept that remains the same in all situations. Yet this assumption blinds us to our personal experience of this moment, which is about what is true and alive for us now, and is unique to each situation and individual. Being removed from our direct experience like this means that we have no way to navigate life except to try to live up to some standard or follow some prescribed formula.

In order to understand spiritual transformation, it may help to redefine truth. Instead of thinking of truth as a finite idea that most of us agree on, we can see it as personal information that is only relevant to us in this moment. This is a more accurate way to describe the idea of truth because, in reality, we never reach an absolute conclusion about anything using rational thought. In perception everything has an opposite, so any "truth" that we come up with necessarily invites an opposing opinion.

Insight or revelation, on the other hand, is instant and accurate and requires no comparison of opposites. This is a knowing that does not involve language or images and may not be able to be shared with others. It is personal and immediate, and simply informs us of what we need to know in this moment. These personal insights may not apply to other people.

Most of us are entirely unaccustomed to this way of knowing and so it simply does not occur to us that it is possible. We think of truth as an absolute conclusion that applies to all people at all times. We are used to accumulating information, storing it, comparing it with other information, and packaging it to provide proof of our theory.

We usually do not trust that the knowledge we need will come to us in the moment we need it. We cram our brains full of information that may be useful to us at some future time, fearing that if we don't do this we will be left ignorant and defenseless. This tends to be the main focus of our formal system of education, and it tragically crowds our minds with endless amounts of abstract data while teaching us not to trust our inner knowing.

Our Fear of The Absolute

One reason that we may be so afraid of absolute knowledge is that we can only conceive of this in the form of an all-knowing ego. The ego, or image of a separate self, appears to be the only thing in our world that could be whole and complete. And in this world of separate individuals, where we measure ourselves by comparison with everyone else, there appears to be room for only one of us to achieve this state. If one of us is complete and whole, we think that the rest of us will forever be incomplete and less than whole.

Most of us have learned to distrust the idea of complete and whole knowledge coming to each of us individually. The idea that we could trust our inner knowing, and not have to continually check our perceptions against those of other people for verification, seems to be the ultimate heresy. In a world where everything is compared with everything else, and there is no absolute reference point for anything, trusting our individual intuition appears to be irrational and irresponsible.

The problem with this paradigm of a separate self, struggling for its existence in a world of competing individuals, however, is that this is not who we actually are. Our minds are programmed to believe this small self is our identity, when actually we are the larger whole. This concept is impossible to put into words, because the idea of us being everything at once does not fit into our paradigm of all things being separate and apart.

All or Nothing

In our programmed comparative thought system, we can only see ourselves as more or less than other people. Therefore the notion of completion can only appear to us as being at the top of the pile, better than everyone else. Anything less than that is usually seen as failure or a lack of completion. In relativity there is only one who wins and gets to rule over all of the rest of us.

Although most of us would say that we believe in democracy, and many of us come from countries founded on the principle that every person is equal, we do not seem to be able to apply this ideal in our day to day lives. We still turn to leaders to make decisions for us, especially during times of crisis, and we tend to establish hierarchies whenever two or more of us are together.

This is why the idea of kings and queens ruling over common people has been so prevalent in human history, and why democracy is often so difficult to realize. It is impossible to fully believe or invest in the notion that all of us are equal and can share power and recognition while we are in the paradigm of duality. Here, there is a top and a bottom, and infinite grades in between, and we do not understand or relate to the possibility of each one of us being whole and complete within ourselves.

The closest that words can come to express our true situation may be that we are both the whole and a part of the whole at the same time. We each exist within a whole that encompasses all life and material form, and *we are that whole*. In the science of physics this is expressed as the idea of a hologram. A hologram is an image that can be broken into individual pieces, with each piece capable of reproducing the whole.

We cannot conceive of this because our minds are programmed only to see opposites or fragments of the whole. Using the mechanism of perception we can never see reality as a complete whole. We can only see individual pieces in contrast to other individual pieces. So, we naturally deduce that reality is made up of all these separate units. Yet, this is simply a limitation of perception. In a similar way, our ancestors deduced that the earth was flat because this is what they could see with their eyes.

Most of us see a world of separate things, yet we long for it to be whole. If we consider the story of the Garden of Eden, this makes sense. Perhaps we carry an ancient memory of everything being connected with nothing opposing us and no danger or lack. This world seems to have so much that threatens us and we are constantly anxious about meeting our basic needs. So we naturally would want to make everything complete and connected again.

We try making our world whole using our rational thought process because this is the only method we know. The problem with this approach of course is that the rational thought process has to take things apart in order to be able to perceive them. The result is the perennial sorting out that goes on in our mind and never reaches completion.

We are continuously trying to bring our thoughts to some conclusion that will define the whole of reality for us. Yet the process that we are using requires us to divide and organize everything into separate categories. We delude ourselves into believing that this process of categorizing and labeling everything will enable us to put it all together into a complete whole, yet just the opposite is true.

The process never reaches a conclusion, and cannot reach a conclusion. The reason is simply that reality is already whole and does not need to be assembled by us. All of our efforts to construct a whole reality only interfere with our capacity to be aware that *it is already complete*.

The Movement Toward Individuality

The ego is simply the idea that each one of us can be a whole, complete, and fully independent self, separate from the rest of the world. The ego will continuously seek independence if given the resources to do so. Its movement is always toward greater and greater autonomy and individuation, because this is the way it thinks it can achieve completion.

If we take this strategy to its natural conclusion, the ego is trying to eliminate all other beings and have itself as the only one remaining. This appears to be the ego's plan to ensure its own survival, and realize the wholeness that it longs for. The result is that we are all unconsciously in competition with each other to be the one whole, complete person.

This longing for completion can be seen in our historical progression toward greater individual autonomy. Our ancestors once lived in tribes where everyone was dependent on the group, and they could not survive alone. As tribal societies were overtaken by organized civilizations, the village gave way to city-states. Intimate relationships then became reduced to extended family units which more recently shrank to nuclear family units.

Today, it is common for many of us to live alone as fully independent individuals. As our technology and accumulation of resources has increased, so has our capacity for independence from each other. Western culture, and especially the United States, epitomizes this movement toward individuality.

For a time, I lived on an old homestead by myself in a rural mountain town. When the place was originally settled, it would have been impossible for one person to live there by himself because of the enormous amount of work it took to simply survive. Yet now, with gasoline engines, electricity, telephones, computers, and readily available food and heat, it was possible for me to manage the place and survive there comfortably on my own.

Now that it is possible for one person to live alone, we don't need each other the way we once did. We naturally are choosing more personal space rather than dealing with the conflicts inherent in relationships, and even the nuclear family is splintering into pieces as we find it increasingly difficult to share our lives with just one other person. This seems to fit the ego's plan of realizing total autonomy. And it offers us an opportunity to experience how dysfunctional our ego really is.

The ego sees total independence as freedom and a chance to realize itself as all powerful. However our actual experience of being independent is permeated with loneliness and fear. The plan of the ego to free us from all external constraints has led us to abandon community and family and disconnect ourselves further and further from nature. Many of us find ourselves in a situation where we can do anything that we want, yet we feel empty and disconnected from everything around us and our lives are filled with anxiety.

Our Program of Self-Destruction

The reason that the ego's plan for the dominance of the individual self is not working is that we are inherently connected to each other and all of life. As we experience ourselves less and less connected to everything around us, the pain of this unnatural separation grows stronger within us. We then have to find more powerful ways to distract and numb ourselves from our feelings so that we can continue pursuing the independence which we think is the answer to our problem.

It should be clear to us by now that this course we are on is leading to our own demise. While the ego battles everything outside of itself to ensure its dominance, it blindly destroys the natural infrastructures required to sustain life. In the name of our own independent existence, we are undercutting the very systems that we need for our basic support. This is like standing on the branch of a tree while cutting the branch off. The inevitable and tragic conclusion is obvious.

The precariousness of our current situation is one of the clearest indications that we are under the influence of an unconscious and dysfunctional program. Our mental conditioning only tells us how to continue to support and enhance the individual ego, and cannot see anything beyond this. If we blindly follow our familiar patterns of thought, we are like lemmings racing to the edge of the cliff without ever stopping to consider what we are doing.

We can see this pattern playing out in our personal lives in the ways that many of us pollute our bodies with unhealthy food, alcohol, tobacco, drugs, and any number of substances that may give us a moment of feeling good in return for some long term illness or disease. And we see it in the way that we abuse the earth and destroy our basic resources such as air, water, and soil, which all of life depends on for survival.

As I began to meditate, I became aware of how I treated other people and had hurt people that I cared about without realizing what I was doing. I thought of my younger brother and how mean I had been to him at times when I was younger, for no reason. I had vivid, painful memories of taunting and teasing him until he cried, and I felt sick with remorse and regret.

I then began to be aware of how I treated the earth and had been careless with the resources that were supporting me. This awareness took a bit longer to develop because the immediate consequences of disregarding the earth were not as plain to see. It seemed easier to overlook my responsibility for an environment that is shared by all of us and to see this as someone else's task.

Our mistreatment of the earth is rooted in this same dysfunctional programming that makes us see our individual self as independent from the whole of life. As long as this programming is active within our thought system, we will continue to destroy and deplete the very elements that provide our basic support. This is why our environmental crisis continues despite decades of awareness that we are fouling our own nest.

Realizing our Natural Connection

We cannot treat ourselves, each other, or the earth, any differently until we free ourselves from the programming that makes us believe that we are separate and independent from each other. We can educate ourselves about the damage that we are doing, but this will not change our basic attitudes or behavior because these are determined by the central premise behind our thought system. We essentially see ourselves pitted against everything else here on earth, in competition to see who will win. And as long as we are in the paradigm of duality with everything in opposition to something else, our destructive behaviors will continue.

In some way the fragility of the earth may be our greatest teacher. The earth and its ecosystems are the tangible proof of our connectedness with each other and all of life. Despite all of our attempts to be independent, we each are still completely reliant on the basic elements of air, water, earth, and fire, for our existence. And as these fragile resources become more polluted, depleted, and scarce, we will all experience a direct impact on our lives.

The nature of the earth and our dependence on it will eventually bring us to recognize the destructiveness of our paradigm of individuality. Our belief that we are independent from one another and removed from the source of life will fall apart once we fully understand how the earth beneath our feet provides our common foundation.

This is not obvious to many of us now simply because the resources of the earth have been so bountiful as to appear infinite. Yet, as we blindly destroy and deplete these resources, their finite nature becomes more apparent. We begin to see plainly how interconnected we are, each of us depending on a delicately balanced, self-renewing, natural environment that we all share.

We are heading rapidly toward any number of crises that could result in enormous damage to life on earth. It still may take a tragedy of great proportions to awaken us to an awareness of our common source. If this disaster occurs, those of us who survive may finally see how we are interconnected with all beings. Perhaps it will be clear to us then that we cannot remove ourselves from the whole without causing our foundation to collapse.

This recognition can threaten our sense of individual self and appear most unwelcome. It seems to bring a crashing halt to our notion of independence and the idea of finally completing the ego. Yet, in reality, it is the best news we could get, as it frees us from isolation. It is the realization of our interconnectedness that answers the plaguing question of the meaning of life and our place in it, and finally relieves us from our painful anxiety and despair.

The completion that we are so desperately seeking here can never manifest within the paradigm of the individual self because that story was made to *replace* our natural state of wholeness. The story of us as individuals struggling for our place in the world has to fail and come undone to reveal the natural connectedness that has been here all along.

We cannot recognize the whole, or our part in it, until we give up trying to complete ourselves by piecing together fragments. Once our strategy fails and the disintegration of the fragments becomes apparent to us, we have a chance to look past the individual pieces and see the whole that is already there.

A Light in the Darkness

While it looks as though we are headed into dark times, it is important to recognize that the light that can show us the way through is already here with us. At the same time as the movement of the ego toward complete autonomy threatens to undermine the foundations of our existence on earth, we can see around us acts of selfless giving that demonstrate an entirely different paradigm. While the dominance of capitalism and the value that we place on material wealth seems to have elevated greed and selfishness into qualities that we admire and reward, our society is still held together by acts of altruism and good will.

I once spent some time in a remote Himalayan village in Nepal where there are no cars and the streets are walkways paved with field stones. I was watching several young men walk through the village and marveled at how self-assured and carefree they were. Suddenly one of the young men stopped and bent down in the middle of the street.

There was a stone that had been kicked out of its place, most likely by a passing donkey or horse. The stone was lying in the road where someone could trip over it, and next to it was a hole that someone could step in. The young man carefully put the stone back into its place and then went on his way, laughing and carrying on with his friends.

This scene left a lasting impression on me. I was sadly reminded of how we in the West have lost our sense of community and responsibility for the whole, trading it for hardened self-interest. In my life in the United States, I had never stopped to fix something that did not belong to me personally, nor had I seen anyone else do so.

I had been raised with the idea that someone else was responsible, and I learned to ignore holes in the road, homeless people, other people's children, stray dogs, and anything else that did not belong to me personally. We weren't supposed to interfere in other people's privacy. That was someone else's business. Watching those young men fix the street in that village, I wept for all that we have lost in the name of progress.

I have lived over twenty years now in a small rural mountain town of less than two hundred people. I moved here in part because I saw how the increasing scale of our industrialized society has alienated people from each other and our communities. Our cities, roads, malls, and shopping plazas are so enormous that a person feels insignificant and powerless. In this kind of environment, few of us are inspired to take responsibility for the whole because it all seems so large and out of our hands.

The overwhelming size of our infrastructure breeds an apathy that allows us to stand idly by as our industries and corporations deplete and pollute the basic elements required for life. It is easy to assume that someone else will take care of the problem and to see ourselves as powerless to do anything about the tragedy of our ailing planet.

Spending time in an "undeveloped" country like Nepal and traveling through self-sufficient mountain villages on foot, I saw how different the scale of things was there. The roads and villages were made for people and donkeys to move through, not cars or huge semi-trailer trucks. People and animals provided the power for meeting basic needs, instead of electricity, oil, and mega-machines. As an individual person, I felt important and integrally part of things. In this kind of environment, it is natural for each person to assume some degree of responsibility for the whole.

Our Need to be of Service

Some time after moving to this small rural town where there are still no paved roads, I was asked to take an office in town government. People already serving in different offices explained to me that our town was so small that everyone had to do something just to fill the different positions we had to fill. I was hesitant because I had never been involved in my local community in this way, but after some time, I finally agreed to be on the select board. This was an elected body of three town residents who oversaw the governing of the town including road maintenance, schools, budgets, and taxes.

Once on the board, I was astonished to discover how much our system of government depends on the volunteer efforts of so many citizens. I realized that the price of democracy is that everyone has to participate. It does not work to have a "government of the people" if the people do not step up to govern. I spent nine years on the select board, going to meetings twice a month and overseeing the business of the town, and I received one hundred dollars a year in gratitude for my service.

If you look around, you will see examples everywhere of work that is done out of a sense of service and not for personal gain, recognition, or financial reward. We are used to thinking in terms of money and weighing our exchanges with other people with our own financial interests in mind. In this atmosphere, everything becomes a trade and we are constantly evaluating what kind of deal we are getting. A lot of us have been trained to think of life in terms of economic exchange because our world has become so dominated by business and financial concerns. Yet, our daily personal life does not work this way at all.

There are many interactions that we participate in which can never be calculated in terms of exchange. Think of all the time, effort, and money that goes into raising children, taking care of a home, or maintaining a family and community. Much of this energy we simply give away with no accounting involved, and never see it returned to us in material form. We assume these responsibilities in many cases by choice because we get some satisfaction out of nourishing and giving to others. Think of your relationships with family, friends, and community, and you will find many examples of time, energy, and money that is freely given and never gets accounted for on a ledger or balance sheet.

True Inspiration

We may get a charge or feel some envy when we hear about a corporate executive or star athlete being paid one hundred million dollars a year. There may be a certain boost of adrenaline when we consider competing for this level of wealth and status. Yet, the thrill of this kind of achievement and the mystique that surrounds it is always short-lived. There will always be someone else who appears to have a better deal or who is more famous, and our ego will never be satisfied with any amount of wealth, power, or celebrity.

All this attention that we give to fame and money tends to obscure our deeper longings for inspiration and purpose. Few of us can claim that we are truly inspired by the unconstrained greed and personal ambition which seem to dominate so much of our society today. Our need for inspiration and meaning is not met by winning the most money or attention.

This is good news because only a few of us can be billionaires or celebrities, while all of us can find inspiration or meaning. We don't have to compete with each other to find purpose, and each one of us can be inspired in our own unique way. Most of us can admit that what genuinely inspires us is not personal greed and ambition, but acts of selfless giving, courage, and love. This is why being part of a family, raising children, or giving to our community can nourish us in a way that material wealth or celebrity cannot.

To better understand this, it may help to differentiate between a celebrity and a hero. A celebrity is popular because something about their image captures our attention. They may be beautiful, witty, or wealthy, or they may be a winner. However, celebrities often have tragic personal lives and rarely inspire us to be better people. Celebrities tend to make us feel worse about ourselves because *we* are not getting the kind of attention that *they* are. They are people who seem to be in a realm above us that we can never reach.

Like so much of our affluent Western culture today, celebrity worship is for children. Children are attracted to celebrities because they love to be part of a popular trend. While idolizing a singer, actor, or model feeds our ego, it does nothing to nourish or support our growth or happiness. Celebrated stars are the result of elaborately-scripted facades created by a profit motivated entertainment industry. Investing in them is like eating junk food made of sugar, salt, and fat. While it may satisfy our need for drama and excitement, it does not give our lives a deeper sense of fulfillment.

Heroes, on the other hand, are people who we admire and aspire to be like. There is something they have done or a message they teach that we think is worthy and noble. A hero is someone like us who tends to inspire us and give us the courage to follow our higher dreams. Heroes encourage us to face our fears and move through them so that we can realize our deeper longings. We all need role models who inspire us to stretch ourselves to get beyond the bounds of our ego and find meaning and purpose in our life. This is the kind of inspiration that is truly nourishing.

———————— •◆• ————————

Think of someone you envy who is popular, wealthy, beautiful, or a winner. Perhaps part of you wants to be this person or have what this person has.

Notice how this feels in your body, and what kind of thoughts this engenders.

———————— •◆• ————————

Now think of someone who you admire and look up to. Perhaps you find this person inspiring or appreciate them for something that they have done to help you or to make the world a better place.

Notice how this feels in your body, and what kind of thoughts this engenders.

———————— •◆• ————————

20

Restoring Your Integrity

The rational mind cannot recognize our natural integrity because it only knows how to break things into separate pieces and compare them with each other. Awareness, however, can recognize the integrity that exists within and around us immediately. That is why a practice that exercises our capacity for direct awareness is so healing. As we allow ourselves to just be present, with no mental commentary, the struggle to make sense of the world dissolves. We begin to realize that it is actually our habit of interpretation that disrupts the flow and obscures reality.

The Means *are* the End

The beauty of meditation as a kind of medicine for our fragmented state is that the means and the end are one and the same. As you develop your capacity for direct awareness, you can use your comparative evaluation process to recognize the difference between awareness and perception. This is the last evaluation that you need to make, and it is where a spiritual path is intended to take you. Once you can distinguish direct awareness from the process of perception, you can see that your own thought system is the cause of your problems and begin to let it go.

As you develop awareness through a practice like meditation, it begins to replace perceptual thought and you see that awareness itself is the solution you have been searching for. You do not have to learn anything new, or develop a skill that you do not already have. You simply need to learn to trust your own presence. A true spiritual practice takes you out of the world of conception and replaces all the ideas that you have accumulated *about* reality with your own direct awareness of what exists in this moment.

The challenge that most of us face in awakening is to learn to rely on this present moment awareness. Our work is merely to allow our full presence to be enough, and to become comfortable now, without needing to constantly recreate our past or project our future. This requires that we let the past be gone and do not dwell on trying to change it or find the meaning in it. It also requires that we allow the future to be unknown and let go of our attempts to predict, plan, and control what will always be unknowable to us. As we do this, our natural integrity becomes restored and we "wake up" from this dream of separation.

Substituting Our Integrity

In order to recognize and maintain our natural state of wholeness, it is useful to take some steps to protect it. Our personality does not recognize our natural integrity and sees it primarily as a threat. The ego has appointed itself the task of constructing a replacement for our natural state of wholeness. That is why it is constantly engaged in trying to patch pieces of perception into a whole belief system.

Our natural integrity exists whether we recognize and nurture it or not, and nothing can ever destroy or diminish it. However, by relying exclusively on the process of comparative evaluation to establish an *image* of ourselves, we continually override and obscure our own wholeness.

We then spend our lives searching for a sense of completion in terms that perception can recognize. And perception can never experience completion because its formatting automatically breaks everything into pieces in order to understand each of them separately. We simply cannot get there from here because perception is not able to process anything that is unified or whole.

Redefining Morality

Perception cannot work without fixed reference points, and because these are not to be found here, we make them up. This often takes the form of social rules, moral codes, conventions, and laws.

The problem with this kind of morality, as we looked at earlier, is that it does not work to control our destructive impulses and in the end only makes us feel trapped. The price that we pay for relying on a universal morality to enable perception and give our lives a sense of stability is that we have to deny our uniqueness. We have to fit ourselves into a tight little box of someone else's rules, and inevitably we feel suffocated and just want to break free.

In the famous counter-culture revolution that shook the United States in the 1960s and quickly spread around the world, morality and law were seen as evil, and anyone promoting them was the enemy. Many of the young people leading this rebellion believed that too many laws and moral codes were stifling individuality and producing a deadening conformity. And, in the dramatic social changes that followed, many of our established rules and moral codes were thrown away.

While they may have been right in recognizing the way moral systems and laws feed hypocrisy, fuel conflict, and diminish our integrity, many people who were part of this radical movement ended up "throwing the baby out with the bath water." By rejecting any notion of rules as bad, they created a world with no sense of direction or purpose. They failed to realize the part that *healthy* boundaries play in the process of maintaining integrity and accelerating personal growth.

In rejecting the strict and overbearing morality of our parents, we often hesitate to make rules for our children, and the result is a generation of young people who have no idea of healthy limits. Consider the kind of offensive pornography freely available on the internet today, the common occurrence of school shootings and public killings, the wide spread phenomena of violent gangs, the tremendous peer pressure that young teenagers face to be sexual or try alcohol and drugs, and the lack of respect that young people have for themselves or society, and it is clear that we have lost all notion of responsible boundaries.

It is no surprise that there is a strong politically conservative movement in the United States and other nations to go back to a time of strict morality and religious fundamentalism. Many of us are understandably disturbed by the lack of discipline and order in our youth and think that the solution is to go back to the way things used to be.

Yet, we have come too far to go back. Few of us would welcome authoritarian religion, government, schools, or parents, and it is not possible to manage the chaos in our society today by simply making stronger rules.

Using rules and laws to establish a universal right and wrong and create a sense of certainty in our life obscures the true value of boundaries. It is a misuse that destroys the whole notion of limits and makes it difficult to see how they can serve us in a healthy way. An alternative to this authoritarian approach is to redefine morality and understand how boundaries can be used to nourish and support instead of merely contain or confine us.

Personal Morality

I suggested earlier that a healthy morality only has meaning on a personal level. There simply is no absolute right or wrong for every person in every situation. However, it is essential that each of us develop our capacity to distinguish what is right and wrong for ourselves in this moment, if we want to maintain our own integrity and be fulfilled.

We may call this new approach a personal morality, and this was the intention of some of the disciplines suggested by spiritual teachers like the Buddha and Christ. The perceptual mind naturally takes teachings like these and formulates a set of fixed rules from them. Once we have a religious authority that determines what the rules are, our ego can orient itself and define its place. In this way, we tragically turn a spiritual teaching intended to dissolve our ego into a subtler means of maintaining it.

In contrast to religious morality, a spiritual path includes guidelines for behavior and thought which merely limit and contain the patterns of our perceptual mind *so that we can see them*. Healthy boundaries make the patterns of the mind visible and give us a chance to become aware of our programming. These guidelines usually involve limiting things like sensual pleasure, accumulation of possessions, consumption of food or stimulants, and our behavior toward other people. They are not meant to be moral values to judge ourselves by, but rather personal limitations undertaken for the purpose of increasing our self-awareness.

Personal boundaries do not apply to all people in all situations. They are different at different times for different people, depending on the lessons that each one of us needs to learn. A teacher or guide may suggest certain limitations for certain people in certain situations; however, it is up to each one of us to determine what limitations we need because we are the only ones who can know that.

When we cross a personal boundary, we compromise our integrity. As long as our integrity is overshadowed by institutionalized morality or laws, it does not mean much to us. That is why people can easily violate each other and atrocities are so common in our world. However, once we let go of our dependency on some authority determining what is right or wrong for us, our personal integrity becomes much more important to maintain.

Crossing a boundary and violating our own integrity is not a sin worthy of guilt and punishment. Rather, it is a mistake to learn from. If we are self-aware, we see how hurting another person or acting out of greed or fear divides us internally. We sense that we have disrupted our own integrity and we feel this as a sense of uneasiness.

In contrast, when we act out of generosity, without fear or greed, the result is a sense of joy, lightness, inner strength, and certainty.

From Morality to Integrity

Personal morality is a private affair that is between us and our own conscience. We tend to scoff at such an idea because we think that if there is no outside authority to measure us, then there is no accountability and there is nothing to limit our destructive nature. Many of us really believe that without clear rules imposed on us, all hell will break loose and we will destroy ourselves and each other. In fact, just the opposite is true.

Look around at what is happening today between people in our world, and to the earth itself. As I suggested earlier, there is no end to the conflict, violence, hatred, and war. We don't seem to be able to get along with each other at all without fighting bitterly. We are quickly destroying the natural systems of our planet that we all depend upon for survival. Our laws and moral systems have not stopped us from this headlong rush toward self-destruction, and often the law or morality itself is the cause of conflict as we fight over whose way is right.

There is no need to be pessimistic, bitter, or resigned about this. It does not mean that we are rotten to the core and doomed to extinction, or that there is nothing we can do to change the situation. However, it can help to look honestly at what our attempts at regulation through authoritarian systems have accomplished. They have in reality created much more conflict, violence, and destruction in our world than they have resolved.

The Limits of Laws

The tiny rural town that I live in is too small to have our own school or post office, and I was surprised to discover after living there a few years that we also have no local police force. Our town is officially covered by the state police, whose nearest post is forty-five minutes away.

My neighbors told me that if we needed police, we could call them, but they would not come unless it was possible to catch a crime being committed. With at least a forty-five minute delay, the state troopers were often reluctant to respond to calls. This meant in reality that we had no real police protection. Yet, I have never lived in a safer place, and it is rare to hear of any kind of crime committed in our town.

Because we have no local police to do it for us, everyone in town looks after everyone else. We all become more responsible for ourselves and our neighbors. No one wants crime, and everyone knows that it is up to us to prevent it because there is no outside authority to do it for us. One time, there was a small rash of burglaries that everyone was talking about, and everyone in town seemed to know who was doing it. When the police finally came to investigate, they were directed to those people's house and found most of the stolen items there.

A strong, authoritarian police force like those in our large cities could not be as effective in stopping crime as the system in my town. Having laws and police may certainly help establish a sense of stability, order, and safety in our communities, and I am not advocating that we do away with these. Yet, as the main strategy that we have for making people honest, it appears to be failing us.

We can always hide our thoughts or disguise our behavior and pretend to be following the rules so that no one will know. Most of us do this, and some of us even take delight in seeing how much we can get away with. We love to find our way around systems.

Even if we know the rules are right and for the good of all, we still bristle at the idea that they apply to us. Look at our complex legal system which is so ineffective that it can allow huge corporations to deplete our natural resources and dump enormous amounts of toxic waste into our air, water, and soil, while it can prevent a person from composting kitchen scraps in their own backyard.

The legal system that we have enables people who have enough wealth and resources to find a way around the rules, or make their own rules. Governments that make the rules and the agencies responsible for enforcing them are often influenced and beholden to the corporations or individuals who support them financially. Corporations hire teams of lawyers who specialize in finding ways around the rules, or writing their own rules and getting them made into laws.

This doesn't mean that we should blame or condemn corporations for seizing control of our political or legal system. They are only acting out of the inherent fear and insecurity of their ego, and trying to ensure their own survival. However, we can be honest with ourselves and admit that our system of rules does not work very well to control the destructive tendencies of people and keep us all safe.

Perception requires fixed values and clear rules in order to function, yet the personality that we create through the process of perception scorns them. The ego will immediately set about finding a way around rules or limitations imposed from the outside, as its function is purely self-perpetuation. So morality and human laws become a game that we play with ourselves and each other to see who can get away with the most.

We can see this acted out on a global scale in the way corporations function. The mandate of a corporation is only to make money for its owners and investors, just as the mandate of the ego is self-preservation. Few traditional capitalist corporations genuinely care about the good of the whole because that appears to be beyond their limited scope and defeats their purpose. So we have these privately-controlled institutions which are immensely wealthy and powerful and are mandated to avoid or alter any rule or law that restricts their ability to make more profit.

Most of us believe that we need rules and laws; however, we despise being restricted by them. So we make it look as if we are following the rules, while privately we do our best to avoid any kind of outside limitation. In the end, we do not see them as helping us, but only constricting our freedom. We accept morality and law as necessary, yet we resent and resist them, believing that they are for everyone else but us.

Personal Boundaries

In contrast to a fixed morality, personal boundaries which apply only to ourselves in this moment can help free us from the restrictions of our conditioning. Personal boundaries are limitations that we place on ourselves consciously in order to reveal our mental programming so that we are not restricted by it.

It may seem contradictory that we have to limit ourselves so that we can be free. Yet, what we are limiting when we set personal boundaries is not our true self, but our ego. By limiting this false idea of our self, we erode its power and control over us and allow it to fall away, revealing our true unlimited nature.

Personal boundaries are disciplines that we assign to ourselves for the purpose of our long term happiness and sense of fulfillment. Their function is to maintain our own integrity, and thereby to ensure our *real* safety and security. Without personal boundaries, the ego maintains control over us and we are hostage to its insane strategy of dominance and exclusion.

An example of a personal boundary from earlier chapters is letting go of desire. When you feel an intense desire, it can be useful not to act on it but rather to simply be with it. You might feel an urge to eat when it is not a meal time, and if you decide *not* to respond to this desire, you may notice that it simply goes away. It is not that eating is wrong. We all have to eat something to stay alive. It is just that our programmed pattern of wanting what we don't have obscures our body's natural hunger signal and we end up confused about our real needs.

Another example is not defending yourself when you think that someone is threatening you. This is often difficult because you have to let go of one of your most basic survival instincts. However, if you can be with the fear and anger for a moment without reacting, you may notice that these strong emotions subside, and then you can more intelligently asses the real danger and respond accordingly.

I have been on the receiving end of several minor law suits in which my instinctive defenses were triggered, and despite my best intentions, I reacted impulsively. One case involved my former wife asking for a large sum of money, and another was a neighbor who was upset about traffic on a public road caused by our retreat center.

Each time I was flooded with fear and anger and thought that I *had* to do something to protect my property and prove my innocence. In hind sight, I wished that I had responded differently. My reactions only made the situation more threatening to the other people involved, and more frightening and painful for me. I realized that I could have maintained calm clarity instead of resorting to panic, and simply waited until my fear subsided a bit before responding to the situation.

Setting a personal boundary could mean that we decide not to eat between meals, not to act aggressively toward someone whom we think is trying to hurt us, or not to react defensively when we think that we are being attacked. These intentions are merely a way for us to become aware of unconscious habits that do not serve us. Without boundaries such as these, we cannot tell if we are caught in a mental pattern. Then we easily become fooled into believing that our perception of the situation is real.

When we limit our ego in this way, it sets up a marker for us to become more conscious. When we cross a boundary that we have established for ourselves, as I did in the story above, we are more likely to be aware of what we are doing instead of blindly following our automatic impulses. This recognition allows us to see the unconscious programming at work in our lives and realize the impact of it so that the next time we might have the presence to respond differently.

Our Capacity for Self-Regulation

Better than any law or morality, a more precise and effective system for limiting the destructive tendencies of the ego is personal integrity. Underneath the false front of an isolated individual personality, we are already whole and complete. When we think or do something harmful to ourselves or someone else, we can feel it immediately. It is like cutting off a finger or a toe. Our system knows that it is not in integrity with itself.

As I suggested earlier, this capacity that we have for self-regulation has been called our conscience. It is a subtle awareness that we all possess, which we cannot block out or destroy entirely. Many of us try to silence our conscience, because it seems to always want to limit us. We try to get away from it by ignoring it or numbing ourselves so that we don't feel it anymore. However, it is always there, and part of us always knows when we have made a mistake.

For spiritual growth, this facility of knowing what is true for me is my greatest ally. It enables me to have a precise guide at all times. As I become more attune to it, I learn to feel immediately when my words or actions are out of alignment with my whole being. And I learn to value my integrity above all else, because that is what gives my life certainty, resilience, and stability.

The ego feels threatened by anything that does not directly enhance it, and I often act in harsh ways toward myself and other people as I unconsciously try to protect and shore up this fragile sense of self. Meditation helps me to become conscious of how painful these actions are and see how defending my ego often damages my integrity. Practicing direct awareness strengthens my capacity to maintain my wholeness. When I act in a way that cuts a part of myself off, I feel it and am able to stop and make space to include it again.

I sometimes lose my temper with one of my children when they do something that seems disrespectful toward me or another family member. I have noticed that some degree of anger is effective in getting their attention and letting them know how their behavior impacts other people. Yet if I go too far with my reaction, I frighten them and then I don't feel at peace with myself afterwards.

There are no set rules for parenting, just as there is no formula for how to behave in life. Each one of us has to figure out for ourselves how to respond in a genuine and effective way. I find it helpful to know how to use basic relationship skills such as setting healthy boundaries, being assertive, and listening empathetically. And it is useful to me to establish personal principles around parenting which include treating children with respect while providing them with clear boundaries.

In the end, however, parenting is an art that we have to learn by trial and error. When I make a mistake and violate my own principles, I generally feel it as sadness, disappointment, or frustration with myself. These are helpful signals that I have done something unskillful or ineffective, and they tell me that I need to try something different next time. If I condemn myself or take on the guilt, shame, or judgment that often accompanies strict moral or legal systems, I diminish my capacity to grow and miss an opportunity to learn from my mistakes.

Genuine Security

I tend to think of security as protection from something that threatens me. My ego is vigilant against any possible threats and quick to defend me from them. Yet, as I suggested earlier, it is through struggling against an opposing force that my ego establishes and maintains its identity. As long as I identify with my ego, therefore, I will require an outside force opposing me in order to validate myself. The kind of security that I gain from defending myself from these perceived threats is always fleeting because as soon as I have dealt with one threat, my ego will find a new one.

Real security is to be found in my own personal integrity, or sense of wholeness. It is only my own thoughts and actions that can obscure my inherent vibrancy from me so that I feel weak, vulnerable, and afraid. When I feel insecure, therefore, the remedy is always to regain an awareness of my own internal alignment. And this is what personal boundaries can do for me. They help to maintain my integrity by signaling when I am out of alignment with myself.

My true self is infinite and encompasses all of existence. This may be impossible to understand because I have identified myself for so long as a small and vulnerable individual. And this is exactly why I feel confined and suffocated so much of the time. I am essentially keeping myself trapped inside the small container of this body and the limited scope of my conditioned mind, when in reality I am infinitely larger.

Finding my way back to my original self is the intention of a spiritual journey. It is the only thing that will finally resolve the struggles and dilemmas that I face in life. This is simply because these obstacles only exist for me here in the world of perception. In reality nothing opposes the whole, and this is what I am.

In order for me to recognize this, it helps to withdraw myself from the fragmenting process of perception. This automatically restores my inherent wholeness simply by making it apparent to me again. In order to realize my true unlimited self, I can think and act in a way that connects me to the whole, instead of continually separating myself as my rational mind is programmed to do.

My true security lies in maintaining awareness of the integrity of the whole. When I am aware that I am inherently part of something that is much larger than my individual being, my fear disappears. There is nothing that can threaten or harm me because I am identified with everything there is. All of reality is a part of who I am, so there is nothing outside of me to compete with for survival.

This is what it was like in the Garden of Eden, before we knew of good and evil.

Recognizing our Whole Self

Waking up and recognizing ourselves as whole and complete is similar to the way infants learn to recognize parts of themselves. They need to learn that the tiny hand in front of their face and the wiggly toes down below are part of their own body. They may have to feel pain or other sensation when they bump or hit themselves in order to realize that all these parts belong to them.

The reality of our existence is that everything in our world is connected as part of one whole being. Most of us cannot see this in the state that we are in now because we have come to think of ourselves as this separate body and mind, in a world of other separate people. In a similar way, people could not see that the earth is round and orbits around the sun, or that microscopic organisms cause disease.

We could not see for sure that the earth was round until we were able to travel beyond our atmosphere into space and look back at our planet from a distance. We did not know of the existence of tiny organisms until we developed a microscope capable of seeing them. And we could not know for sure how our planet aligned with the sun and other planets until we developed a telescope so we could see directly how it is.

In a similar way, it can help us now to get beyond perception and away from our definitions of space, time, and personality, to see that things are not separate as we thought. Once we relax our reflex to protect and enhance our separate self, we begin to see all the ways we are similar. Gradually, it becomes obvious that we come from the same source and are like branches of the same tree. As this "re-membering" occurs, we begin to feel happy, safe, and secure again. We recognize that we exist without question as part of a whole that includes everyone and everything around us.

Integrity begins as an internal process of coming into alignment within myself and quickly expands to include the world around me. Where perception divides and excludes parts of our world, integrity unifies and includes. As I feel integrated in my own being, I naturally experience my connection with all of life and realize that I am part of the whole world and the world is part of me.

As I become more conscious, I recognize that my integrity is the most valuable thing that I have. It is like the physical body's immune system. As a separate individual, I often feel vulnerable, weak, and powerless. But as part of the whole, I immediately regain a sense of being durable, strong and powerful.

This is a very different sense of power than that of the individual ego. The personality tries to attain power by taking it from other people and controlling its surroundings. The awakened mind knows that power comes only from being in integrity with the whole.

Expanding our Edges

A spiritual practice involves expanding my edges. It is a deliberate examination of the limitations that I have put up around my true self in an attempt to maintain my identity and achieve security. Growing spiritually means being willing to stretch these limitations. This process is similar to what happens inside the body when I stretch in a yoga posture and relax into it. As I consciously breathe in and out while holding the stretch, I can feel muscles and tissue gently relax and let go a bit. Afterward, my body feels more alive and connected to all of its parts.

I know when I have found an edge in my body because it is difficult to move in that direction, and my impulse may be not to move my body that way. Yoga, or stretching practice, shows me the benefit of challenging myself to move where my body does not feel comfortable, and doing it with awareness and care. Finding the edges of my inner being and stretching them gently is much the same.

In meditation practice, I let go of everything that arises in my mind and body except the object of my awareness. I usually use the sensation of my body breathing as an object because it is continuous, involuntary, and simple. As I try letting go of thoughts, I notice that certain ideas, memories, or fantasies seem to stick. These are my edges. It is the thoughts that I give more importance to that I use to define who I am. And ultimately it is these thoughts that confine and limit me the most.

As with physical stretching, it is not wise to judge the thoughts as bad, or force them away. It works much better to simply lean into them with your awareness, the way that you might lean into a stiff muscle when doing yoga. The idea is to soften, relax, and widen around your sticky thoughts, so that you simply become bigger than they are. After a while, they loosen their grip on you because you have experienced yourself in a larger context and no longer need them to give your life meaning.

Seeing our Shadow

Integrity is not an ideal with which to compare and measure myself against others. This would merely lead back to the slippery slope of morality and feed my false sense of self. It is a personal commitment that I make to my own growth and long-term happiness, and the only measure of integrity is the way that I feel inside. If I take the time to recognize my real feelings and notice a sense of peace, then I am in integrity with myself.

Integrity is not a goal that I finally achieve, but rather it is a continuous practice. It is easy to lose my integrity when I feel threatened, scared, or angry. I was on a family vacation recently with my mother and we were invited to go to another family's house to socialize before dinner. I agreed to go, yet I felt a bit uneasy as it meant leaving our children home alone.

When the time came to go out, I mentioned that we would not stay long at the party, and my mother became visibly upset.

Something about the way that she responded to me triggered some old buried emotions, and in a moment I found myself yelling at her, telling her to mind her own business. I was overwhelmed with anger and resentment and just dumped it on her.

After I took a time-out and calmed down a bit, I realized how shaken I was by my outburst. My energy felt scattered and I felt sick to my stomach. There was no peace and I was clearly out of integrity with myself. I realized that in defending myself so aggressively, I had hurt my mother, and possibly damaged our relationship.

I knew that I had to restore my integrity and the way to do this was by talking to her. As soon as I found a moment to meet with her alone, I told her that I was sorry for my angry outburst and recognized that it must have scared her. I expressed regret for talking to her in this way and admitted that I had not treated her with respect.

I also explained to her that my reaction was due to anger I had built up for years in response to a certain way that she talked to me. I told her that I did not like being told what was right or wrong in social situations, and that I was capable of coming to these conclusions on my own. In this way, I established a healthy boundary with her in a more respectful way.

I instantly felt better inside, and I learned from this to pay more attention to my emotions around my mother so that I did not end up disrespecting her and feeling awful afterwards. My self-awareness grew so that the next time I was with her and had a strong emotional reaction to something that she did, I was able to stay calmer and try to express my feelings to her in a more constructive way.

———————— •◆• ————————

Think of a situation where you acted in a way that hurt or frightened someone else. Take a moment and remember the details of what you said or did, and how you felt afterwards. Perhaps you can recognize feelings of inner turmoil, anxiety, or confusion after it was over.

Breathe deeply and see if you can accept what happened without judging yourself or the other person. Notice simply the way that it made you feel, and how your response displaced your serenity.

How can you be at peace with this situation now? If you find yourself in a situation like that again, how can you take care of yourself without hurting someone else?

———————— •◆• ————————

21

The Existence of God

When I returned from my stay in Sri Lanka, I became curious about the notion of God. I had grown up in the Christian religion, yet I did not have a clear sense of God. As I explored the teachings of Christ, I found the concept of God helpful as a way to understand the idea of the whole. It became clear to me that when Jesus used this concept he was referring to the source of all of life.

I began to understand the idea of God as the notion of a complete universe resulting from one creative source. It is a concept that points to one unified whole that includes all the fragmented parts that we perceive in our idea of the world. As such, it is the one absolute in our world of relativity, and the one stable and real reference point that we can count on. This is why it became such a central idea in the teachings of Jesus.

Our Idea of God

The problem with the idea of God is that perceptual mind can only conceive of it as an individual, all-powerful personality. It is common to picture God as a super human being with supreme powers of judgment and a capacity to know and control everything. In order to understand the concept of God, perception has to have some opposing force to compare it with. So we have the idea of Satan or the devil as a force opposing God. We usually say that God is good and Satan is bad.

We often attribute to God human qualities of jealousy, envy, anger, judgment, retaliation, and vengeance. And we end up with an image of an all-powerful, super-human being who has ultimate control over our lives and can reward or punish us. This story is one way that some of us try to explain the suffering that we experience in life and make sense of the seemingly random way that our lives take extreme turns from pleasure to pain, and good fortune to bad.

We often bring the concept of God into our paradigm of perception and use it as a way to explain many of the mysteries that we cannot otherwise comprehend. The power which God has over us has become a myth that we use to explain our predicament. We tend to think of God as someone who knows everything and is orchestrating every detail of our lives. In this way, our story of God is no different from any of the more primitive myths and superstitions that cultures have used over the course of human history to explain the unexplainable.

Even those of us who claim not to believe in God have a notion of some all-powerful force that is controlling our fate and keeping us from getting what we really want. We may alternate between being afraid or resentful of God's overriding authority, and trying to please God and supplicate him so that he will give us what we want. We have made God to be like us. This is the only way that we can bring the concept of one ultimate source of life into our world where everything appears to be separate and individual.

Dealing with God

Our humanized concept of God leaves us with the choice to try to placate this ultimate Father figure in order to get what we want in life, do battle with him to try to gain control of our lives, or reject the existence of God altogether. Many of us try all of these approaches, and none of them seem to work in the end.

Our attempts to please God always have mixed and unpredictable results. We tend to make up elaborate rituals to try to influence this supreme authority in our favor. We use bargains, prayers, pleas, and sacrifices, and still our fate seems to have no rhyme or reason to it. We may think that we are God's chosen people and that we have God on our side against our enemies. And we perpetuate war and do unspeakable violence to each other in order to prove our exclusive claim to God's love.

These are all merely ways in which our ego attempts to use the concept of an all-powerful God to support its charade of a separate and vulnerable self. If we really are this one small individual in an ocean of other individuals, then we surely do need an all-powerful God to take our side and defend us against everyone else if we are to survive. So, many of us develop elaborate beliefs and superstitions about how to get God to come to our rescue.

Some of us ultimately get fed up with this process and try to oppose God directly. We challenge God to a duel of wills, and compete with him for the position of ultimate authority. This is yet another angle that the ego takes to enhance the notion of our separate self. There is perhaps no higher glory for the ego than in triumphing over God. In the end, however, we always seem to be losing, and this often leaves us feeling depressed and defeated.

Some of us finally reject the notion of God altogether, simply choosing not to believe that there is any one supreme intelligence behind life. The existence of our source can never be proven using the mechanism of perception, because there is nothing to compare it with. It remains invisible to us as long as we are using our conceptual mind. So, we end up either believing in God, or not believing in God, with no way to verify the truth. To the rational mind, this is enough to prove that God is simply an idea and not a reality.

The idea that God is merely a fantasy feeds the ego's ultimate aim of being its own source. The ego is the embodiment of the idea that we each are our own creator. This gives the ego credibility and grants it the independent existence it exalts. Yet it also cuts the ego off from any connection with the larger whole and leaves it weak, trembling, and afraid of everything.

Cutting Ourselves Off

When we acquired the knowledge of good and evil in the Garden of Eden story, we lost our awareness of our connection with God and believed that we were cut off from our source. As soon as we entered the realm of opposites, the whole became invisible to us.

This is usually translated as our loss of innocence, or the original sin. From our perspective, it appears that God has rejected us and we are now separated from the whole, thrust into the world to fend for ourselves. We believe that we did something wrong and God is now punishing us for our mistake.

The reality is that it is *we who are rejecting God*. Each moment that we judge something as good or bad we are trying to replace God with a mechanical system of perception that we think will give us power and authority greater than our source. We are trying to become our own reference point and sever ourselves completely from the whole. We think that this is the only way in which we can be complete, and we believe that our capacity for rational judgment will get us there.

The temptation that Adam and Eve faced in the Garden of Eden story was to use their capacity for perception to become greater than God. They were asked not to touch the fruit of the tree of the knowledge of good and evil; however, they finally could not resist. They thought that if they had this capacity, they could become the final authority, instead of God. This is what we have been doing ever since, and our task now is simply to recognize that it is not working.

There is no sin in rejecting the authority of God, and we are not being punished for doing so. That is why no amount of placating God with our good deeds will relieve us from loss, suffering, sickness, or death. We cannot resolve our dilemma here by accumulating enough good behavior to outweigh the sin that we have committed, because we have committed no sin. We simply made a mistake by assuming the capacity for rational discernment. The remedy for us is to recognize that our judgments are not making us happy or keeping us safe, and forego judgment to rely instead on simple awareness.

There is a humbling that happens when we do this which can feel to the ego like failure. Accepting an overriding intelligence that we are inherently part of but cannot own as ours exclusively means that the ego has not accomplished its mission of dominance and ownership of the whole. Yet, it is also the greatest relief that we can experience, because it means that we do not have to be the judge and final authority of reality.

God, Buddha, and Christ

Once I was sitting a ten day intensive Buddhist meditation retreat, and during an open question period I asked the teacher what the Buddha had said about God. The room of about eighty people, who had been in silence for a week, suddenly erupted in laughter. The Buddha's recorded teachings generally do not use the concept of God, and Westerners who follow these teachings tend to reject the notion of a supreme being or singular intelligence.

I was in a sensitive place emotionally, and the response in the room shook me. The teacher himself broke into laughter when I asked my question, as if the answer were too obvious to bear serious attention. But then, he became quiet and thoughtful for a moment. He said that, according to the Buddhist scriptures, the first words uttered by the Buddha after his enlightenment could be translated as "I have found God." After hearing this, everyone in the meditation hall became profoundly silent.

Christ and Buddha were two humans who realized the whole of reality and knew their intrinsic part in it. They each chose different words to explain their experience and point the way for others to follow. The Buddha used the concept of emptiness to describe the experience of totality, because to the conceptual mind this is exactly what it appears to be. This mind cannot perceive reality as a whole, and so the closest concept that could describe the experience is emptiness. Reality is certainly not empty, but there is nothing in it that can be recognized through our process of perception.

Christ used the concept of God to describe the same reality. His teachings point to God as the original source of all existence. He never intended to present an image of God as a super-human being controlling our lives. Rather, he was presenting God as the single intelligent creative force from which all life emanates. Christ's teaching is that we are creations of God, and at the same time we share the creative force with God. He tried to show us that we are inseparably part of creation and that our completion lies in simply remembering our fundamental connection with all that is.

Jesus was killed for asserting that "I and the Father are one." From our perspective, such a thing cannot exist. The basis of our paradigm is that everything here is separate and apart. Above all, God has to be separate from each of us, with no one of us having access to such concentrated power and authority. The Catholic Church reinforced the notion that God stands apart from all of us, and thus they obscured the real message of Jesus and made God a force that we had to serve, but could never unite with.

It is inevitable that the perceptual mind would turn the concept of God into a supreme authority figure who enforces moral laws. In a world of relative opposites, a singular source of reality would naturally be someone who determines absolute right from absolute wrong. So the concept of God has been used by religions and authority figures throughout history to try to establish the fixed reference points that perception requires. We refer to a finite moral law determined by an all-powerful God who uses guilt and fear of punishment to enforce that law.

It is also understandable that many of us would come to reject any notion of such a punitive and terrifying God. With the ideal of democracy and advent of science weakening the grip of authoritarian governments and religious institutions, we are beginning to have some degree of personal choice about what we believe. Many of us are choosing not to believe in a God that judges us according to some invisible laws and uses guilt and punishment to teach us right from wrong.

Tragically, though, many of us are imprisoning ourselves in the world of perception by our complete rejection of the notion of God. Without some idea of a source that is infinitely larger than ourselves, or a singular intelligence behind reality, we are at the mercy of the whims of the ego and the fickle judgments of our conceptual mind, with no anchor in reality. Ultimately, this leaves us feeling isolated and afraid, having to fend for ourselves in a threatening world.

God is Everything That Is

I see no conflict between the teachings of Christ and Buddha, and am comfortable using the concept of God as a reference point for spiritual awakening. For me, God is the sum total of everything there is in the universe, and I find it helpful to imagine that we are all part of this one infinite being. The idea of God represents the whole that includes all of life, and it offers a vision of unity and completion that is painfully absent in our world.

This idea of God does not define our source as male or female or assign it human attributes and capacities. It simply gives a name to everything altogether, and suggests that as a whole we share an intelligence and consciousness with all life and all matter. The reason that we find it difficult to describe God is that this source of consciousness is entirely outside of perception. It would have to be because it is *what perception depends on.*

God could be described as the creative force behind consciousness itself. It is the infinite intelligent source that enables our process of perception. We cannot access God through conceptual mind because our mind is *using* God to conceptualize. We can only imagine what God is and try to describe that using concepts.

In a similar way, we could never actually *see* the earth in its entirety and understand what it is as long as we remained on the earth. We were simply too close to it to have any perspective. The first people in Western civilization to suggest that the earth was a sphere suspended in space had to piece together their theory from fragments of observable data, none of which were conclusive or convincing. It was not until we were able to travel around the earth in sailing ships and eventually leave the earth in a rocket traveling to the moon, that we were able to finally see and fully recognize our planet as it is.

God is Unity and Completion

The word God gives us a simple way to express wholeness or completion. It is impossible for us to see or describe God because it is what we *are*. I don't mean that our ego is God, but our real self. From our normal perspective as a separate personality, this is blasphemy, because it means that our individual person is greater than any other. This is the only way that we can understand such an idea.

However, we are *not* this limited and separate self that we believe ourselves to be. We are intrinsically part of something so much greater than our ego. This is what I meant when I suggested earlier that we are both the whole, and part of the whole at the same time.

Far from making our individual self greater or more special than any other, this makes us inherently equal with every other person, all other life forms, and everything that exists. To put it another way, *everything* is part of our self. Our perceptual mind can never understand this because it is outside of its limited paradigm.

At first, this idea appears to deny our individuality and force us into conformity. From the perspective of our ego, to have everything connected as one means giving up our unique existence, and most of us are unwilling to do that. Even if we believe in God, we fight against the ultimate authority figure that we have made God into because this concept threatens our ego.

It is vital for our spiritual evolution that we question the idea of an authoritative, overriding God. In truth, God is the solution that we have been searching for, and experiencing God for ourselves can resolve each of the crises facing humanity today. Once we recognize the existence of God as the source within each one of us, our kinship with each other and all of life becomes obvious.

The answer to our quest for completion is a paradox that can hardly be explained in words. Each of us is a unique expression of God, as are all life forms, matter, and energy. All of this comes from God, is part of God, and therefore *is* God. Once we realize that God is who we are, the whole notion of separation or competition between us disappears because it has no meaning. As we recognize ourselves as God, we instantly recognize everyone and everything else as God also.

Imagining God

We have to stretch our language and the nature of perception itself to even begin to imagine God. Think of a perennial flower in a garden that has many stems coming up from one root under the earth. We see only the many different stems, and may easily conclude that each is a separate plant. However, when we dig under the stems, we discover that they all source from the same root. This describes our relationship with God as the invisible source beneath each individual expression of life.

We could also conceptualize God as the body of the universe, with each one of us and all life forms being individual cells in that body. In this way we are all connected, yet all separate, at the same time. We each have some individual destiny, yet we cannot exist without the whole. Whatever happens to another individual also impacts us because we are part of the same body. The health and well-being of the body is also our health and well-being.

A simpler way to imagine God may be to think of the whole of earth and everything contained within it. We have been acting as though we each are separate here and our survival depends on controlling our own individual resources. Yet it is becoming tragically obvious that this is not so. We are able to see today that we all depend on the same resources, and the health of the earth is essential for our own individual health.

Having faith in God means that we believe there *is* something much larger than any of us which is whole and eternal. There is nothing that we know of now, in all of the material universe, which is like this. Everything here, even the earth, sun, moon, and stars, has a lifespan and eventually dies and changes into something else.

God is the idea that all matter and life force energy springs from a single eternal source. The existence of God does not deny science or undermine our ideas about the physical world around us. Science has never been able to even guess about the source of consciousness itself because it is so far outside the realm of perception.

To put this in terms that the Buddha might have used, don't believe in God, but rather find out for yourself if such a thing exists. Do not discount the existence of God simply because you have no way to verify it. Perception is limited by its need to separate everything from everything else, including God. Outside of perception, there is no separation and instead of conceiving of the world, we *are* the world. This unity is God, and it is what we long for most.

In the direct awareness that can be cultivated through meditation practice, everything is experienced as one unified presence with no distinctions or boundaries. I experience this as my own presence, yet it is clearly much more than my personal attention and energy that I find there. In the stillness of pure awareness, I enter a field where all of awareness exists, and all of us are there together with our individual presences merged into one infinite, conscious whole.

The Buddha called this state the unconditioned mind and described it as emptiness, because it is void of any conceptual distinctions. He used the word Nirvana to describe the condition of dwelling in this place. Christ described it as God, and used the word Heaven to describe this state of being. Our old creation myth in the Bible called it the Garden of Eden. This state of unification with everything, whatever we choose to call it, is clearly the purpose and ultimate destination of our human experience.

———————— •◆• ————————

Imagine that you are completely alone here, with no connection to a larger source. What does this feel like?

Now, imagine that you have an eternal source that you are always connected to and part of. Do not try to picture what this source looks like or define it in any way. Simply notice what it feels like to belong to something much larger than just yourself.

———————— •◆• ————————

God and Evolution

With the age of reason and development of science, Western civilization has increasingly found new explanations for things that people had previously looked to religion to understand. When Darwin famously presented his theory of evolution, it naturally caused a controversy with the established Christian church. The leaders of the church saw themselves as the authorities on creation as presented in the Old Testament of the Bible, and Darwin's theories seemed to contradict this story. One hundred and fifty years later, this historical drama is still playing out.

In the biblical version of creation, God took six days to create the earth and all of its life forms, including humans, just as we see them today. This story is similar to the myths of other cultures who describe the creation of our earth and life as we know it in some miraculous way, often at the hand of a creator. The fact that this story was the primary way that we explained our origins in Western civilization until just a century and a half ago demonstrates how little we actually know about where we come from.

From our modern scientific perspective today, the biblical creation story seems to be a simplistic myth based on fantasy and imagination. We cannot conceive of a single super-human God who put all of this together in a week. This obviously was an imaginative attempt to explain our origins in the absence of any other facts or theories.

The story of creation as described in the book of Genesis implies a static situation that was put into place all at once. One of the limitations of this simplistic creation myth is that it leaves little room for spiritual development and does not give us much direction about what to *do* about our predicament.

The teachings of the Christian church suggest that our task here is to be perfectly moral and good so that we can gain entrance to heaven after we die. The alternative is that if we do not attain moral perfection here we will be condemned to eternity in hell.

While the harshness of this message may provide some motivation for personal improvement, the nature of such an abstract and absolute judgment being placed upon us when we die is more than many of us can handle. Putting the goal of heaven off in a future after life seems to effectively put it out of reach and does not provide much comfort or guidance now. Some of us become morally fundamentalist while others give up trying to be good at all because it seems impossible to get it right.

As Western civilization increasingly looked to the rational observations of science instead of traditional religious authority to understand our world, it was natural for someone like Darwin to investigate how life came to be the way it is. Our age of reason demanded a logical explanation that relied more on observable data than superstition, and the theory of evolution fills this need. However, it seems that in our urgency to find a rational explanation, we have eliminated the possibility of a singular intelligent cause or source of life because we have not yet been able to identify what that is.

We understandably may shy away from the biblical version of God as an all-powerful being with human characteristics who can punish or reward us. Yet we can surely come up with a more creative concept of God which includes the possibility of an intelligent source behind the complexity of life. Consciousness itself must have a source, and because we are conscious, we must be connected to that source. When we find God, it is because we have become identified more with pure consciousness than with perception.

The reason that an experience of God is so vital now is that when we recognize this source, we realize that it can never be damaged. It is only perception that splits everything into pieces and thereby destroys its integrity. Beyond perception, everything is whole and complete, as it always has been.

A Way Out

While the theory of evolution appears at first to contradict the existence of a creator God as described in the book of Genesis, it lends credence to the idea that we are all part of a whole, interconnected system of life. Darwin's idea establishes a common source for all of life by suggesting that all living things on earth, including ourselves, evolved from the same raw materials and the original single-cell organisms.

Previously, I suggested that creation myths often include coded messages that show us a way to get beyond our limited human condition. As if consciousness itself had a hand in constructing them, each one tends to have hidden within it some clues that point the way out. I have already demonstrated how the biblical story of Eden presents such a message.

Our modern creation myth of evolution also suggests a way out. This story is based on the idea that all life changes form through incremental genetic shifts in physical development motivated by the urge for continued survival. According to this theory, life forms that appear to be static and finite here are actually in a constant state of flux. All life forms are changing into something better and more suited for their environment, and it is the pressures of living in their environment that inform these changes.

Similar to the way that our eyes cannot see the earth as round because of its immense size, the great extent of time and space does not allow us to witness directly these evolutionary changes. We can only look back and suggest a theory about how we came to be in our current human form by studying ancient fossils and skeletons of animals who we presume to be our ancestors.

As in all of science, the theories that we develop to explain how things work are approximate and subject to change. The profound message in our theory of evolution is not to be found in the exact details of how we developed from monkeys to humans, for that will always be subject to speculation. It is that all life forms are continually changing, therefore, *we are now in the process of becoming a new species*. This is simply happening at such a slow rate that it is beyond our capacity to notice.

Conscious Evolution

More interesting and significant than where we came from is the question of what we are becoming. Christ, Buddha, and other people who have realized their true nature, may well represent the next evolution of humanity and provide living examples of the new species that we are to become. The experience of becoming fully conscious changed their fundamental nature and they became something beyond human, with capacities that we can only imagine.

Buddha is reported to have had mental powers of clarity that could see past and future lives and a whole cosmos of beings that are normally invisible to us. He spoke about matter being made up of minute particles of energy that are invisible to the human eye, over two thousand years before Western science presented the theory of atoms and molecules. Christ is said to have turned water into wine, walked on water, healed incurable illnesses, brought the dead to life, and arisen from the dead himself.

More profoundly, these teachers presented us with an entirely new model for being human. Perhaps the simplest way to describe the significance of the shift that they made is their absence of fear. Those humans who have awakened show us the possibility of transcending human nature in order to be inspired by love instead of motivated by fear. They showed us by their example that we are not limited by our body, mind, or anything external to us. And they provided us with guidance so that we may follow their lead and do what they did.

The process of transformation that these teachers have undergone could be referred to as *conscious evolution*. They recognized the limitations of their current form and discovered a way to expand themselves beyond it. Using the power of their own conscious awareness they saw past the veil of illusion presented by perceptual mind and realized the true nature of themselves and reality. And in so doing they may have consciously assisted in their own evolutionary process.

Pressure to Evolve

The model of evolution that we are most familiar with has each species developing new physical forms and capacities slowly over long periods of time in response to changing conditions around them. We tend to think of this as a purely mechanical process of random genetic selection that takes many generations and is something that happens *to* us, instead of something that we participate in.

Yet, this is only one way to approach the process of evolution. Another way to explain our place in evolution is that as humans we have a unique capacity to consciously evolve. We have the ability through our conscious awareness *to be actively involved in our own species transformation.*

To make this angle more compelling, consider the pressures of our situation now on earth. I suggested earlier that the magnitude and variety of the crises which we face today appears to be beyond our capacity to resolve. Our most advanced scientific processes are much too slow and cumbersome to learn enough about each situation in time to prevent catastrophe. There seems to be a demand now that we change with much greater speed and agility than has ever happened before, or perish altogether.

Our current theory of evolution suggests that species change and adapt in response to environmental or social pressures. Because the environment of the earth and the social structures within species tend to change so slowly, the process of evolution normally has ample time to make adjustments in each species to make them compatible with the changes around them. When environmental changes happen too rapidly, however, some species perish. A common scientific theory asserts that the dinosaurs did not have enough time to evolve when dramatic changes took place in the earth's environment in a relatively short amount of time, and so they all died out.

We now seem to be poised on the brink of environmental and social pressures that will come fast and hard and may pale in comparison to what the dinosaurs went through. The combination of environmental pollution, depletion of natural resources, exhausted petroleum reserves, a human population explosion, proliferation of nuclear weapons, global climate change, world-wide economic instability, and increasing conflicts within and between nations, points to the perfect storm for life on our planet. If you are paying attention to our situation here, this much should be obvious; we are facing a crisis of extreme proportions that could threaten the very existence of humanity, and much of life on earth as we know it.

Many of us do not want to look directly at our current predicament because we end up feeling hopeless and depressed. We are in a massive state of denial that anything is wrong with our current situation. We rationalize that science and technology will save us before it is too late. Meanwhile we feel a sinking helpless sense of dread inside that we are frantically trying to pretend is not there.

We are under perhaps the greatest pressure ever experienced by a species here on earth to evolve. And given the slow rate of evolution that appears to have occurred up until now, the chances of Darwinian evolution adapting us to survive these catastrophic changes seem very slim. Yet, there is a possibility which many of us have not considered – that we may be able to accelerate our own evolution.

The theory of evolution suggests that pressure for survival motivates a new adaptation. The impending crises facing humanity today surely present us with ample pressure, and could be just the motivation that we need to become involved in our own evolution.

The severity of our predicament is putting pressure on us to awaken. And the way to do this has been presented to us by spiritual teachers like the Buddha and Christ. We have the capacity to recognize who we are in reality, and as those who have awakened before us have demonstrated, this recognition changes our fundamental nature.

A human being who does not refer to ideas of right and wrong in order to get a handle on reality, and is not motivated by fear, is as different from us as one species is to another. This is both the challenge and the hope that we face now. As terrified as we may be of leaving behind the familiar world of perception, we surely will find our own extinction more dreadful.

While it may be impossible to conceive of ourselves evolving into a new species, it is equally impossible to imagine that we can learn how to survive this crisis given the current constraints of our human condition. Consciously assisting the process of evolution may be the only way out that we have.

Cooperation

In nature, most species rely partly on competition and partly on cooperation for survival. Some, such as carnivorous predators, depend heavily on their capacity to compete, and survive better on their own. Eagles, hawks, lions, sharks, wolves, and other animals establish personal or family territories that they defend aggressively in order to ensure their food supply and personal security. These solitary animals are not entirely competitive, however, and also practice a great degree of cooperation within family or small group units.

Other species, such as ants or bees, depend heavily on their capacity to cooperate and can only survive in large colonies. These creatures display a remarkable loyalty and dedication to their colony and queen, fulfilling their functions tirelessly and being willing to die for the survival of the whole. While these insects demonstrate a high level of cooperation, they also are capable of competition and aggression when defending their colony, fighting with other colonies, or in some cases killing for food.

As humans, we span the entire spectrum from competition to cooperation. Our diet can range from carnivorous to vegan, and our lifestyle can vary from a high degree of competition and individuality, to a strong preference for community and cooperation.

In Western civilization, we have emphasized and relied on our capacity to compete, to the exclusion of our ability to cooperate. This approach has allowed us to conquer much of the earth and become the dominant culture. Yet the price that we are paying is a painful sense of isolation and disconnection from community, family, and our natural environment.

While it once may have appeared that being skilled competitors increased our chance of survival, it now seems that our unchecked predatory habits may cause the collapse of the life systems that we depend on. Our enhanced capacity to compete, which Darwin presented as a compelling force behind evolution, appears to have run its course and is now directing us headlong toward our own extinction. Our survival may now hinge upon our capacity to change our fundamental human nature so that cooperating for everyone's benefit becomes more compelling than competing to see who will win.

22

From Competition to Cooperation

Our population is multiplying exponentially and the industries which have enabled and supported this explosion of people are rapidly depleting or contaminating the basic resources that we all need to survive. At the rate that we are using oil, the primary energy source on which most of our technology depends, we are set to deplete the earth's reserves within this century. Industrial chemical farming practices leave us vulnerable to massive crop failure and world-wide famine, and our dependency on cheap energy and technology has rendered many of us overweight and unhealthy.

We have created such powerful weapons like nuclear bombs and chemical or biological toxins, that to use them against each other would ensure our own destruction. Meanwhile war continues to be the primary way in which we respond to conflicts between nations. Add to this the disintegration of our communities and families, global climate change, and an international financial crisis, and it is clear that we have every reason to be afraid.

Our usual response to situations that threaten us is to try to contain the shadowy and destructive impulses of human nature through force or persuasion. We spend an enormous amount of energy trying to get other people to change, because from our perspective *they* are the ones causing the problem. And this either leads to escalated conflict or leaves us feeling frustrated and powerless.

If we do succeed in controlling other people's greed or aggression, it lasts only a short while. Passing laws that make some behavior illegal only tend to push it underground and encourage secrecy and manipulation. Most of the time our attempts to change other people only make the situation worse. Instead of enlightening others, we make them more determined to carry on with their destructive behavior in secret.

The obvious lesson here is that change does not happen this way. We cannot alter other people's basic human nature, and the more we try, the worse the situation becomes. This is because we are using the same means to try to solve the problem that is causing the difficulty in the first place. When we see other people as the ones doing the damage and we try to stop them, we inevitably see them as bad and ourselves as good. This increases our sense of opposition and separation from the whole and feeds our habit of competition.

Trying to be Good

When we aren't focusing on what other people are doing wrong, many of us feel uneasy about our own self-centered impulses and try to overcome these by being good. Religion often teaches us to be selfless by establishing moral codes of behavior that suppress or deny our survival instincts. They tell us to put other people's needs before our own and act in a generous and caring way.

The limitation of morality, however, is that we are following someone else's script. We are trying to live up to a standard of goodness, and often all that changes is our outward behavior. We end up trying to *look* good by helping other people, while privately we are still afraid and insecure about meeting our own needs. Our old habits are hidden but remain intact, only to surface again when we are pushed beyond our edge and lose control of ourselves.

Suppressing our own programmed impulses does not work anymore than pushing against those of someone else. Morality or rules of behavior do not by themselves change anything. We may think that we have changed because we have a new idea of what is right, but often all that we have done is to push our fear and aggression underground. This makes real growth and change more difficult because we can no longer see the shadow parts of ourselves that need healing.

After a while, it seems impossible to live up to the ideals of perfection inherent in moral codes of behavior, so we either spend our lives tying to fake being good, or we throw out the entire idea of goodness. Mistaking morality for truth is so common that our only choice seems to be struggling to get it right, or not caring at all. Either way we are stuck with no way out except trying to change other people. In the end, this cannot work because real change is an inside job. So even those of us most ardent and passionate about making things better often end up feeling hopeless, discouraged, aloof, or cynical.

The Way Out

Throughout history, a few people have managed to transform their own basic human nature. They have shifted their orientation from focusing on their individual desires, to looking after the good of the whole. The presence of these saints and their teachings in our world is a great gift and blessing. Without an example to follow, we would surely be lost here, bound by our human instincts to self-defeating behaviors. These individuals may have made the next evolutionary leap for humankind, and are demonstrating what our species can eventually become. They are showing us a real way out.

If we can see how our basic human nature is responsible for each one of the impossible situations that we face today, and recognize that the only control we really have is over ourselves, it may occur to us that the answer to our survival lies in self-transformation instead of self-preservation. This crisis demands that we have to grow and evolve, and this is a process that begins within each one of us and requires our active participation.

This kind of evolution is not a physical change or adaptation in the way that we are used to think of it, but an evolution of consciousness that happens within each one of us individually. The process could be called conscious evolution because we have to actively participate in our own transformation. The essence of this shift is that instead of being concerned primarily with our individual survival, our self-definition expands and we become more concerned with the welfare of all of us together.

A change like this is not something that can be forced, faked, or learned in the ways that we are accustomed to learning. We cannot get there by merely suppressing or disguising our self-preservation instincts, and we cannot *learn* how to care for the whole as much as we care about ourselves. These efforts merely override our basic instincts and are temporary fixes.

Spiritual transformation is quite different from accepting moral limitations or trying to be good. As discussed earlier, these efforts may be necessary in order to reveal the programming of our mind. However, they are not an end in themselves because by themselves they do not change anything. Rather, morality keeps us locked into the world of perception and duality – the world of the ego.

Realized beings such as the Buddha and Christ surrendered to a *transformation* of their ego. They allowed their fundamental human nature to simply fall away and reveal an eternal self that is beyond personality or limitation of any kind. We each can make a similar choice to undergo a transformation of our most basic orientation and allow our fundamental perspective on life to shift. We can unlearn our habit of self-preservation and surrender our automatic defenses in order to see that we are not vulnerable and isolated as we imagine, but are an integral part of one infinite and eternal whole.

An Impossible Situation

When we look at the enormity of the global disasters looming ahead of us, the idea of focusing on transforming ourselves can seem hopelessly inadequate and even irresponsible. Even if we *could* change our own nature, it makes no sense that this would have any impact on the world around us other than making us a better person.

Many of us discount the impact of spiritual growth and view the idea of self-transformation with a bit of skepticism. It may seem absurd that our individual attitudes or assumptions could affect anything but ourselves, and the notion of personal growth looks like merely a selfish indulgence. If we are concerned about the state of our world, it appears obvious that we can only serve the greater good by actively being involved in changing things around us.

However, all of these reasonable arguments are merely smokescreens hiding a much larger issue. When we try to challenge our own basic nature and grow beyond our self-centered instincts, we realize that it is *nearly impossible*. Many of us finally conclude that even if there were some merit in doing so, changing human nature is just too difficult to be realistic.

It is also common among people who want to make a difference that we find ourselves divided between focusing on our own needs and trying to help the world. We assume that our personal needs and the needs of the greater whole are at odds with each other. And this common assumption lies at the very root of our problem.

Solutions can be Simple

Inherent in any problem is often an obvious and simple solution, if we can only shift our perception enough to see it. So it is with these mega-problems we face today. Consider that global climate change is caused by too much carbon being released into our atmosphere, due in large part to our burning of fossil fuels. Also consider that the technologies which we depend on to meet our basic needs use these same non-renewable fossil fuels, and these ancient stores of energy are going to run out soon, rendering much of our technology useless.

Both of these are impending disasters that threaten all of us and may undermine our survival as a species. And if we look at them together, a single, simple, inevitable solution is obvious. We have to learn to support ourselves again, as we did for thousands of years, without the use of fossil fuels.

I do not presume to know the best way to achieve this, and am not suggesting that letting go of our dependency on fossil fuels will be easy. I am simply noting that this is what we need to do if we want to survive. The solution to an impossible situation is often obvious if we step out of our ordinary way of thinking and see things from a new angle.

Finding the Cause

I have suggested that the root of all our problems is basic human nature. The primal instincts responsible for our nature are founded on the assumption that each of us has to look out for ourselves. These basic impulses propel us toward ever greater independence and personal armoring. And a consequence of focusing so much on our autonomy and individual defenses is a painful sense of isolation that ultimately results in a feeling of deep anxiety and insecurity within each of us.

When we think that we are alone here, we naturally become afraid. And in our desperate attempts to overcome this fear, we have ransacked the earth and pitted ourselves against each other. So we find ourselves now locked in a fatal competition for greater material comfort and physical security that seems to promise personal safety, yet in reality makes our world ever more threatening.

Just as with all problems, the deeper cause underlying our current predicament reveals a remarkably simple solution, once we see clearly what is happening. Consider that the root of this problem lies in the way that we think of ourselves – as independent people each having to secure our own welfare. Our advances in civilization have steadily increased our capacity for living independently from each other. Yet, in striving for greater individual freedom, we unknowingly have increased our anxiety and insecurity by eroding our sense of belonging and further disconnecting ourselves from the whole.

As this anxiety increases so does our need to resolve it. And many of us have been trying to subdue this fear of being alone by increasing our material comfort and security. The chronic sense of isolation that results from our insatiable drive for independence creates a vacancy inside of us that we try to fill by getting more goods and services for our personal comfort and protection. The result is rampant over-consumption and hoarding of resources that causes personal illness, massive destruction to our environment and violent conflicts between us.

While we have been aware of the damage that we are causing to ourselves and our environment, and are beginning to realize the obvious implications of depleting the natural resources that we require for our sustenance, we have not been able to stop ourselves. This is because we are trying to fix our most basic problem by addressing the *symptoms*, and not the cause.

We have been trying to control our ego-centrism without questioning the basic assumptions that underlie it. This leaves us trapped in a place of irresolvable tension. On the one hand we are frantically trying to support and feed our individual ego because we believe that our survival depends on it. And on the other hand, we are trying desperately to suppress and contain our ego impulses because we see how destructive they are.

Resolution

The resolution to this impossible situation is to begin to see ourselves as part of one whole system of life, instead of as separate beings fending for ourselves in an often hostile world. We have to realize that we are all dependent on the same natural resources, and whether we like it or not, we share these resources with every other person and all of life. Fighting over air, water, or soil becomes meaningless once we realize that none of us can control these resources or keep them only for ourselves.

The very nature of the earth's most basic elements is that they recycle themselves endlessly through every life form, and this is how they continue to be available to all of us. We breathe in oxygen and breathe out carbon dioxide, and plants breathe in carbon dioxide and breathe out oxygen. Our natural waste products such as food scraps, feces, and urine, when composted, become food for plants. And the plants in turn provide food for us.

While it may seem that we have nothing in common with plants, in fact, we completely depend upon each other and have an amazing degree of compatibility and interdependency with them. If we take the time to look carefully at our relationships with other forms of life, and other people, we can find the same sorts of interconnectedness and synergy.

We each have our unique part to play in the whole of life, and without every individual life form, the whole of life is incomplete and less sustainable. This startling realization led the allied countries who won World War II to agree to rebuild Germany and Japan and recognize them as sovereign nations. They realized that if they took one element out of the mix, they risked destabilizing the whole.

Realizing that we all belong to the earth and our physical needs come from the earth, we begin to see how we are connected to each other in such a fundamental way that we can never be fully separate. And this recognition of our interdependency begins to dissolve the existential anxiety that arises from thinking that we are alone here, fighting for our survival against everyone else. The more that we realize our inherent connection with each other and all of life, the less isolated we feel, and the urgency to protect our personal interests naturally begins to dissipate.

Instead of trying to suppress our individual ego and its insatiable hunger for power and control, we can learn to replace the emphasis on our individual personality by identifying instead with the whole of humanity. At first, this takes a clear intention and sustained effort. However, it begins to happen spontaneously as soon as we realize the relief of knowing that we are part of something much larger than ourselves.

The Meaning of the Crisis

In the last several centuries, human civilization has moved rapidly from being dominated by the forces of nature, to dominating them. In our perennial search for greater comfort and security we are discovering that we have the capacity not only to impact the earth and the other life forms here, but also perhaps to damage them beyond repair.

It is finally dawning on us through startling realizations like global climate change, the rapid depletion of ocean fish populations, and the pollution of our water and air, that we may be able to destroy the living systems upon which our own lives depend. We have come to a point where the primitive nature of our individual ego is revealing itself to be self-destructive in a way that we cannot ignore. While our self-preservation instincts may have once served us, they have now become the largest threat to our survival.

The concept of the earth as a contained and limited life-support system is also now becoming clear to many of us. Just a generation ago in our Western civilization, this idea was relatively new. We tended to think of the earth as unlimited and indestructible because it is so enormous. Now the signs are everywhere that this is not so. Our capacity to mine the earth's resources and our insatiable appetite for greater wealth, comfort, and security have combined to tragically deplete or pollute the land, water, and air that we once assumed were infinitely renewable.

The lesson of living on a finite earth, upon whose resources our life depends, is that no one of us here is truly independent from everyone else. We are all on the same ship called earth, and what each of us does affects the integrity of the whole. These crises which we face now are demonstrating that we are all connected - every one of us dependent on a fragile and limited earth that we share, and thereby all of us dependent on each other.

As we recognize that our desire for personal security is causing our own life support systems to collapse, we are forced to look at ourselves from a whole new angle. We see that ordinary self-interest does not work in the long run because our individual lives depend on resources that can only be sustained if we share responsibility for them.

Enlightened Self-Interest

In Buddhist teachings, this concept is called "Enlightened Self-Interest." Once we become sufficiently aware of our situation here, and see how intrinsically our fate is connected to that of everyone around us, we realize that it is truly in our best interests to be concerned about the welfare of all beings and living systems.

The miracle in this simple recognition of our inherent connection with each other is that it finally resolves our fundamental need for safety and security - a need which has not been met by all of the "progress" that we have achieved in humanity's two hundred thousand years on earth.

In spite of our recent rapid advancement in industry and technology, most of us feel more insecure and uncertain than ever before. Yet the moment we recognize that we are part of one whole, instead of merely isolated individuals, the weight of our chronic fear and anxiety begins to lift. We realize that we are not alone, and could never be alone.

Fortunately, we do not have to choose between trying to do good for others, or focusing on our own personal growth and development. The very idea that our individual self-interests are in opposition to those of other people is what is causing all of our problems. The solution lies in questioning the assumption that we are separate and have to compete with each other for our own survival. We can expand our perspective enough to recognize that our interests are connected to everyone else's. Then it becomes obvious that it serves us to serve the whole.

23

Meditation Instructions

An awareness practice like meditation is a kind of medicine which can resolve our chronic fear and anxiety at its source because it enables us to experience ourselves as part of the whole. Understanding this concept does not change anything because we are still in perception. However, believing that the discipline of meditation might help can motivate us to practice. When we practice direct awareness and allow our small-self to melt into an infinitely larger whole, it gradually dissolves our defensiveness and enables us to relax into sustained contentment and peace.

I sit in silent meditation daily as a way to ground myself in this moment and remember the stillness that exists within me, below the chatter of my perceptual mind. It is a way for me to visit my source, which is also the source for all of life. It is part of how I care for myself, like brushing my teeth or having a good night's sleep, and if I miss it for some reason, I feel off-center and out of touch.

Following Instructions

Receiving and following clear instructions for meditation is important because you can quickly develop habits that may be difficult to break later on. In a similar way it is good to have a piano teacher demonstrate which fingers to use to play which keys, in order to develop fingering which will enable you to play complex compositions more fluidly.

It may be better to receive instructions in person with a teacher. Each teacher of meditation will add their own unique style to the practice and it is usually a good idea to follow the method taught by whatever teacher you happen to resonate with, and try that for a while. You will also be able to ask questions early in your practice that may clear up misunderstandings and help make the process more effective.

For those of you without access to a teacher, I am including this chapter based on my experiences practicing Insight meditation (also known as Vipassana or Mindfulness) for the past thirty-six years, and teaching for the past twelve. Please keep in mind as you read this that there is no right or wrong way to teach or practice meditation, and we each have to find a way that works for us.

Body Posture

The most important part of a sitting position is having your spine self-supported. As soon as you lean back onto something for support, the body begins to slump, constricting the natural flow of breath and lowering your overall energy level. This is difficult for some of us as we are not used to supporting our spine in this way, however, with practice, it often becomes easier.

The importance of this physical self-support became clear to me as my wife was teaching our daughters how to write. She had read about teaching children to write on paper without lines, and was asking them to learn to write in straight lines across the page. This proved to be difficult for them at first and required a lot of practice before they could do it.

The children kept asking for lined paper and we kept insisting that they write in straight lines on blank paper because it teaches them how to support themselves and not rely on outside guidelines. While this exercise involved a physical process, it was presented in our home-schooling books as a way for children to develop support from inside of themselves, which would later translate into being more self-reliant.

As I watched our children struggle with getting their lines of writing straight, I saw that they had to develop a strength inside of them. When each one could finally do it, their personal character was more developed and they had a new sense of confidence in themselves. I finally understood some of my mother's old-fashioned insistence on sitting up straight and not putting our elbows on the dinner table.

To support the spine being upright and enable a deeper natural breath, it is helpful to tilt the pelvis slightly forward. This can be assisted naturally by putting more cushions under your seat if you are sitting cross legged on the floor, until you get a feeling of sitting on an incline, slightly leaning forward. Other sitting options that naturally tilt the pelvis forward include the short wooden kneeling benches with an angled seat, or the higher backless "computer desk chairs" that have a tilted pad for your knees and a higher one for your seat.

The four positions I have used include sitting cross legged on the floor, kneeling on the floor with the aid of a sitting bench or large cushion between the legs, sitting in a kneeling chair, or sitting on the front edge of a regular chair, with a small cushion to help tilt the pelvis slightly forward. Any of these positions can work well and I suggest that you experiment to find one that can work best for you.

I discourage people from sitting in "backjack" floor seats, or lying down for meditation because it usually results in drowsiness or lack of focus. The main idea with a sitting is to get the body in a position that it can take care of itself. No position will be entirely comfortable, and the longer your sitting period, the more likely it is that your body will experience some discomfort or pain.

Physical Pain or Discomfort

If you think that the goal of meditation is simply to discipline the body or endure pain, you are missing the point and will likely end up unconsciously feeding your ego and possibly damaging your body. As I have already discussed, our false sense of self loves to be the martyr, especially for the purpose of becoming more spiritual or holy. Spiritual practice often conjures up images of wearing itchy hair shirts, lying on beds of nails, or bathing in ice cold water. These practices may contribute to a sense of humility, and if used wisely can restrain the ego in a useful way. However, they are just as likely to increase a sense of self-righteous piety. Training the body to sit still is not the same as hardening ourselves to endure self-inflicted pain.

Sitting still is not an end in itself, but rather a means to become more aware of the subtle movements of your mind. You will notice as you begin to develop a sitting practice how the body constantly demands your attention and requires you to do something. This itch needs to be scratched, that leg moved, or this shoulder rubbed. Often, you simply feel restless or agitated and want to move to release some of this built-up energy.

Meditation practice begins with learning to let the body take care of itself. This is quite different from neglecting the body, or causing additional pain. As you try to sit still, you will likely notice a layer of restlessness just below your normal level of awareness, which you probably endure and generally explain as "just the way life is."

Everything is uncomfortable on some level, and no matter how much you try to adjust or control your situation to relieve that tension, often nothing seems to work. If you remain unconscious of this low level anxiety or discomfort, it can color your life experience with a layer of resentment. You might end up expressing your dissatisfaction with life as a resigned callousness or sarcasm, and it may come out as anger directed at the people closest to you. Many of us try to mask this discomfort with stimulants or distractions, which can easily become addictions.

As I described previously, meditation is about facing your uneasiness and confronting it directly. You are not adding anything painful, but simply allowing yourself to notice the discomfort which is *already there*. Normally when you face something unpleasant, you might harden yourself, bracing for the pain and meeting it with force. In awareness practice, you meet your discomfort by simply feeling it for a moment without any reaction.

You can begin by accepting the uncomfortable sensation, experiencing it directly (instead of thinking about it), and softening the body around it. This takes some practice for most of us as our habit has been to try to ignore or get rid of anything painful as soon as we notice it. Be aware of your impulse to turn away from discomfort and try gently receiving it instead.

Simply feel the moment to moment sensations that you are inclined to push away, and notice how they shift. Many of us fear that pain is solid and permanent and will never change. In reality, even the most intense physical pain is made up of momentary sensations that keep moving. As you learn to simply observe ordinary discomfort such as pain in the knee or an itch on the nose, you begin to experience it as merely sensations coming and going.

Rather than identifying an unpleasant sensation as "my pain" and building a story around it, include it as part of your experience. By relaxing and softening around it you may notice that it passes and realize that the discomfort in the body is merely a passing phenomenon that has nothing to do with who you are. In this way you can learn to accept a certain amount of physical pain without taking it personally. When you do not see yourself as a victim trapped in a painful body, you become more flexible and free, and the ordinary discomforts of life do not bother you as much.

Coming Into Your Body

Meditation practice is about coming into your body. Instead of denial of the body or bodily impulses, as some people believe, becoming more awake means receiving all sensations fully, and with equanimity. In being aware of sensations in your body and how they change moment to moment, your body becomes more alive and energized.

In sitting meditation it can be helpful to "breathe into" parts of your body that feel tight or painful. As you become more focused on breathing, you can fill your whole body with the breath, or direct it to some part of your body that needs to expand, relax, or heal. In imagining your breath going throughout your body, you connect yourself with your body and it often feels lighter and more free.

Being with pain or discomfort in the body in a conscious way *is* meditation. You do not have to get rid of the pain in order to meditate. Use whatever sensations arise as a way to focus your attention and develop mindfulness. The aim of meditation is simply a fuller sense of presence which includes everything in your experience of this moment, and nothing else.

As you sit in meditation, keep coming back to the body and taking it in as a whole, or in part. Notice where you are tensing up or contracting, and consciously relax and soften that area. This may be a constant task in the beginning, however, with time it becomes automatic, and relaxing tension can become a healthy reflex. As you are aware of tightening, you naturally feel the discomfort or pain of contracting yourself and your response can be to relieve the strain by simply letting it go.

Attachment to Pleasure

The Buddha talked about our basic mental conditioning as an aversion to pain and attachment to pleasure. We often think that the antidote to pain is to do something that gives us pleasurable sensations. While sitting meditation is not about causing more pain, it is a way to be with ordinary discomfort without immediately trying to drown it out with pleasure.

It is common to believe that becoming spiritual means giving up pleasure. This way of thinking often reinforces the ego by setting up an unconscious exchange. We think that we become more advanced spiritually the more pleasure we are willing to forego. I explained earlier that giving up desire is not an end itself, but simply a means to become more conscious of the conditioned impulses behind wanting what we do not have.

There is nothing wrong with pleasure. The problem arises when we automatically seek pleasure to drown out pain or relieve tension. This is how we become addicted to pleasant sensations and enter an endless cycle of pain and pleasure which ends up confining us.

As you learn to investigate painful sensations with simple awareness, and allow them to unfold naturally, you can apply the same process to pleasure. Notice how it feels to smell a flower, taste something sweet, feel hot water on your body, or drink something stimulating or relaxing. As you bring awareness to pleasant sensations, notice how they change, and see if you can allow them to pass, just as you do with pain.

The problem that most of us have with pleasure is we don't want it to pass. We often try to do the same thing that brought us pleasure over and over again, and in trying to hold on to it, we end up numbing ourselves to the pleasant sensation. Then we need more and more of whatever brings us pleasure in order to feel some degree of satisfaction, and this is the basis of most addictions.

As you apply mindfulness to pleasure, you develop the capacity to be fully with a pleasant sensation in this moment, and then allow it to pass. In so doing, you recognize that the pleasant sensation is not who you are either. This is not "my pleasure," it is merely another passing sensation.

Your consciousness stands apart from both pleasure and pain. This is the great freedom that comes with awareness. As you learn to identify as the witness, you see that pleasure and pain are not as different as you assumed. They are both temporary sensations in the body, and beneath them is a steady awareness that does not change or depend on outside conditions.

This core consciousness does not automatically recoil from pain or lunge after pleasure. It is free from the idea of a self that is either threatened or pleasured by outside circumstances, people, or events. Not being affected by pain or pleasure may seem dull and boring. Yet, in reality, it is full of a wonderful tranquility, stability, and sense of security that all of our worldly pursuits can only approximate.

Relaxing the Body

I often begin basic meditation instructions with a guided relaxation of the body. Guided visualizations can be helpful to get your body to settle and begin to calm your mind, however, these are quite different from what I would call meditation. I find it helpful to distinguish meditation as an act of complete surrender where you are not *doing* anything apart from directing your attention. I will say more about this later.

This guided visualization is usually done by listening to someone else say it while you close your eyes and follow the instructions. You may be able to get the idea from reading it here, and then try remembering the steps as you sit to meditate. Alternatively, you can access a voice recording of this visualization, and the meditation instructions that follow, on our web site: www.SkyMeadowRetreat.com

———————— •◆• ————————

Imagine that there is a large balloon filled with helium gas floating above your head, and a string is tied to the balloon which is also attached to the crown of your head. You can feel the balloon pulling your body so that your head, neck, and spine all extend upward. As you allow the balloon and string to carry some of your weight, imagine that the balloon is being pushed around by the wind and allow your upper body to sway with the wind as well.

Holding this image of the balloon gently pulling you upward, begin relaxing your body from your head downwards. Relax your face around your eyes, cheeks, and jaw, and let your whole face go. Allow your head to rest lightly on your neck, and your neck to rest lightly on your shoulders. Pick up your shoulders for a moment, and then let them drop, allowing any weight that you are carrying to slide off. Shake your shoulders out and let them relax. With your hands resting in your lap or on your legs, allow your arms to relax from your shoulders to your fingertips.

Imagine your spine as the trunk of a sapling tree, upright and strong, yet flexible and naturally curved. Allow your spine to carry the weight of your upper body, and relax the rest of your muscle tension, using only what is necessary to hold yourself up. Drop your shoulders back slightly so that your chest is open, and breathe deeply into your belly, letting go on the exhale. Allow the belly to be soft, open, and full. If there is anything constricting your abdomen, loosen it so that your belly can fully expand and contract with the breath.

Bring your awareness to your hips and rock the pelvis forward slightly so that you are sitting up on the edge of your seat. Notice how your belly sticks out, there is a curve forward in your lower spine, and your body has a slight lean forward. Feel how this posture allows your breath to flow naturally all the way down to your lower diaphragm. Then, let yourself sink into your seat and feel the support of the solid floor and earth beneath you.

Pay attention to your legs and notice if there is any pinching or constriction that you can alleviate by making an adjustment. Then relax your legs from your hips down to your toes, letting go of any tension. Notice how your lower body is supported from below and trust the earth to carry your weight, allowing yourself to sink into the floor beneath you.

Imagine roots growing down into the earth from all the points of contact between your body and the floor. Feel yourself being nourished and held secure by these roots going deep into the earth below you. See your upper body as the stem of a plant growing out of these roots, with your head as the flower reaching up toward the sun. Then let your body be, and allow it to take care of itself.

Mindfulness of Breathing

Once your body is upright and relaxed, focus your attention on hearing sound. Notice just the quality of sound, how it becomes louder and softer, and includes spaces and different tones. See if you can hear sound as simply vibrations coming and going, without thinking about or naming the source. Pay attention also to the sound of silence. What do you hear in the absence of sound?

Now bring your attention to your abdomen and feel the subtle rise and fall of your belly with each breath. Allow your body to breathe naturally, without holding or pushing your breath. Wait for your body to breathe, and notice what happens. On the exhale, allow the breath to go all the way out and pause a moment, letting the body decide when to take its next breath.

As the body breathes, pay attention to the skin and muscles in your belly stretching and expanding, and then contracting. How do you know that you are breathing? What are the sensations that you can feel with each breath? When does the in-breath or out-breath start and finish? These are not questions to be answered once, but rather a way to direct your attention to the moment-to-moment experience of the body breathing.

————————— •◆• —————————

If you cannot feel the movement of the breath in your belly, try adjusting your posture so that your spine is upright, with your pelvis slightly tilted forward and your belly hanging loose. Sitting your body up in this way can often open the channel for the breath to go down to the lower diaphragm. Allowing your diaphragm to do the work of breathing makes the process much easier and enables naturally deeper breathing and more complete relaxation.

It may take some practice to allow your body to breathe and your diaphragm to do the work. Often you might be tight in your belly or cut off from your lower diaphragm. Many of us tend to breathe primarily in our chest because we are stressed and trying to take in air quickly. Relaxing the body may begin with taking time to breathe fully and deeply. This step alone can benefit you greatly by increasing your oxygen supply and releasing built up tension.

If you cannot consistently feel the breath in your belly, you can find another place in your body where the sensations of breathing are clearer. You may be able to feel the air passing in and out of your nostrils, or your chest rising and falling, more than your belly moving. It does not matter where you place your attention as long as you can feel the body breathing there. Once you have chosen a place to put your attention, stay with it for a while and the sensation of breathing will grow stronger and clearer.

This type of meditation is often called mindfulness of breathing. It teaches you how to direct your awareness and keep it in one place, and this is the objective. You are not trying to understand or do anything with the breath. You are simply using the natural rhythm of the body breathing as a way to focus your attention.

Letting Go

Most of us have little experience with consciously placing or holding our attention. We learn how to focus on a task, a problem, or a game, as long as necessary to accomplish what we are trying to do. When we are not motivated to engage in this way, our minds tend to wander endlessly, jumping from one thing to another with no clear direction.

The practice of meditation teaches you how to stay focused and not dissipate your energy by the constant proliferation of thoughts. It is different from other pursuits as the aim is simply to stay focused, not to accomplish anything. You are not trying to become an expert breather or learn about the breath. You are using breathing as a way to practice paying attention to the present moment.

The breath is an excellent vehicle for learning awareness because it is simple, ordinary, involuntary, and continuous. Your body is always breathing, even when you are asleep or unconscious. If your body stops breathing for more than a few minutes, it will die. You do not need to tell your body to breathe, or make it happen. It just happens continuously by itself.

Focusing on an ordinary process like this, which is essential to life and self-perpetuating, enables you to experience a deeper level of surrender. This allows you to recognize that much of life happens without requiring any effort on your part. You can then see how much you have been trying to control or manage processes that do not need your oversight. And this insight enables you to let go further.

A simple surrender happens when you allow the body to breathe and become a witness to the process instead of a manager. This release of control encourages you to let go of other aspects of life that you may think you have to direct. It teaches you how let go of the rest of the body, and eventually release the mind itself. Seeing the impersonal, self-regulating nature of breathing enables you to see your mental thought process in a similar way. The mind is just thinking, with no effort or participation needed on your part.

Letting Go of Thought

Once you see that thought comes and goes, as does sound and the breath, it is easier not to get caught up in each thought and identify with it. Your thinking mind may have you hooked because you react to thoughts impulsively, assuming that you have to engage with them. In a similar way, you may be unconsciously making your body breathe when this is completely unnecessary.

The first thing that you may notice as the body settles down and you try to focus on your breathing is how easily distracted your mind is. As soon as a thought or image appears, you usually become engaged with it and can end up many minutes later realizing that you have lost contact with your body and breath completely. The thing to do at that moment is simply bring your attention back to the breath.

It does no good to chastise yourself or become upset for losing track of the breath. This is not a contest and no one is evaluating your progress. It does not matter how many times you find yourself distracted by thought. The point is simply that by establishing the intention to be aware of your body breathing, you create a container for the mind that enables you to notice when you are lost in thought.

Noticing that you are engaged in a thought process is what the practice of meditation is about. Without meditation, you would not be aware of your mind in this way at all.

There is nothing that you can do about thoughts, just as there is nothing that you can do about your breath. The mind will think, as that is its habit. All that you can do is to give it space and let go. In this way, meditation is about making room for thought, rather than shutting it out. If you try to shut out thought, you will only proliferate more thought and make the process more difficult.

The way to be with thought is just the same as with the breath. Simply allow a thought to be, without doing anything with it. See if you can simply be aware of a thought without adding or reacting to it. Notice what happens to the thought if you simply watch it.

For most of us, witnessing our thoughts dispassionately in this way is more difficult than releasing control of the body or breath. This is because we usually are more identified with our thoughts than with our physical experiences. As I suggested earlier, we think that our thoughts determine who we are, and so we become attached to them.

Your thoughts may determine your personality, however, your personality is not who you are. As soon as you can witness your thoughts with a bit of neutrality, you begin to see how the thinking mind is constantly engaged in building up this sense of individual self. Your personality and your thoughts are dependent on each other, and as you witness this process you begin to realize that part of you is not engaged in it. Some part of you is able to just observe.

Neutral Witness

Meditation is a tool for strengthening your capacity to be a neutral witness. At first it can seem that this part of you is weak, ineffective, flat, and boring. In contrast, your personality is full of drama, passion, and emotion. Yet, as you recognize how the dramatic, passionate, and emotional swings of your personal story infuse your life with fear, anxiety, and insecurity, the steady certainty of the neutral observer becomes more appealing.

In meditation practice, you are familiarizing yourself with the still point that lies in the center of the drama of your life. You are cultivating your capacity to see events and experiences from the perspective of this still center, without becoming involved. This may sound like you are missing all the fun, however, the experience of being the stillness around which all the drama spins is actually quite satisfying.

As you become more familiar with this quiet place of non-reaction, you can feel the rich sensuality of it. There is a sweet luscious quality to this "empty" place that is deeply pleasant and nourishing in a way that the dramatic swings of your personal story can never be.

Meditation becomes fun and interesting as you allow your mind to dwell in this place of soothing calm. There is a great satisfaction in allowing this moment to be complete and this breath to be enough. The mind then naturally gravitates toward the present because it feels comfortable there. This experience is like coming home to a place that you forgot was there, but have been yearning for all of your life.

Cultivating Insight

In the practice of Insight Meditation or Vipassana as taught by the Buddha, you bring your attention back to a present moment experience again and again in order to develop a steady field of awareness that you can rest in and refer to. This is similar to the way a person might hold a melody line in singing, a steady note in chanting, or a base rhythm in drumming which others can harmonize or improvise from.

Once enough people are singing the melody together or drumming in the same base rhythm, a field is created that holds all the musicians and lifts them up effortlessly. A similar kind of buoyancy happens in traditional group activities such as folk dancing, or musical chanting. This is the uplifting experience of singing, chanting, drumming, or dancing together that so many cultures and spiritual groups have repeated throughout human history.

Once you learn to steady your awareness in the present moment, this creates an energy field that lifts you up a bit and gives your mind a place to rest which is free from fear, worry, or anxiety. From this perspective you can look at situations in your life from an entirely new angle. As I explained earlier, seeing your usual life dilemmas from a new perspective is often enough to free you from their heavy weight. This is what happened to me in the monastery when the big life questions of meaning and purpose suddenly lifted from me simply because I was seeing them from the perspective of present moment awareness.

The goal of meditation is presence. As you develop presence, the stories running through your mind which shape and control your life lose their urgency and meaning. There is a certainty in the stillness of this moment that puts to rest doubt and fear and answers your deepest longings.

Many of us are disillusioned with life and carry a deep sense of disappointment about things not going the way that we wanted them to. The Buddha says that if you are feeling this sense of disillusionment, there is nothing wrong with you or your situation. Disillusionment means that you are paying attention and are on the right track. He points out that nothing here is stable or solid, and in that sense nothing is real. Therefore, all worldly pursuits eventually lead to disappointment, loss, and grief.

However, the Buddha's message does not end here. This is not where you finish, but rather where you begin. He continues to point out that all of your disappointments result from looking in the wrong place for contentment. You are caught up in a story about a world that is not real, and imagine yourself to be an isolated character in this story, constantly looking for something permanent and solid in a universe of ephemeral things.

Meanwhile, the contentment that you seek is already here with you. It is as close as each breath and as immediate as this moment. You simply have to relax the conditioned thought patterns that keep you looking in the past or future. Then true contentment appears and you discover that it is the very ground you have been standing upon all along.

This kind of insight has a much different quality than most of our ideas about the way things are. You can think about the world being an illusion fabricated by your mechanical perceptions, yet until you experience this directly for yourself, it remains merely an idea that you either believe in or not. When you glimpse the ephemeral nature of this world and are mindful of how each experience arises and passes away, that is insight. After such a revelation, you can never see yourself or your surroundings in quite the same way again.

Living Without a Story

Meditation is a way to cultivate insights which reveal a reality that is beyond perception, and therefore is stable and sure. It is a gradual process for most of us simply because revealing the fleeting nature of our world too quickly would cause us great distress. So we build a base of mindful awareness which enables us to refer to the present moment instead of to the elaborate story about our past and future. As our unfiltered experience of this moment becomes more stable, it becomes possible to release our story with less fear, because we are already standing outside of it.

The freedom, peace, and security offered by meditation comes from being grounded in your body in this present moment, instead of caught up in your thinking mind. As soon as you experience yourself without a story, your whole world changes. You see that the stress, fear, anxiety, doubt, and pain that you were struggling so hard to overcome only existed within that story. In that sense, they were fabrications of your mind and were not real.

To many of you, this may sound too simple to be realistic. You can only imagine your problems going away by doing something about them. The idea of simply letting them go sounds like denial, avoidance, or fantasy. Yet this is only because you have not experienced your own full presence.

It is your thoughts which are perpetuating a fantasy of you as an isolated personality having to struggle to get your needs met in an often hostile and unforgiving world. The resolution that comes from standing apart from your thoughts is not superficial or make-believe. Once you stand in full awareness of the present moment, you will feel a sense of certainty that reveals the story you believe in now as nothing more than a random set of conclusions with no basis in reality. In your own presence no thought can substitute for what you already know, and perception is not necessary to interpret reality.

24

Establishing a Meditation Practice

Meditation can be a difficult discipline to develop and it is particularly challenging to do so on your own. You may read a book like this and want to start meditating, so you try doing it by yourself. While it can be useful to sit silently and begin to feel your body breathing, this also may be the most difficult way to begin. It is easy to become discouraged and give up after a few attempts because your body hurts and your thinking mind proves to be so unruly.

Meditation Retreat

It can help to begin a meditation practice with an intensive retreat. In the tradition of Insight Meditation, which originated in the Buddhist monasteries of Southeast Asia, it has become a common practice to do intensive silent retreats with a group of people, guided by a teacher. The benefit of this is enormous. There is the support of the community of other people meditating, and a teacher who has gone through many such retreats and can offer inspiration and guidance.

Sitting in silence for a number of days can appear overwhelming. Yet, this is merely the way it looks from your rational perspective. You can only imagine the extreme boredom and discomfort that would arise, and the whole idea seems quite impossible. However, when you actually sit still for this long, something shifts inside, and the experience usually turns out to be quite different than you thought it would.

The beginning of an intensive meditation retreat is often the most difficult time. Your body may be tight and uncomfortable and your mind scattered by thoughts of every kind. It can take a few days of sitting still before the body and mind calm down. However, once the mind surrenders to the limited conditions of a structured retreat, things generally become easier and you usually discover a great joy in the silence and stillness that you could not have imagined. This is the experience of your own presence which many of us overlook and undervalue in our race toward becoming somebody in the world. It is quite beautiful and satisfying and can fill you with a light that you never knew existed inside of you.

The most difficult part of a retreat can be just staying with it, no matter what the mind tells you to do. It certainly does not seem that sitting still in silence with a group of people for days could result in such a pure experience of satisfaction or joy. Yet, that is exactly what can happen when you commit to stay and participate in the schedule of an intensive retreat. It is an experience that you have to do for yourself before it will make any sense. It is one of those things you just have to try on faith, and not think about it too much.

Dealing with a Restless Body and Busy Mind

Most of us find our body restless and unable to sit still because we simply are not used to sitting quietly in one position without moving for this long. As discussed earlier, it helps to be patient with your body and approach it by softening, rather than tightening. I find it useful to breathe into any tight or painful place in my body and gently soften the muscles as I notice discomfort.

Try responding to your body's agitation as part of the practice, rather than merely an obstacle to be overcome in order to meditate. Indeed the process required to quiet the body is exactly the process that you are trying to learn. Instead of giving it orders, making demands, or trying to control the body, simply be present with it. Work with your body, befriend it, and make it into an ally.

If you stay sitting even though you are uncomfortable, and keep softening instead of tightening, the resistance of the body gradually diminishes and sitting still becomes easier. This gentle approach to discipline is not just to get the body to behave. It is teaching you new way to approach life.

It is the same with the mind. You may see thoughts as enemies invading your peace, or temptations luring you away from your purpose. You might attack them with force, trying to make them go away, or judge yourself harshly for becoming lost in thought so often. Yet, if you see thoughts as another obstacle to overcome on your way to enlightenment, you are missing the point.

Meditation is simply the practice of being fully present with what is. Most of us don't know what this is like because we only know how to *think about* what is. You may imagine that meditation means stilling the body, quieting the mind, or achieving one pointed concentration. This goal oriented thinking uses your programmed mind, however, and you cannot use the program to undo the programming.

Accepting What Is

It is difficult to just *be* with what is because there is nothing familiar about it. Yet, it is actually the most natural and ordinary thing that you can do. It simply means accepting everything that comes into your awareness, each body sensation or thought, without *doing* anything about it. In order to accept each experience as it is, it helps to stop identifying with the body sensation as *my* pain, or the thought as *my* thought. It is the practice of bringing your attention back to a simple experience like the breath that enables this to happen.

It is important to understand, however, that focusing on breathing sensations is not an end in itself. Most of us find it impossible at first to be aware of the breath with any consistency because the thoughts are so compelling and overwhelming. So, begin by simply being aware that you are thinking. That is all. Notice the thoughts and simply be aware that *these are thoughts*.

Just be aware of a thought and notice how compelling that thought is. Then notice the next one in the same way. You can soon notice the vast array of thoughts that run continuously through your mind at any moment and their random and chaotic nature. Then see if you can loosen your grip on an individual thought, and gradually let it go altogether. This may take some time, so be patient. There is no rush. There is nothing else to do. This *is* meditation.

It is easy to become discouraged because the flood of thoughts is so overwhelming and you may only occasionally be able to interrupt a thought in order to focus on the breath. At that point, just widen your focus to include the thoughts. Instead of trying to get rid of them so that you can return to your breath, let the *thoughts themselves* be the focus.

When you get caught up in the content and become emotionally involved in a thought, you will find yourself slipping back into a sleepy sort of trance. This is where the simple form of meditation can be useful. The fact that you are sitting still and upright with an intention to mediate offers you a perspective that you don't usually get in the busy rush of your daily life. When you come out of your thought-induced trance again, you are able to recognize that you were in one.

To meditate, you don't have to force yourself to pay attention to just one thing. This kind of one-pointed awareness helps focus the mind and strengthen concentration in order to access wisdom and insight. Yet, this level of focus is not the goal of meditation. It is a capacity that grows gradually, out of your desire to be more present and fully alive.

Coming Out of the Trance

When I go into a movie theatre and watch a good movie, I become drawn into the story and entranced by it as though it were real. I like movies because they offer a virtual world that takes me away from my normal one. Watching a movie is especially appealing when my life feels stressful or I am in emotional pain. Stepping into another world like this and watching other people's lives can feel like a relief from the pressure and stress of my life.

The next time that you go to a movie theatre, pay attention to your experience of coming out after the show, walking back onto the street, and interacting with real people again. Notice how you feel when the movie ends and you re-enter your world. I often experience a strong sense of disorientation accompanied by some uneasiness at being back in the world. There is a sense that I was dreaming or somehow asleep, and am just waking up again.

This is the same experience that I have when I am meditating and realize that I have just been deeply engaged in thought. I first remember my body and realize that I am sitting, and then remember my breath. Once I do this, I am able to see the trance-like state of thinking for what it is. It may be more dramatic and attractive than the discomfort or boredom of sitting still and being aware of my breath over and over again. Yet, it is *not real.*

The aim of meditation is simply to show you that your thoughts are not real. And it is the virtual nature of thought that ultimately makes you lose interest in it. In meditation you are simply isolating your thought process so that you can see how limited it is. With a movie this is easy because it is not running continuously and sooner or later you leave the theatre or turn off the television. Your thoughts are more difficult to escape because they are continuously with you and you have no way to turn them off.

Gradually by becoming aware of thoughts instead of always caught up in the content of them, you can develop a taste for reality. Imagine that you lived in the movie theatre or in front of your television and once a day you walked away and went outside. You would slowly get used to the idea that there is a world apart from the one on the screen that is more real. And eventually that real world would become more interesting to you because it is *alive.*

Daily Meditation Practice

Once you have sat through an intensive silent retreat for a number of days at a time, a daily sitting meditation practice becomes easier and more satisfying. You may find that you look forward to and are drawn to meditate, rather than dreading it and having to force yourself to sit. I encourage students new to meditation practice to lower your expectations for how long you sit each day, and suggest that you begin with short sittings which you are more likely to complete. Once you have sat an intensive retreat with a group and a teacher, and have received detailed instructions and support, try sitting for just five or ten minutes a day on your own.

It may help to designate a sitting place and a regular time of day so that your mind and body become used to being still when you sit there at that time. Make your sitting place comfortable using cushions, a bench, or chair, and find a place where distractions are minimized.

We each have different circumstances in our living situations, so do not try to make your sitting space fit some model of perfection before you can begin. Do the best you can with what you have, and trust that the situation will present you with exactly what you need so that you can become more aware. The most important part of a daily sitting practice is your own intention. If you want to learn to be still, you certainly can, regardless of the circumstances within or around you.

I recommend that you set a timer for the amount of time that you intend to sit, and then stick with that time, no matter what. Regardless of how much time you determine to meditate, your mind will likely tell you to get up and do something urgent before the allotted time is up. That is why it is not as important how long you sit, but that you sit for the entire time that you commit to. Every time you stay with your commitment instead of reacting to the commands of your perceptual mind, you weaken the control that mind has over you. This is a significant step toward freedom.

Sitting for longer periods can be useful to deepen the stillness and train yourself to be comfortable with your own presence. This will come more gently and easily if you approach it gradually. Forcing or pushing yourself is a habit that comes directly from the conditioning of perceptual mind. This mind only knows how to manipulate and control through domination, yet awareness does not respond to such pressure.

If you try to approach awareness using your usual ways of making things happen, you are likely to realize a sense of defeat and give up on meditation altogether. For this reason, I suggest that you start with a shorter time which is manageable for you given your daily schedule. You can increase the time that you sit once you feel more comfortable and confident and feel a natural urge to meditate longer.

Our Habit of Evaluation

When you take on a spiritual practice like meditation, and make an internal commitment to it, your perceptual mind will naturally want to measure your progress and establish levels of proficiency. It will try to compare your ability to meditate with that of other people in its constant struggle to establish itself as worthy. This unconscious habit can make meditation just another arduous task to master.

While evaluating yourself may strengthen your discipline, it leaves you back where you started in the end. This is because you are using the practice of meditation to feed your sense of self by setting up another obstacle for the ego to conquer. Instead of releasing your concept of self, you unconsciously enhance it, and this is not what meditation or spiritual practice is for. It is simply for letting your false sense of self dissolve in the light of direct awareness.

It is important to be aware of your habit of evaluation and need for measurements and comparisons, and pay close attention to the way that these thought patterns can take control of your spiritual practice. Any comparison or evaluation on a spiritual path is likely to lock you more deeply into the very perceptual mechanism that you are trying to free yourself from. It is not easy to let go of the habit of comparative measurement, and there is no need to judge yourself harshly when you notice your mind doing this. However, it is important to drop any system of evaluation as soon as you notice yourself getting caught up in it.

Meditation has no levels and there is no body of knowledge to memorize or set of skills to master. It is much too simple for all this. It has to do only with being fully present in each moment, with no past or future, or any idea of what should happen next. This is actually the easiest and most natural thing for you to do. However, it can feel difficult and strange because your habit for so long has been to continuously review, plan, and rehearse your life.

The only evaluation that I think is useful in meditation practice is to know if you are fully in the present moment, being aware of your direct experience, or if you are engaged in thought. Once you can feel the difference, you have a choice to stay with the thought or become present. And this is a choice that you did not have before.

After a while, it becomes a habit to let go of thought and return to a present sensation. You won't lose your ability to think. Your thoughts will merely cease to dominate your experience, and reality will become more interesting than your conclusions *about* reality.

Expanding the Practice of Meditation

You can expand your meditation practice by bringing awareness into every moment of your life. This is not a task to accomplish, it is merely a natural progression toward being more fully conscious and awake. You can stretch the edges of meditation by taking it out of retreat, off your sitting place, and into daily life activities. This can be as simple as recognizing the sensation of breathing while walking down the street, driving the car, or talking on the phone. You can notice the taste, smell, and color of the food you that are eating, and feel your feet touching the ground and the weight of your body against the floor throughout the day.

————————— •◆• —————————

Right now, see if you can feel your hands, feet, head, and neck. Notice where they are and how they feel.

Notice the simple sensations of pressure, heat, heaviness, or lightness in your body. What is the feeling of this book in your hands, your bottom on the seat, and your feet and legs underneath you?

What does your belly feel like right now? How are your shoulders, or back? Especially notice any tightness or holding, and gently relax and soften that place.

———————— •◆• ————————

Meditation is simply bringing your attention to what is happening in this moment. This kind of awareness contains no thought, as it occurs before thought can happen. It is simply the knowing of a sensation without any judgments about it or concepts explaining what it is.

Awareness can happen while you are in life and doing your daily routine. After a bit of practice you don't need to stop what you are doing or make any changes other than perhaps slowing down a bit, remembering to notice, and breathing. Simple awareness slowly becomes more familiar and replaces the debilitating habits of worry, fear, planning, and remembering. Your own presence becomes more interesting and satisfying than any of these, and what is happening in this moment increasingly holds your attention because it is real.

Breaking Habits of Thought

You can extend your meditation practice further and help yourself grow in consciousness by noticing when your mind is fixing its attention on something that you want which is not here now. Try interrupting this habit and replacing it with simple gratitude for what is right in front of you at this moment.

It becomes easier to notice when you are craving what you do not have once you learn what this feels like in your body and recognize the emotions that accompany this thought. There is usually a feeling of discomfort and uneasiness with what is going on, and a strong pull to be somewhere else. I feel it often as a tight place of resistance in my body, and a sense of agitation or unrest inside of me. In these moments I cannot accept the situation that I am in and want to change it.

When I first notice this internal unrest, before I get caught up with focusing on what I want that I don't have, I have a chance to stop, breathe, and relax the tight place inside me for a moment. This is usually enough to interrupt the pattern so that I can see it more clearly. Once I can see that I am in this unconscious pattern again, I can choose to respond differently. This is where it gets interesting and fun. I realize that I don't have to do what I have always done in this situation, and I don't have to let my perceptual mind dictate my response.

It can also be a bit frightening at this point because I suddenly find myself in new territory. I am off the beaten track of my unconscious mental habits and there is both the sense of freedom, and the fear of the unknown. Suddenly there are new possibilities before me that I did not know existed, and with these is the potential for real change. This is what makes it exciting. There is actually the possibility for something completely different to happen in my life.

Cultivating an Attitude of Gratitude

Once you recognize that the pattern of desiring what you don't have is running in your thoughts, you can refocus your attention on what you have right in front of you that *is* working. No matter what the situation, there is always something that is working well for you in each moment. Cultivating gratitude is simply learning to find something good that you have now, and focus on it for a moment. These are usually small and ordinary blessings that you may overlook because your habit is to focus on the big and dramatic events in life.

———————— •◆• ————————

Stop for a moment now, and notice something that is working for you. It doesn't have to be earth-shaking, and it does not have to affect anyone other than you in this moment. It could be the way that you are sitting, the light in the room, the clothes that you are wearing, or the feeling of this book in your hand. It may be what you just ate, or the fact that you have time to sit and read, or something in this book that strikes a chord in you. It can be as simple as the relief of taking a breath of air.

Don't look for a new thrill or peak experience. Simply try to identify one thing in this moment that you don't want to change. Set this book down, look around you, feel your body from the inside, and find one thing that is O.K. as it is, right now.

Once you find something to be grateful for, just feel it for a moment and do not concern yourself about whether it is going to last or if anyone else thinks it is good. This is personal to you, and only for this moment. It may all change in the next moment, and in fact it likely will. Just be with the feeling that this one thing is alright. Then simply be thankful that it is so.

———————— •◆• ————————

If you have just done this simple exercise, you will likely notice a subtle sense of ease and satisfaction. There is usually a lightness and joy that just *is*, with no strings attached to it. This is the result of interrupting the mental habit of always wanting what you do not have.

Once you step away from this pattern, there is the possibility of appreciation for what you *do* have, and an opportunity for contentment with this moment. You may notice that right now the situation in front of you is not so bad. And this takes your focus off of what your mind is telling you that you need to fix or change in order to be happy.

Cultivating gratitude in this way does not mean that you cannot have new things or experiences, or follow your desires. Too often, spiritual practice becomes defined by perception as a sacrifice of what we want or need in life. As discussed earlier, many of us conceptualize spirituality as a linear exchange where we have to suffer in order to be worthy and holy. Yet, this merely feeds the ego by giving it the identity of the one who is making a noble sacrifice.

On a spiritual path, you still have urges for change or things that you want or need, and all these can happen. Being grateful and content with what you have does not mean that is all that you ever get. In fact, my experience is that as soon as I am content with what I have already, there is a natural opening for me to receive more.

All that you are learning to do with this simple practice of appreciation is to be fully with what you have. You are cultivating the capacity to receive and feel the fullness that comes from getting what you want. If you don't stop to let this in, you just blindly go on wanting the next thing with no ability to take in what you get. The tragedy of your conditioned mind is that there is no possibility for satisfaction in this cycle of endless wanting. You just keep on wanting more and it can never be enough because you don't know how to appreciate what you already have.

Undoing Opposition

Another conditioned thought pattern that you can approach more consciously is your need for an enemy or opposing force in order to define yourself. Once you notice how this habit of opposition keeps you focused on imagined enemies, you can more easily interrupt it and make new choices.

For many of us our conditioning keeps our attention on resisting opposition and maintaining a rigid defense system in order to keep others from hurting us. This can be one of the most difficult habits of mind to uproot because we really believe that if we do not defend ourselves, we will be destroyed.

We have already looked at the notion of being defenseless, or "turning the other cheek," as Christ is said to have taught, as a way of interrupting this unconscious pattern. A further step toward freeing yourself from this habit of creating enemies is to look at people who you think are opposing you with compassion, instead of fear and hatred.

Abraham Lincoln is reported to have said; "I destroy my enemies when I make them my friends." This is not a formula for being spiritual or accumulating credits for entrance into heaven. It is the only way that really works to undo opposition. Look at human history and your own experiences with those whom you have seen as your enemies. When you enter into a battle of wills for control and dominance, you often feed a struggle that never ends.

Many of us have an instinctual approach to protecting our security by destroying our opposition. Yet once you engage in this kind of war with your perceived opponent, you only add to the sense of instability and danger in your life. By attacking your enemy, you increase the likelihood that they will attack you back, and in the end this only serves to make you less secure.

Your completion lies in recognizing yourself as inherently part of the whole, not as a separate individual fighting for your personal survival. The separation of this whole into competing parts always undermines your larger self and makes you feel more vulnerable and isolated. Instead of unconsciously feeding this habit, you can learn to see it as a programmed response that is useful only in maintaining the illusion of a separate ego.

Setting Down Defenses

You can help yourself move in this direction by stretching to open your heart to those who appear to threaten you with harm. This will naturally seem counter-intuitive and even foolish at first. It takes courage and a leap of faith to risk being vulnerable in the face of opposition instead of striking out against it. Yet, if you refrain from striking back, you may begin to see your imagined enemies as wounded people who see *you* as *their* enemy. They are merely attacking you in order to defend themselves because they are afraid and think that you mean to do them harm.

Think for a moment of how you might respond to a two-year-old boy who is trying to hit you. Most likely, you would not try to hit the child back. You would notice that he feels hurt, frustrated, or angry, and is striking out at you because he does not know what else to do. And you would probably respond by having compassion for the child and trying to soothe his hurt.

However, if the person trying to hit you is a man, your response tends to be entirely different. This man is also hurt, frustrated, or angry, and thinks that striking out against you will somehow solve his problem. Yet it is much more difficult not to defend yourself or attack back when another adult seems to be threatening you. To shift your response pattern, you can consciously focus on the other person as someone who is wounded and in need of healing. This can help you to feel a sense of understanding and compassion for his pain.

This does not mean that you become a doormat and never stand up for yourself. You can still say "no," and protect yourself from harm by asserting your personal boundaries. When you think someone is attacking you, simply chose not to feed violence with more violence. There is a way to maintain a healthy boundary with other people who seem to be threatening you that also allows you to keep your heart open to them.

Loving your enemy, or turning the other cheek, will not work to shift your perspective if you approach it as a formula. Then it becomes a morality that you try to follow outwardly in order to be righteous or more holy, while inside you are still threatened by the other person. It is wise to approach this gently without trying to be good, and simply see if you can stretch yourself a bit beyond your normal comfort level.

You can start by finding one thing about a person who seems threatening that you like or can relate to. Don't try to accept every part of them. Simply look for some quality or characteristic that you can appreciate, perhaps something they once said or did. Just sit with that and allow yourself to feel the small spark of goodness in them.

Closing your heart to someone who appears threatening does not make you safer. It only tends to fragment and constrict your world and make you feel more cramped and divided. By leaning into your edge of comfort you invite real change. You stretch yourself beyond what you think you know, and often discover something entirely new. When you are willing to challenge your basic assumptions about what is safe and what will make you secure and happy, you make space for yourself to grow, and your life becomes more full and complete.

Re-Membering Yourself

Being with someone who has hurt or upset you without defending yourself or attacking them is not for the purpose of being good or holy. It is not about overriding your defensive or judgmental responses and trying to be more accepting. It is about remembering who you really are.

If we are all individual cells in a single body, then shutting another person out of your heart ultimately damages yourself, because it keeps you from being whole. Most of the time we cannot see that we are connected in this way because of the limits of perception. Yet, if you could see, you would no sooner make someone an enemy than you would cut off your finger or ear.

In the end, stretching yourself and challenging your habitual ways of responding is for your own good. There is no "other person" who is separate from you. God is all of us together, and if you separate someone out, you simply make God unavailable to you.

You cannot really fragment or destroy the whole. You can only imagine that you are separate and fighting against others for your survival. In reality, your survival is never in question because you are part of an eternal, infinite whole. You simply have to recognize that this is so.

25

Spiritual Growth

The idea of spiritual growth is that we each contain the seed of a unique being that is part of the whole we might call the universe, or God. Our essence longs to grow into its complete form, just as a kernel of corn wants to grow into a corn plant. If we provide the right conditions for the corn, giving it earth, water, warmth, and sunlight, it grows into a plant by itself. It has within it all that it needs to do this. And, what an astonishing miracle that a large corn stalk could grow from a small kernel!

Just so, there is a potential greatness that lies dormant inside each one of us, waiting for the right conditions to grow into its completion. In our case, "growth" means stripping away our illusions in order to reveal what is real and true about ourselves. We already *are* in our whole state, and are merely asleep to this fact, dreaming an illusion of a limited, vulnerable, and isolated person inside a fragile body. There is no way to describe this reality because of the limits of perception, so the idea of a seed growing into maturity gives our mind an image of the process of completion that it can relate to.

If you look at a corn kernel, and then look at a corn stalk, there is no similarity. The corn plant is an entirely new being, with nothing visible left of the seed. We see other examples of this in nature all around us. A frog begins as an egg, turns into a tadpole, and then sprouts legs, loses its tail, and jumps out of the water to live on land. A butterfly begins also as an egg, becomes a caterpillar, and then spins itself into a cocoon, out of which emerges a mature butterfly.

In all these miracles of nature, one being is transformed into an entirely different one. The corn seed, tadpole, and caterpillar likely could never imagine themselves as a corn plant, frog, or butterfly, just as we cannot imagine the beings that we are becoming. We can only surrender ourselves to a process that we do not understand, and be willing to let go of the form that we have now in order to become something larger and more complete.

Transformation

In the summer, I often find beautiful black and yellow caterpillars feeding on the wild milkweed plants growing in the fields around my farm, and I usually bring a few of them inside to watch their transformation. I give them fresh milkweed to eat and watch them grow larger until they become big, fat, and long. Then they climb to a high branch or leaf and attach one end of their bodies with a strong, silky thread. At this point they simply hang upside down with their head curled under in the shape of the letter J, often for days. Suddenly one day, their whole body begins to shake, and in a matter of fifteen minutes, they shed their outer skin and transform into a beautiful, translucent, emerald green chrysalis with intricate gold leaf designs on it.

The chrysalis hangs still for ten days or so, and gradually becomes almost black in color. Then one day it begins to move, and out emerges a fully formed Monarch butterfly with its wings tightly furled. The butterfly hangs upside down for some hours to allow its wings to unfold and become rigid enough to enable it to fly. And then, in one miraculous moment, this stunningly beautiful creature takes wing and begins to float and fly in the air. I love to watch this moment and imagine how terrifying and ecstatic this entirely new experience must be for this butterfly that used to inch its way slowly over the ground as a worm.

Watching the caterpillars turn into butterflies helps me to remember my own process of waking up. The most significant part that I have to play in my own transformation is simply allowing it to happen. Like the caterpillar, my part is to know when to surrender my former self in order to become something larger, with more beauty and capacity than I could ever dream of.

In the teachings of the Buddha, he suggests that it may take lifetimes of struggle and suffering in different forms before a human becomes willing to undergo such a radical surrender. Yet, it is the inevitable destiny of each one of us to eventually transform into our whole complete self.

Letting Our Self be Undone

Our life here as separate individuals inhabiting bodies with private minds is like that of the caterpillar. We stretch and grow until we realize that we have gone as far as we can go in this form. The signals for us that we have reached this stage are when we feel disillusioned with the world and it starts to lose interest. We begin to sense that we are going in circles and nothing is really changing. We seem to be repeating the same experiences over and over again. And, indeed, this is what is happening as the programmed perceptual mind keeps repeating the same patterns endlessly, with only the content changing.

This experience of being stuck in a rut, repeating the same thing day after day, is common for most of us. This is why we find so many ways to stimulate or distract ourselves and become so easily addicted to them. When it becomes uncomfortable enough for us that we cannot function well in the world, we call it anxiety or depression. We may then take prescribed medications that diminish the discomfort and allow us to get by without so much emotional pain. Yet, we often do not follow up with a deeper look at how to address the cause of our symptoms.

We don't have an explanation in our Western culture for the experience of feeling blocked in our development and coming to a threshold in our growth. We have few ways to recognize or understand spiritual growth or emotional maturity. So, naturally, when this happens we think that there is something wrong with us, and we often try to make the symptoms or feelings of discomfort go away.

The Buddha described this condition we are in as the wheel of life, and characterized it as an endless cycle of sorrow, loss, and suffering. He was not trying to bring us down but simply to get us to pay attention to the condition that we find ourselves in. His message is entirely positive as it focuses on the idea that all the pain which we experience here is merely the result of our mental formatting causing us to repeat endlessly the same patterns. He teaches that there is a way to be free of this, and therefore free ourselves of any kind of suffering.

The Nature of Transformation

When you begin to understand the nature of the transformation that the Buddha, Christ, and other teachers have gone through, you see that this process cannot be formulated and there is nothing that you can do to *make* it happen. It does not require your understanding and there is nothing that you need to learn or perfect. The caterpillar does not *try* to become a butterfly, the corn a plant, or the tadpole a frog. They somehow recognize their larger destiny and simply become willing to surrender their form, perhaps with no idea of what will happen next.

You cannot learn *how* to transform yourself. It is a process that happens naturally on its own, and is happening to you whether you recognize it or not. All that you can do is to be conscious or unconscious that you are transforming, and either allow or block the experience.

This same idea is conveyed beautifully in the story that we tell about the death and rebirth of Christ. As Jesus hanged on the cross waiting to die, he was heard to exclaim, "Father, why hast thou forsaken me?" It seems that he did not understand at this point what was happening to him, or why he had to go through this painful experience. At the same time, he willingly surrendered to it, riding into Jerusalem on his own, allowing the kiss from Judas, and carrying his own cross without resistance. After he died, his body was sealed into a tomb with a large stone. And when his followers visited the tomb the next day, they found the stone rolled away and his body no longer there.

Shortly afterward, Christ found his disciples and visited them in his new form. He was reported to have told one of his followers not to touch him yet, as he had not fully come into his new being. Then the story goes that he talked and ate and drank with his friends, just as he was before his crucifixion. Clearly, Christ was demonstrating for us the process of transformation that we all must go through to become fully who we are. It is a process of surrendering to what feels like death, and allowing a rebirth into a new realization that we are not this body and therefore cannot die.

This is the freedom promised by spiritual transformation. We are no longer restricted by the body, or any form, and realize ourselves as unlimited beings. While this freedom is a personal choice and cannot be formulated or forced, it is also our natural, unconditioned state of being. It is who we are in reality, and our lives will not feel complete until we realize it.

Conditions for Growth

You cannot make your growth happen through belief in a set of ideals or by following a formula. However, you can seek and find the conditions that support and enable it. A corn seed sitting on a shelf will not grow into a corn stalk, as a monarch caterpillar in a field without milkweed cannot grow into a butterfly, and a frog egg, taken out of water, cannot mature into a frog.

So, a human being who is constantly subjected to the judgments and evaluations of perceptual mind cannot transform into wholeness. Perception obscures the real cause of fear and anxiety, and keeps us chasing one false solution after another, always promising that the one that will work is just around the next corner.

In order to grow beyond perception, it is useful to see that your own thought patterns and unconscious beliefs are the cause of your dilemma. Once you see this, you can explore ways to get out from under the grip of your often harsh and judgmental mind. You may try to do this unconsciously, by numbing your thoughts with drugs, alcohol, stimulants, or medication. Or you might distract yourself from your judgments and evaluations through music, games, or other entertainment.

The problem with these approaches is that they work only temporarily, and so you need to repeat them over and over again. This is how these habits become addictions that you cannot stop, even though you sense that they are hurting you. When you approach the problem of your judging mind from this angle, you are trying to overcome its power over you by weakening your own mental capacity. This, in turn, weakens you and makes you less able to muster the courage and will to break free of the debilitating power of these conditioned thought patterns.

This is similar to the way in which Western medical practice uses chemotherapy to attack cancer. Our approach to problems with our body or mind is often to weaken the whole system. We see that some part of the system is causing the problem, but we cannot isolate that from the rest, so we try to minimize the damage by suppressing the energy that is feeding it.

Many of our medical practices merely seek to reduce or suppress the symptoms, rather than addressing the underlying cause. While this may give us some relief, and can work in some cases to overcome the problem, often the result is that we lose vital energy and diminish our inherent integrity.

Psychiatric Medications

Many of us are constricting ourselves with our thoughts and desperately want to be free. As suggested before, we often do not realize that it is our thoughts binding us, so we don't think to look there. If we do see that it is our mind causing the pain, we often don't know how to deal with that effectively.

Drugs and alcohol are ways that we commonly "self-medicate" when life becomes too overwhelming or stressful. Prescribed medications offer a more studied and thoughtful approach based on scientific research, yet they can have a similar appeal and a similar effect. Our society tends to use medication as a first resource because it seems to make the problem go away quickly and we don't have to interrupt our busy life and take time to deal with our over-active mind.

This thinking assumes that happiness and security are attained through material success or having a normally functioning life. If our mind is a problem and we feel depressed or anxious most of the time, the answer is to get rid of the problem as quickly and efficiently as possible. So we have developed pills that suppress the symptoms and allow us to be productive and fit into the world around us.

To be fair, psychiatric medication may prevent painful mental breakdowns and allow us to function in the world again, and this can provide a wonderful reprieve from suffering. It is possible that medications can give us enough space from chronic fear or anxiety to enable us to explore the deeper cause of our distress. Yet, if we use medication as the only solution, we tend to create an unhealthy dependency.

The development and wide-spread use of psychiatric drugs for treating mental suffering is a natural response based on the assumptions of Western medicine. This approach to healing tends to see pain as the problem and focuses on getting rid of it. Such a response is an obvious and forgivable mistake, as it does appear that suffering is bad and immediate relief is good. However, when we act on this assumption, we miss the meaning and message in our discomfort and often unknowingly perpetuate our suffering by delaying a true healing.

Our Need for Meaning

As suggested earlier, Western civilization lacks a deeper spiritual wisdom. The teachings of Christ have been largely reduced by the institution of religion to overly-simplistic platitudes or moralities that do not effectively address our distress here and now. And science is not capable of addressing our need for meaning or purpose because that is personal and beyond the range of objective inquiry.

While Western medicine has developed amazing technologies for repairing or manipulating the physical body, we have few effective remedies for mental or emotional suffering. We often respond to our basic need for meaning by distracting ourselves with the aspirations of our ego, and simply disregard our longing for a greater purpose.

I searched frantically in my late teenage years for someone in our society who could explain life to me and settle my restless longing. I was fortunate enough to be able to enact a quest which led me to the teachings of the Buddha and the practice of meditation. And I was startled to discover that amidst the simplicity and material poverty of rural Asia there was an ancient and highly-developed remedy for just the kind of mental unrest that was plaguing me.

Once I discovered the source of my distress and began to resolve my anxiety by practicing awareness, I was astonished that no one had suggested to me before that my problem was a lack of meaning or purpose. Our society does not recognize that a large portion of our mental pain is because our lives do not make sense on a fundamental level.

One of the limitations of the rational process of science is that we cannot approach anything that is beyond perception. It simply does not register as real or valid. Western medicine cannot recognize our fundamental problem as a lack of meaning because that is beyond its reach. There is no way to objectively measure the intangible things that we most want such as happiness, security, meaning, or purpose, and so we cannot study and manipulate them the way we can with the material world.

Instead of trying to discover the purpose of life, Western civilization tends to avoid the entire question and focus instead on pursuing more immediate and tangible desires. Western doctors are therefore not likely to prescribe a path of spiritual growth, such as the practice of meditation, as a cure. They are likely to prescribe a pill for mental disease because that is what they know how to do.

I had to leave this culture and find my way to a Buddhist monastery to discover my purpose. Sitting in a cinder block cell with a cement slab for a bed and a bare light bulb hanging from a cob-webbed ceiling, I became aware that my body was breathing. In that simple awareness, which had been obscured by layers of scientific knowledge implanted by years of formal education, my life suddenly made sense and my mind was at peace.

Beginning Where We Are

For those of you reading this who are already taking or considering medications for mental or emotional pain, there is no judgment or advice intended here. I am not in your shoes; I don't know what your experience is like. This is a choice that only you can make for yourself, and it is entirely your business. Some forms of mental suffering are indeed caused by chemical imbalances which may be corrected mechanically in this way.

If you have been told that you are somehow cursed, sick, or different from "normal" people, consider that those around you who appear to be happy and well-adjusted may just be better able to numb, distract, or hide from their pain. No one is without mental or emotional pain. I hope this book makes it clear how mental suffering is built into the programmed thought patterns that every one of us is subject to.

Psychiatric medication is not bad or good in itself. My concern is that it seems to be commonly used in a way that creates a dependency which weakens instead of strengthening us. Think about how you might use a decongestant when you have a head cold to allow you to sleep at night so that your body can get the rest that it needs to heal. I would consider this a healthy use of medicine. An unhealthy use of the same medicine might be to take it throughout the day so that you can push yourself to go to work without having to take time to rest and heal.

A good use of psychiatric medication may be to enable you to focus and relax enough to take up a discipline such as meditation. I am not recommending that you stop taking medication or ignore the recommendations of doctors. I am suggesting that mental suffering is inherent in our human condition, and that the practice of meditation exists in order to address it effectively. The Buddha spoke directly to mental distress as the cause of all pain, and suggested that unless we deal with it at its source, it will haunt us throughout our life. And he developed the discipline of meditation specifically to heal this pain.

If you are not practicing meditation, I encourage you to consider that there is a powerful medicine designed for exactly the symptoms of mental and emotional pain that cause most people to take prescribed medications. It is relatively new and foreign to our Western culture and therefore not commonly accepted or recognized yet. However, that does not mean that it is invalid.

The challenge in practicing meditation is that it requires personal effort and discipline. It is not a cure that someone gives you or a medicine that you can simply swallow whole. Like most real cures, training your mind to stay in the present takes practice and will likely be difficult at first. To see results you have to be committed, stay with it for a while, go through discomfort, and be willing to seek some kind of help and support.

26

Support for Spiritual Growth

Effective conditions for spiritual growth offer you encouragement and support to face your judgmental mind directly. Instead of avoiding your thoughts or trying to drown them out, you can learn to be with them and simply let them go. An awareness practice like meditation can be helpful, and it can be useful to have the support of other people who also want to be whole and awake. A teacher who has traveled the territory of becoming more conscious can be useful to create a safe and nourishing container, and to guide you when you cannot see where you are stuck.

In the Therevadin Buddhist tradition, from which the practice of Insight or Vipassana meditation originates, a teacher is viewed as a "spiritual friend," instead of an authority figure. This helps to minimize some of the common mistakes made in the name of spiritual support, and it sets a useful tone for exploring what real support looks like. The challenge of receiving or offering this kind of support is that awakening is an inside job, and there is little that can be done to help from the outside.

Support for awakening can be as simple as holding another person's hand while they go through emotional pain, or listening to another with empathy and compassion instead of judgment. I notice that, even as an adult man, I can still get scared walking alone in the dark in a strange place. In this situation, just the presence of another person walking with me or holding my hand makes the fear disappear.

The essence of spiritual support is assisting other people by simply letting them know that they are not alone. It is standing with other people in their fear, and neither shielding them from the apparent threat, nor feeding their notion that the threat is real. It is helping other people to find the courage to face their own personal demons, and standing by their side while they discover how to effectively deal with them on their own.

The kind of support that is most useful to me is when someone can listen to me without offering their judgments or solutions. A supportive person is someone to whom I can say, "Help, my mind is attacking me again!" and who will understand and help me become aware of my perceptions and gently let go of them. This person does not encourage or deny my perceptions, but sees them as simply my mind making up stories that are not real. They offer compassion and empathy for my struggle, but do not offer justification or strategies for overcoming my imagined opposition.

Individually and Together

The challenge of supporting ourselves and each other in healing from this dream of separation is that the process is so completely individual. Each one of us awakens in our own unique way. That is the nature of this paradigm of individuality. While the outcome of wholeness and completion is the same for all of us, we each get there by a slightly different path.

While the paths to awakening may share some common aspects, no two are exactly alike. That is why no teacher or person outside of us can tell us what is right or healing for us. Only we can know for ourselves, by learning to trust our direct inner knowing. This is what the Buddha meant when he reportedly said to his students, "be a light unto yourselves," just before he left his body.

Gathering with other seekers is vital for keeping the flame of inquiry alive, yet it carries the risk of creating a new identity based on fundamentalism and exclusion. It is important to find a way to come together for support that allows each of us the creativity and freedom to find our own way, while providing a container that is strong enough to lean into for strength, courage, and inspiration.

This might look like small communities where enough intimacy is possible to know how and when to help each other, while there is still enough diversity to diffuse our habits of exclusion and isolation.

When seeking spiritual support from other people, it is useful to have some sense of what real help is. You may join with others in a spiritual group with the intention of becoming more awake, but end up unconsciously reinforcing your conditioned habits of mind. As we form our groups and define our path to wholeness together, we can offer enough structure and boundaries to effectively limit and contain perception, while not becoming dogmatic and rigid. We can create a container that is strong enough to interrupt the patterns of our conditioned mind, while not defining the process or outcome in exclusive or absolute terms.

True Support

Anytime you feed other people's story of victimization, or support their opposition to a perceived enemy, you are strengthening their illusion of a separate self. If you establish levels on a spiritual path and attempt to measure or recognize someone's attainment of those levels, you are feeding the habit of comparative evaluation. And, if you create a new identity out of being a spiritual seeker or member of a group, you are merely enhancing the ego in a new and disguised way.

Spiritual support does not come in the form of a teacher who offers ideals to believe in or a formula to memorize and follow. These common approaches tend to strengthen your conceptual understanding while neglecting your capacity for simple awareness. The kind of knowledge that sets you free cannot come to you through your process of perception, because this merely feeds the mechanism that you are trying to undo. You cannot learn or memorize awakening because it is your inherent state of being. You can only surrender to it.

In this sense, a spiritual path is an undoing. True spiritual support does not enhance your story of an individual self, struggling to become somebody in the world. It does not encourage your personal dramas but rather offers you gentle reminders that the story of who you think you are is only just a story, and is *not* who you really are. Real support helps you face the fear of losing yourself as you surrender your story.

You will be the one to open the doors of awareness within yourself in order to enable your own awakening, yet having a competent teacher can be very useful. Someone who is familiar with the territory of awareness and comfortable outside of the boundaries of perception can help greatly to overcome the fear and uncertainty that often accompanies the loss of familiar reference points. Such a guide can make the difference between being paralyzed by resistance, or passing through the veil of conceptual thought unharmed.

An effective teacher offers a container for your transformation, rather than directing you or giving you a new ideal. Without the strong containment that comes from gentle yet firm spiritual disciplines, the ego tends to take over the process, as we discussed earlier. A wise teacher suggests limits intended to expose the ego and weaken its control over you, while enabling and strengthening your natural intelligence to guide and direct you.

Using the Map

A spiritual path or map cannot give you a picture of your completion, but it can point you in the direction that will take you there. In a spiritual journey there is no time or distance to be covered, because the reality that you are seeking is already here now. Awakening is therefore unlike anything that you would normally call a journey. It is simply the removal of the veil or release of the programming that has been concealing reality from your experience.

Having a structure to guide you in this process is usually necessary in order to challenge the chronic deployment of the ego as an agent to interpret and distort reality. The key is to be sure that any structure that you use is entirely disposable and does not become an end in itself. Remember that perceptual mind can only see formulas, and cannot directly experience reality. So our habit is to mistake the map for the place that the map is leading us to discover. You can use a map to help you get there, and then you have to let the map go and be fully present to where you are.

The simpler and more direct the practice, the easier it is to let it go once it has served its function. The Buddha instructed his students to be mindful of the bodily sensations of breathing in sitting meditation, of the feet and legs moving in walking meditation, and of each individual sensation that we experience throughout the day. He taught that the rest of the process of awakening would happen on its own as a result of this simple practice of direct awareness.

This practice offers a discipline and focus without dominating the process and becoming an end in itself. The more I practice being present with just what is in this moment, the less of a practice it becomes, and the more it feels like what I am. The focus of the body breathing or walking falls away and awareness becomes a field encompassing all of my present experience. In the end, there is just breathing or walking, and only awareness remains.

The End is a Beginning

The irony of spiritual awakening is that it ends at the beginning. Our journey here as human beings concludes when we are always starting anew. This simply means that we are free of the restrictions of linear time. To our perceptual mind, this will always be inconceivable. The idea that we end at the beginning makes no sense in the way that we are used to seeing the world.

When the mind is free of its habit of comparative evaluation, everything is new all the time. Outside of perception, you do not need to contrast the present with a past memory, or imagined future. The present stands on its own as the only thing that exists in reality. The only time is now, and if you use the concepts of time and space to describe your location, you are simply always at the beginning.

The spiritual journey can seem so difficult to us precisely because we don't understand how it works, and cannot conceive of a way to approach it. To our familiar way of thinking, completion would be an end point from which we could look back at the beginning. However, our completion as humans frees us from the paradigm which requires the contrast of past and future. So, the only way that we have to describe the end point of this process in conceptual language is to say that we find ourselves continuously starting anew.

In the world of perception, the beginning is not a good place to be. It means that I am new and uninformed and have a long way to go and a lot to learn. I tend to dislike being a beginner and try to get past this stage of any new experience as quickly as possible. I sometimes view beginners with distain and try hard not to allow myself to be at this place for long, if ever. This is why becoming fully conscious can be so difficult. It requires dwelling in the very place that I have been trying so hard all of my life to avoid.

Once I get past the stigma that I have attached to being a beginner, and gradually get used to abiding where everything is new all the time, I find that it is a light and joyful place to be. Everything is fresh and full of possibility, and there is no heavy weight of the past dragging me down. The concept of the future has no meaning, and so there is nothing to be anxious or afraid of. This is the state of innocence that we left behind long ago in the Garden of Eden when we decided that we wanted to live by our own judgment instead of by simple awareness.

Christ reportedly said, "unless you be like little children, you shall not enter the kingdom of heaven." This was his direction to us to allow ourselves to be beginners always, and not to think that we have to know anything except what is present for us in this moment.

A Work in Progress

It may appear that I am describing a state of perfection that is beyond attainment to ordinary people. Indeed this is how many people think of the Christ or Buddha. And it is what often leads religious institutions to portray the teachers who inspired them as deities, instead of ordinary people who had extraordinary transformations.

In this writing, it may also sound like I am "above it all" myself and have no more pain or suffering in my life. I began this book with a story about a transformation that enabled me to live in the world with some peace and contentment. I have filled many chapters now with insights and teachings which came out of my transformative experience and are expressed often as abstract ideals. And I realize that you may be wondering what has become of my own personal journey.

I still stumble and fall almost daily, believing the story perpetuated by my ego and succumbing to the fear inherent in maintaining the illusion of a personality. In addition to teaching and writing, I am a husband, an active parent of three children, a manager of a small business, a part-time college professor, and work daily to maintain a hundred-acre rural homestead in a cold, northern climate. While I am removed from some of the stresses of our overly competitive society, my mind still creates plenty of tension and drama.

I often blame my wife or children for doing something that upsets me, or find myself in emotional knots because the situation at hand is not going the way that I want it to go. I still try to force my way at times and think that controlling my surroundings will give me peace or security. And I still cling to beliefs established long ago by my ego that continue to blind and limit me.

Hitting the Wall

A few weeks ago, I ran headlong into a hardened assumption which left me reeling for a moment. It happened during a passionate argument with my wife.

Five years earlier, my wife moved into the house in which I had lived for about fifteen years. When we first began living together, she often talked about how she wanted an uncluttered home and how she liked cleanliness and open spaces. I shared her value of uncluttered space and was delighted to hear how important a clean and open house was to her.

Over the years, however, I began to notice that she had a habit of collecting things in piles around the house. Most days there were seemingly random piles around her desk, on counter tops, on couches, and in open floor spaces, including our kitchen and bedroom. I was getting used to a new level of disorder around the house that came from living with children, and it took me a while to realize that these piles belonged to my wife.

I tried ignoring them for some time, and eventually things came to a head and I voiced my frustration and confusion. It disturbed me to have to walk around piles all over our house because I found it a distraction and missed the open floor space or use of our couches and counters. What bothered me most, however, was that she kept saying she needed open, clear spaces, and implied in her statement that I was somehow responsible for the clutter in our home.

As we hashed this out in a sometimes heated discussion, I heard her state again that she needed open clear space around her – as if something I was doing was preventing her from getting this. When I pointed out in exasperation that the perennial piles were hers, this did not seem to register as significant to her.

This is where I began an internal meltdown. I could not fathom how she could talk so passionately about needing open clear space, suggest that I was responsible for the clutter in our house, and then simply ignore her own unruly piles! Her apparent contradiction threatened my sense of sanity, and shook me to my core.

As much as I wanted to run away from this seemingly impossible situation, my commitment to our relationship dictated that I try to understand her. As I listened to her more deeply, I heard that she was not bothered by the piles and rarely noticed them, and instead was distracted and upset about the wall decorations and shelves full of things in the house. It seemed that in her mind, the wall decorations were permanent, while the piles would eventually move.

It was the static nature of things placed intentionally on the walls and shelves that bothered her, instead of the piles placed unintentionally all over the house. Even if they were there for weeks, the piles were temporary in her mind and she knew that someday they would move. The decorations, on the other hand, appeared permanent and out of her control. Many of them were already there when she moved in, and she did not have a relationship or history with these random objects as I did.

Surrendering Cherished Beliefs

On one level this was a common household conflict representing two different people with two different sets of values and needs. I am a mediator and teach conflict resolution skills, so approaching a negotiation like this feels natural to me. However, at that moment, all I could see was the apparent contradiction in her position. It seemed to me that she was saying one thing and doing exactly the opposite, while thinking there was nothing at all wrong with her approach.

As I took hold of myself and noticed the intense emotions churning through my body, I realized that I was confused and frightened by my wife's behavior. I recognized that I had a need for some sort of rational explanation that would allow me to make sense of what she was saying and doing. She was my closest adult companion and shared most aspects of my life. Hearing that she could openly contradict herself in this way and think nothing of it worried me greatly. I thought that I could not rely on her or trust her capacity for abstract reasoning. This conclusion left me feeling isolated and afraid.

I was very frustrated and wanted her to see and admit to the contradiction that she was presenting. I knew that I could not *make* her see this, however, and I did not want to numb or distract myself from these intense feelings, even though they were causing me so much inner distress. So I did the only other thing that I could do and just sat with my emotional charge for some time without reacting. Simply being with myself and staying aware of my emotional turmoil, something strange and surreal began to happen.

I recognized that at the bottom of my problem was a belief that people, especially those whom I depend on and am intimately connected to, should be rational and make sense. I realized that I held onto that belief without question. And I saw that all the tension and fear in my body at that moment came from thinking that this belief, which seemed so right to me, was being disregarded by her.

Knowing that I could not make her conform with my idea of what was right, good, and normal, I went the other way and looked at myself. I questioned the assumption I held, which I had thought was so basic that it was beyond questioning. And in the light of this inquiry, my belief that my wife had to make sense in order for me to be safe began to collapse.

At first there was a great sense of failure and loss. Something that had identified me was gone, and I was quite disoriented. A granite stone in the foundation of my ego had been crushed and reduced to pebbles, and it seemed like my life was hanging by a thread. I felt empty and vacant.

Then I began to notice an inexplicable sense of freedom and joy rising up from the ashes of my old belief. I recognized that the world had long seemed dangerous and threatening to me on some level because I could not make sense out of other people. I had seen so many people in my life contradicting themselves and acting inconsistently, and this had always made me feel unsafe. In response to this, I had unconsciously hardened and distanced myself from other people, afraid that their irrational behavior would result in me being hurt.

As I let go of expecting my wife's behavior to make sense, I also surrendered my demand that *anyone's* behavior make sense. I recognized many of the ways that *my own* behavior was contradictory and made no sense, and realized that all of us are fundamentally irrational in some way. The pain of coming to the edge of my wife's apparent irrationality led me to dissolve a belief that had isolated me and kept me guarded for most of my life. Letting go of my need for other people's behavior to make sense felt like shedding a skin that was too tight. A heavy layer of fear had been peeled away and it felt wonderful to be free of it.

Imperfection

The spiritual path I am describing here could be summed up as: *seeing the perfection in the imperfection.* This kind of statement makes no sense to perceptual mind, just as my wife's behavior made no rational sense to me in the story above. We have to let go of our habit of linear thought in order to open ourselves to see things from a new perspective. This is how we grow spiritually.

Many of us hold a deep-seated belief that there *is* such a thing as a perfect world. We may bury this belief underneath layers of resignation, despair, or resentment, as the world we experience disappoints us again and again. Or we may say that there is no such thing as perfection and act as though we don't care anymore. Yet, each of us uses some notion of perfection to measure our daily life experiences, and against this standard what is happening now usually looks pretty bad.

As I watch my thirteen year old daughter come kicking and screaming into adulthood, I am bewildered that so many of her experiences receive the designation of "disgusting." Anything and everything seems to end up with this degrading label at some point, including vegetables from our garden, insects, photographs, clothes, her sisters, and so on.

I wonder to myself how someone with so little life experience can already know that all these things are so extremely foul? The answer is that she compares each experience with her ideal of perfection, which is remarkably complex and well-developed, and most of the time what is happening for her now doesn't measure up – not even close. At that point whatever is in front of her ends up in the "disgusting" bin.

Comparing this moment with my imagined perfect moment is how the ego keeps me restless and unsettled. I am always seeking something more and different and thus ensuring perennial employment for my struggling sense of self, which is never quite fulfilled.

The way to get off of this treadmill is to allow my ideals of perfection to be crushed by reality, as happened to me in the story above. This is often a difficult experience, however, the result is a new sense of lightness and freedom that quenches the deepest longings that I have for real growth and change.

I can allow my ideals to be broken apart by reality in order to appreciate fully what is happening now, and disengage from my obsession with what *was* or what *could be*. The only way to put this into words is through a seeming paradox like "finding the perfection in the imperfection." This is not a gimmick or lie that I try to convince myself is true. It is a way that my linear, rational mind can approach reality, which it turns out, is not linear or rational at all.

My mind cannot experience reality directly because it already has a well-formulated ideal of reality that it uses to measure my ordinary experience by. This is the "Achilles heel" of my rational mind. I can never see anything *as it is*, but only in contrast to how I think *it should be*.

In that sense, everything here will *always be imperfect*. Once I understand that my mind can only see imperfection in the world around me and in myself, I can drop my expectation that things be different than they are, and simply accept the imperfection in all things. In this way, the imperfect becomes perfect and I am able to give up struggling to get it to be different.

Our Purpose is to Bless

I was once traveling with a friend in a small tropical country which was rapidly becoming developed and losing its pristine natural beauty to cement buildings and crowded, noisy cities. My friend made an observation common to anyone who is sensitive to the devastation that human development has caused to our natural environment. She bemoaned the fact that people seem to cause destruction everywhere we go, and suggested that we were merely a burden to the planet and life on earth would be better off without us.

My friend seemed to be looking to me for a response, and I began by recognizing her feelings of despair and hopelessness about the destructive nature of people. I then heard myself saying that we simply have not yet recognized our true purpose here. I suggested that our unique gift to the earth and all of life is our capacity to simply witness and appreciate everything around us.

We are conscious and have an inherent capacity for empathy and gratitude. This enables us to feel the suffering of other beings and offer them our supportive presence. It also makes us able to love and appreciate things of beauty that bring us pleasure or joy. We are uniquely suited to recognize and enjoy all the variations of beauty and pleasure that exist on earth. And I believe that our primary function is to witness, honor, and respect all forms of life and all matter.

As I become more conscious I realize how my thoughts affect everything around me. In the light of my appreciation and love, all things become more vibrant and alive. Taking care of the earth does not mean that I cannot use what it offers me. It simply means that I use the earth's abundance with appreciation for where it comes from, and use my conscious intelligence to nourish and support the living systems which nourish and support me.

This may sound like a "new age" platitude, and indeed it is often used in such a superficial and abstract way. Yet the reality which dawns on me as I awaken is that I am not a separate individual as I thought, but am intimately connected with everything else. As I recognize this to be true, my fear dissolves and my impulse to love all things as extensions of myself emerges effortlessly.

Making a New Story

A spiritual path begins with a new story. Without words, images, or symbols, perceptual mind would have no way to access a teaching like this. The irony of a spiritual teaching is that it points to a reality that exists beyond stories and perceptual images of any kind. Yet, because this is the only language that my mind can access at this point, this is where I need to begin.

A spiritual story has to be taken lightly. That does not mean that we make light of it, or treat it as insignificant. Indeed, teachings like those offered to us by the Buddha and Christ are valuable beyond measure, because they enable us to find what we are really seeking here. It is just that when we understand the nature of reality, and know who we are, we recognize that a story of any kind keeps truth at a distance.

None of what is written here is true. Truth is a personal experience beyond words or symbols. The best that these words can do is to create an opening for truth to occur. An effective teaching merely reveals a knowing that is already there, but was simply obscured by your urgency to establish a self in the world of separate selves.

If any of these words have struck a place of truth in you, simply allow that place to resonate. Take it in and recognize that it is yours and did not come from somewhere else. Let the words go, and give up trying to understand the experience of being moved by them. Let the vibration in you settle, and know that part of you is now alive and can guide you further.

Don't be concerned about how you found the truth inside of you, and don't try to remember or repeat any of these words. Keep it alive and pass it along in your own way. It is yours now. Be original and authentic. Make it up as you go along.

If any of the words in this book do not resonate with you, simply let them go. They were not meant for you. They are like water flowing down a river to the sea, all ending up in the same place, only to rise up as clouds and fill the rivers with rain again.

I invite you now to set down this writing and forget everything that you have just read. Go forward in complete confidence that your presence is all you need for your full satisfaction and total security. Any information that you require will be provided to you when you need it, and you do not have to know how this will occur - you only have to trust that it will. Be assured of your own worthiness, for there is no one else here like you, and no one who can be what you have come here to be.

About the Author

Miles learned Insight Meditation in a Buddhist Monastery in Sri Lanka in 1976, at the age of 19. He has lived and attended numerous retreats at the Insight Meditation Society in the U.S. and other Buddhist centers abroad.

He purchased an historic hill farm in Vermont in 1988 and developed it into a working homestead. Ten years later he started a small retreat center there, and began teaching meditation and leading retreats in 1999.

Miles currently lives at Sky Meadow, managing the retreat center and organic farm with his wife and three daughters. He also is a professional mediator and teaches Conscious Communication skills. His first book is: *Conscious Communication* - A Language of Connection.

For more information:

www.SkyMeadowRetreat.com
www.BeyondPerception.org

CPSIA information can be obtained at www.ICGtesting.com
Printed in the USA
BVOW040828230812

298407BV00003B/3/P